Rick and Morty

LIL' POOPY SUPERSTAR

AN ONI PRESS PUBLICATION

[adult swim]

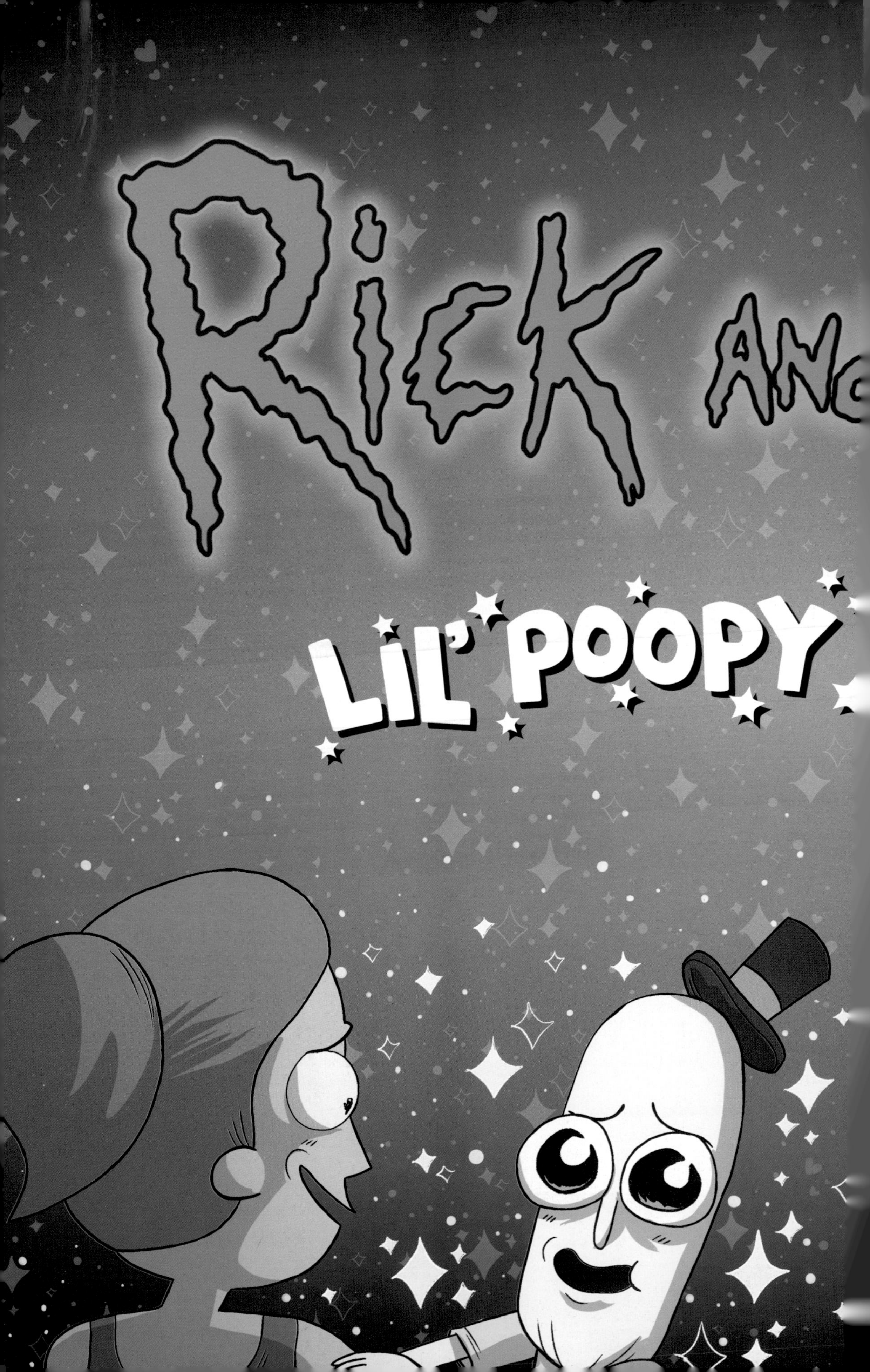
RICK AND
LIL' POOPY

MORTY™
SUPERSTAR

RICK AND MORTY CREATED BY **DAN HARMON** AND **JUSTIN ROILAND**

WRITTEN AND DRAWN BY
SARAH GRALEY

COLORED BY
MILDRED LOUIS

BONUS COMIC ART BY
MARC ELLERBY

LETTERED BY
CRANK!

RETAIL COVER BY
SARAH GRALEY WITH **MILDRED LOUIS**

ONI EXCLUSIVE COVER BY
JULIETA COLÁS

FRIED PIE EXCLUSIVE COVER BY
RIAN SYGH

EDITED BY
ARI YARWOOD

DESIGNED BY
HILARY THOMPSON

ONI PRESS

[adult swim]

PUBLISHED BY ONI PRESS, INC.

JOE NOZEMACK PUBLISHER

JAMES LUCAS JONES EDITOR IN CHIEF

ANDREW MCINTIRE V.P. OF MARKETING & SALES

DAVID DISSANAYAKE SALES MANAGER

RACHEL REED PUBLICITY COORDINATOR

TROY LOOK DIRECTOR OF DESIGN & PRODUCTION

HILARY THOMPSON GRAPHIC DESIGNER

ANGIE DOBSON DIGITAL ART TECHNICIAN

ARI YARWOOD MANAGING EDITOR

CHARLIE CHU SENIOR EDITOR

ROBIN HERRERA EDITOR

BESS PALLARES EDITORIAL ASSISTANT

BRAD ROOKS DIRECTOR OF LOGISTICS

JUNG LEE LOGISTICS ASSOCIATE

[adult swim]™

ONIPRESS.COM
FACEBOOK.COM/ONIPRESS
TWITTER.COM/ONIPRESS
ONIPRESS.TUMBLR.COM
INSTAGRAM.COM/ONIPRESS
ADULTSWIM.COM
TWITTER.COM/RICKANDMORTY
FACEBOOK.COM/RICKANDMORTY

THIS VOLUME COLLECTS ISSUES #1-5 OF THE ONI PRESS
SERIES *RICK AND MORTY: LIL' POOPY SUPERSTAR.*

FIRST EDITION: FEBRUARY 2017

ISBN 978-1-62010-374-6
EISBN 978-1-62010-375-3
ONI EXCLUSIVE ISBN 978-1-62010-382-1
FRIED PIE EXCLUSIVE ISBN 978-1-62010-380-7

PRINTED IN SINGAPORE.

LIBRARY OF CONGRESS CONTROL NUMBER: 2016950329

1 2 3 4 5 6 7 8 9 10

SPECIAL THANKS TO JUSTIN ROILAND, DAN HARMON, MARISA MARIONAKIS, AND MIKE MENDEL.

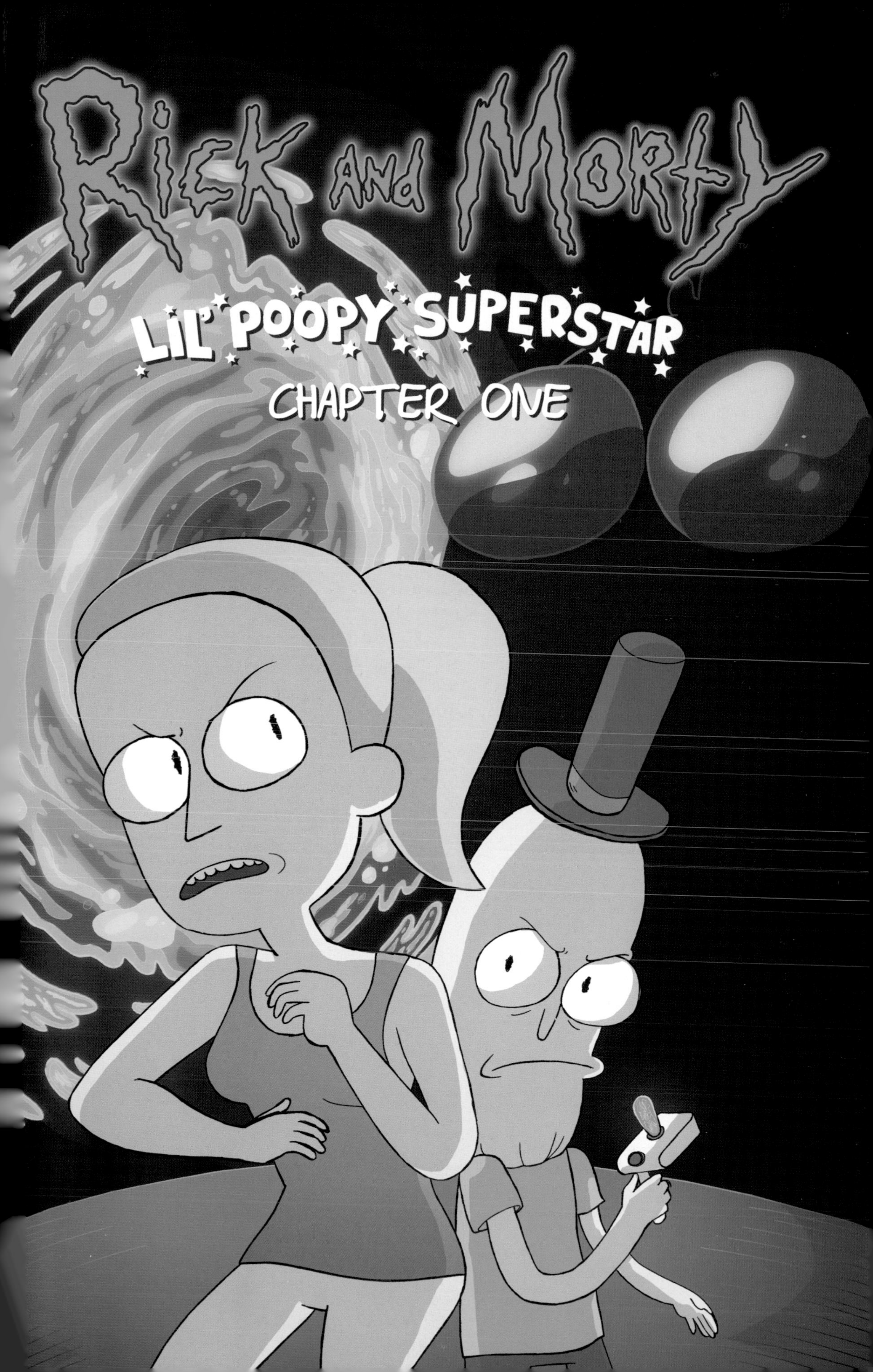
Rick and Morty
LIL' POOPY SUPERSTAR
CHAPTER ONE

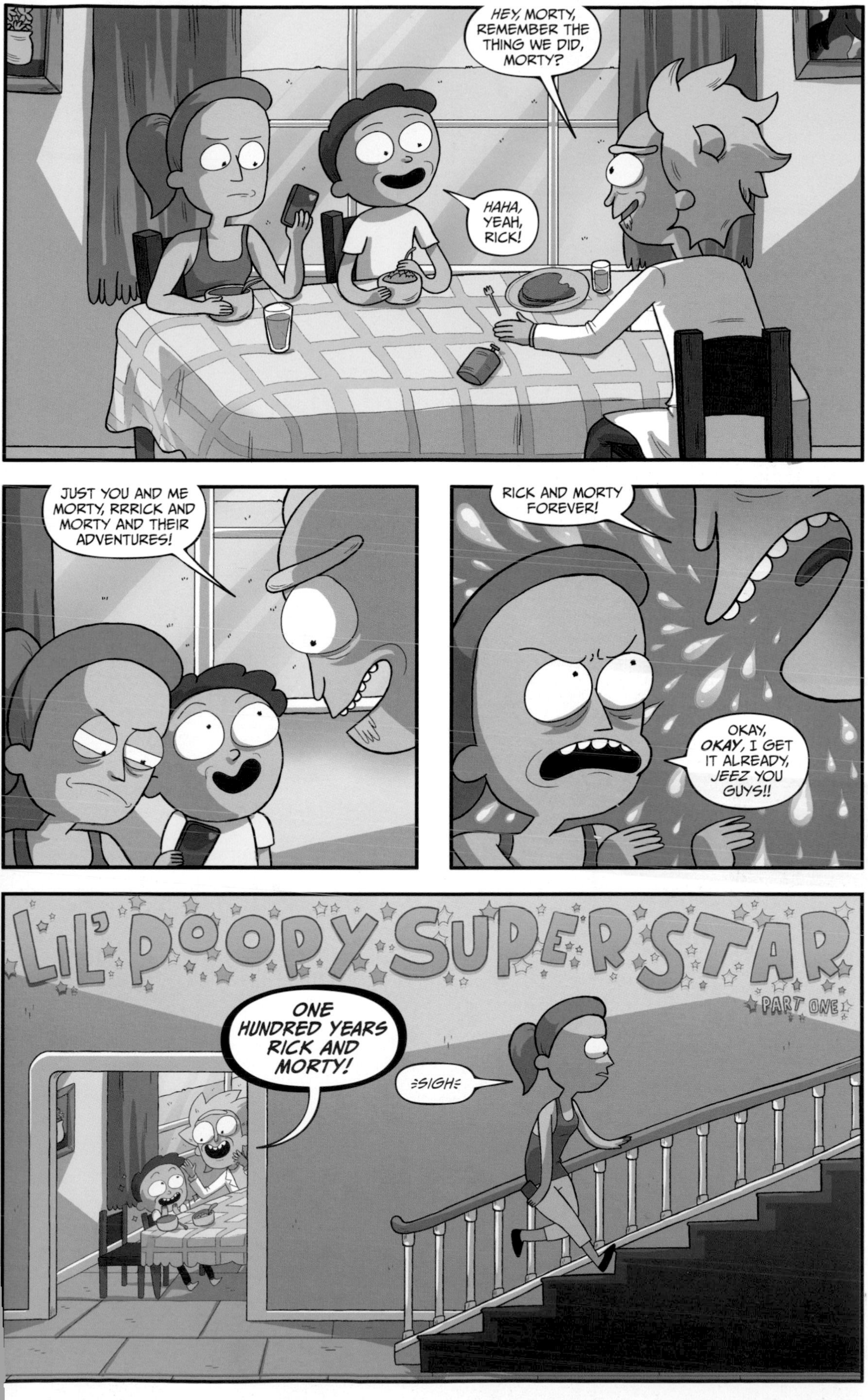
HEY, MORTY, REMEMBER THE THING WE DID, MORTY?
HAHA, YEAH, RICK!
JUST YOU AND ME MORTY, RRRICK AND MORTY AND THEIR ADVENTURES!
RICK AND MORTY FOREVER!
OKAY, OKAY, I GET IT ALREADY, JEEZ YOU GUYS!!
LIL' POOPY SUPERSTAR
PART ONE
ONE HUNDRED YEARS RICK AND MORTY!
=SIGH=

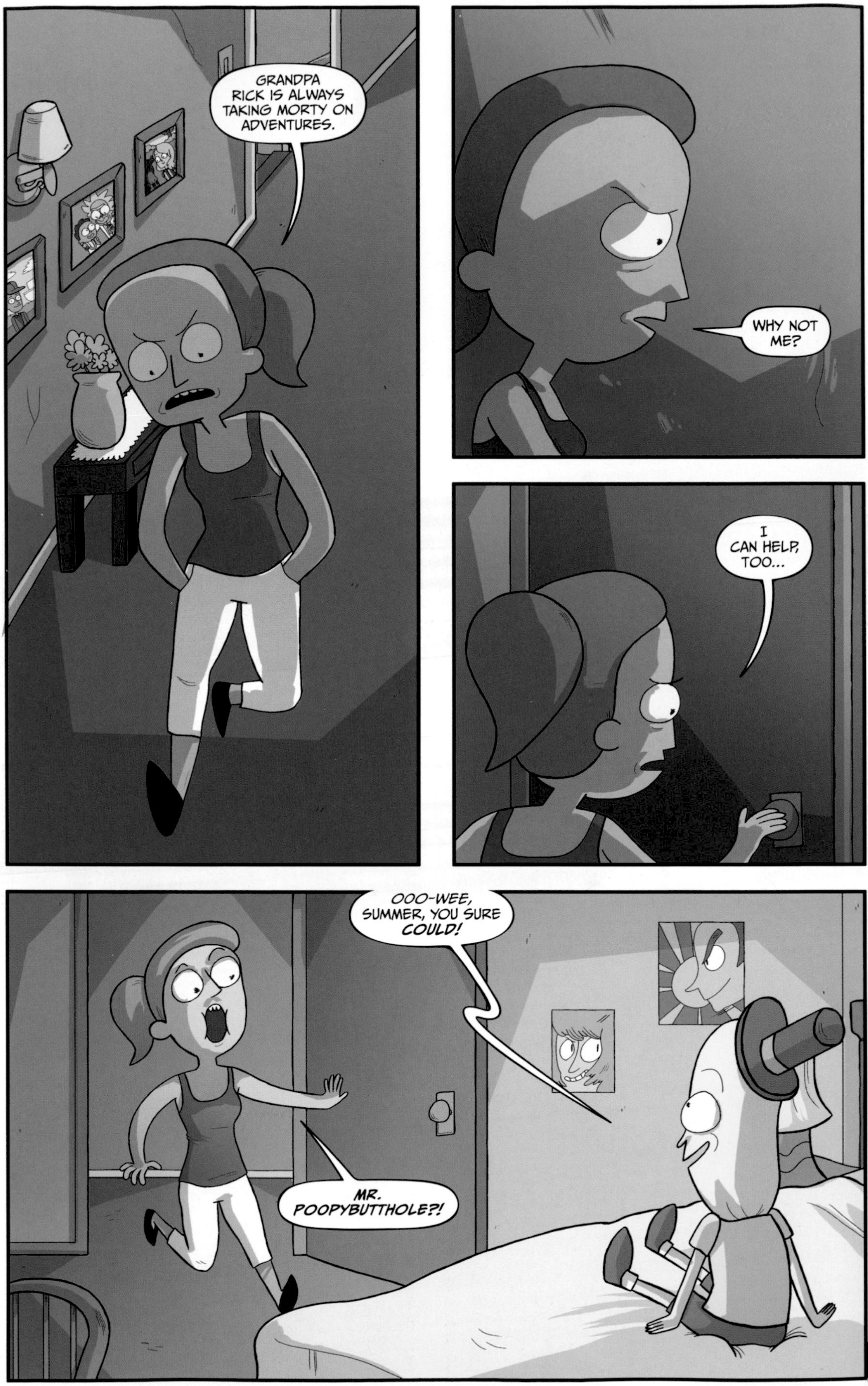
GRANDPA RICK IS ALWAYS TAKING MORTY ON ADVENTURES.
WHY NOT ME?
I CAN HELP, TOO...
MR. POOPYBUTTHOLE?!
OOO-WEE, SUMMER, YOU SURE COULD!

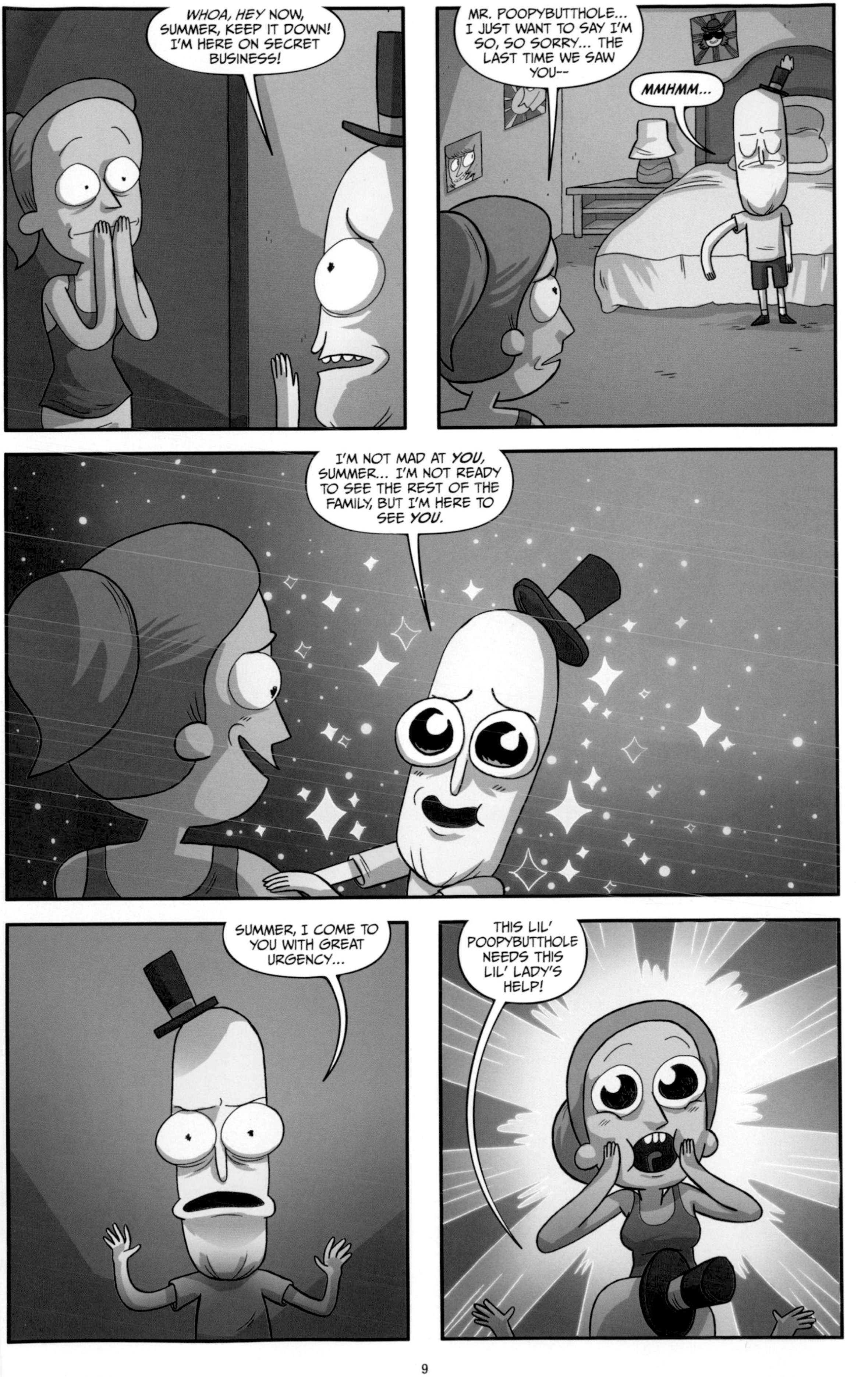
WHOA, HEY NOW, SUMMER, KEEP IT DOWN! I'M HERE ON SECRET BUSINESS!
MR. POOPYBUTTHOLE... I JUST WANT TO SAY I'M SO, SO SORRY... THE LAST TIME WE SAW YOU--
MMHMM...
I'M NOT MAD AT YOU, SUMMER... I'M NOT READY TO SEE THE REST OF THE FAMILY, BUT I'M HERE TO SEE YOU.
SUMMER, I COME TO YOU WITH GREAT URGENCY...
THIS LIL' POOPYBUTTHOLE NEEDS THIS LIL' LADY'S HELP!

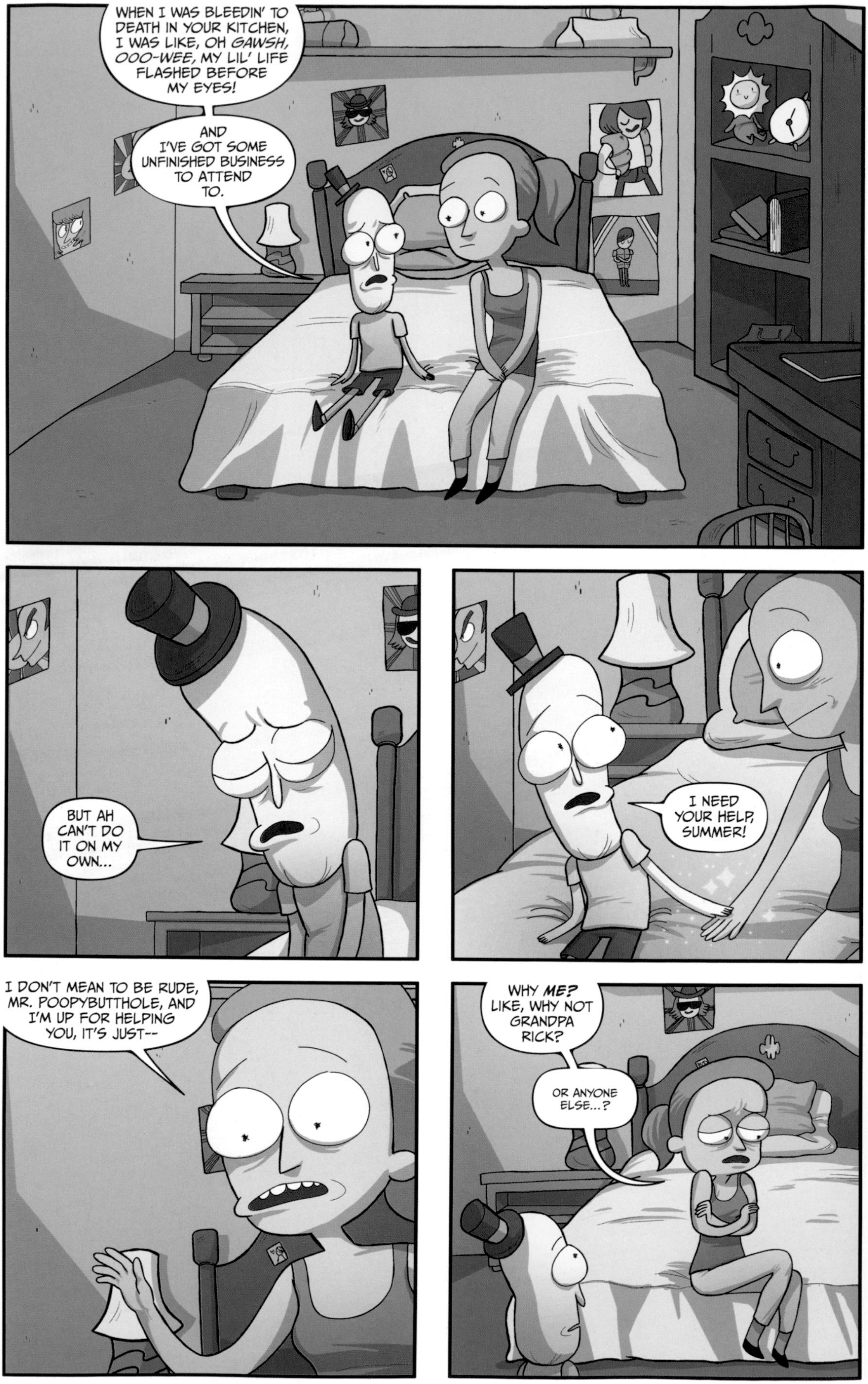
WHEN I WAS BLEEDIN' TO DEATH IN YOUR KITCHEN, I WAS LIKE, OH *GAWSH*, *OOO-WEE*, MY LIL' LIFE FLASHED BEFORE MY EYES!
AND I'VE GOT SOME UNFINISHED BUSINESS TO ATTEND TO.
BUT AH CAN'T DO IT ON MY OWN...
I NEED YOUR HELP, SUMMER!
I DON'T MEAN TO BE RUDE, MR. POOPYBUTTHOLE, AND I'M UP FOR HELPING YOU, IT'S JUST--
WHY ***ME?*** LIKE, WHY NOT GRANDPA RICK?
OR ANYONE ELSE...?

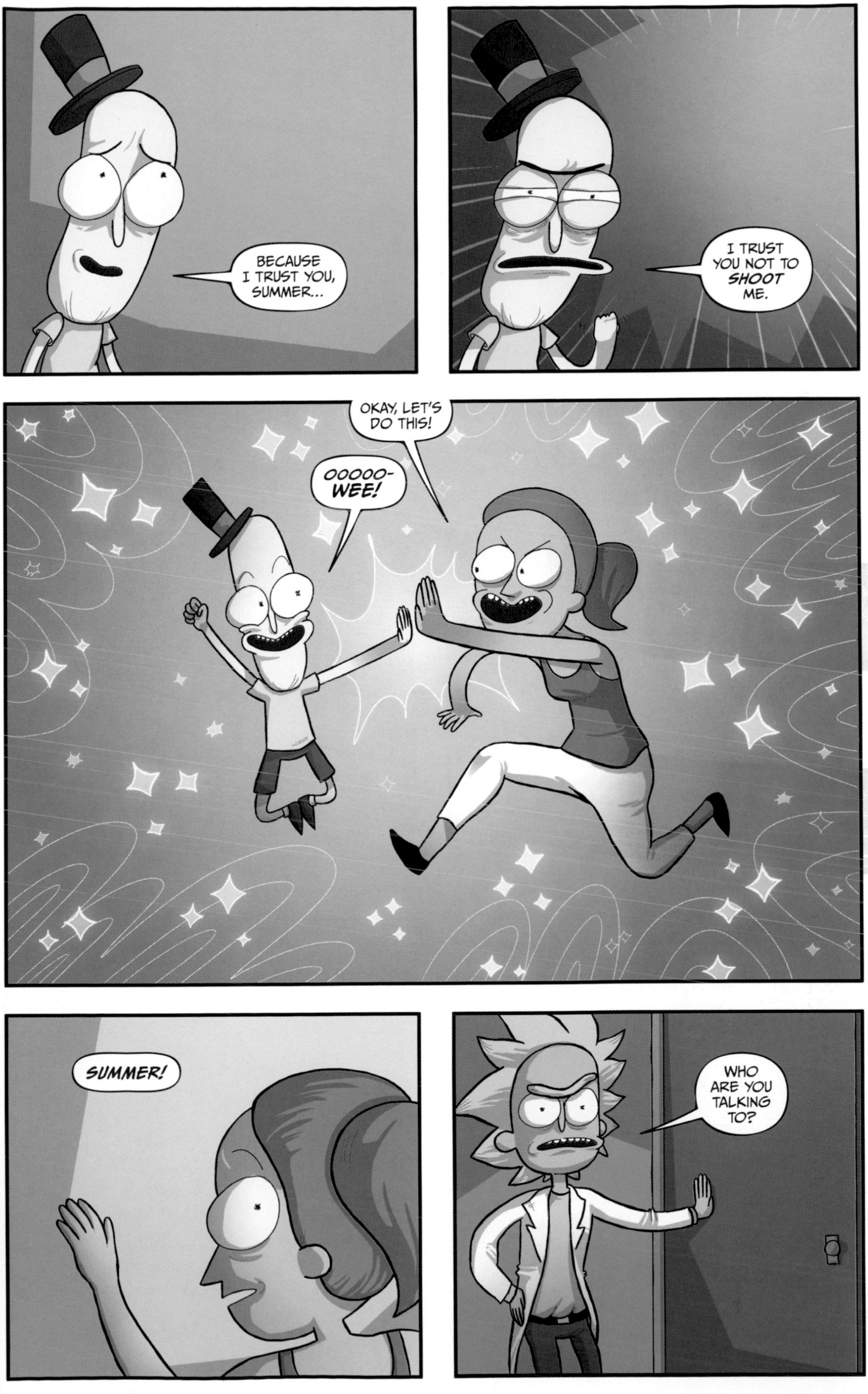
BECAUSE I TRUST YOU, SUMMER...
I TRUST YOU NOT TO SHOOT ME.
OKAY, LET'S DO THIS!
OOOOO-WEE!
SUMMER!
WHO ARE YOU TALKING TO?

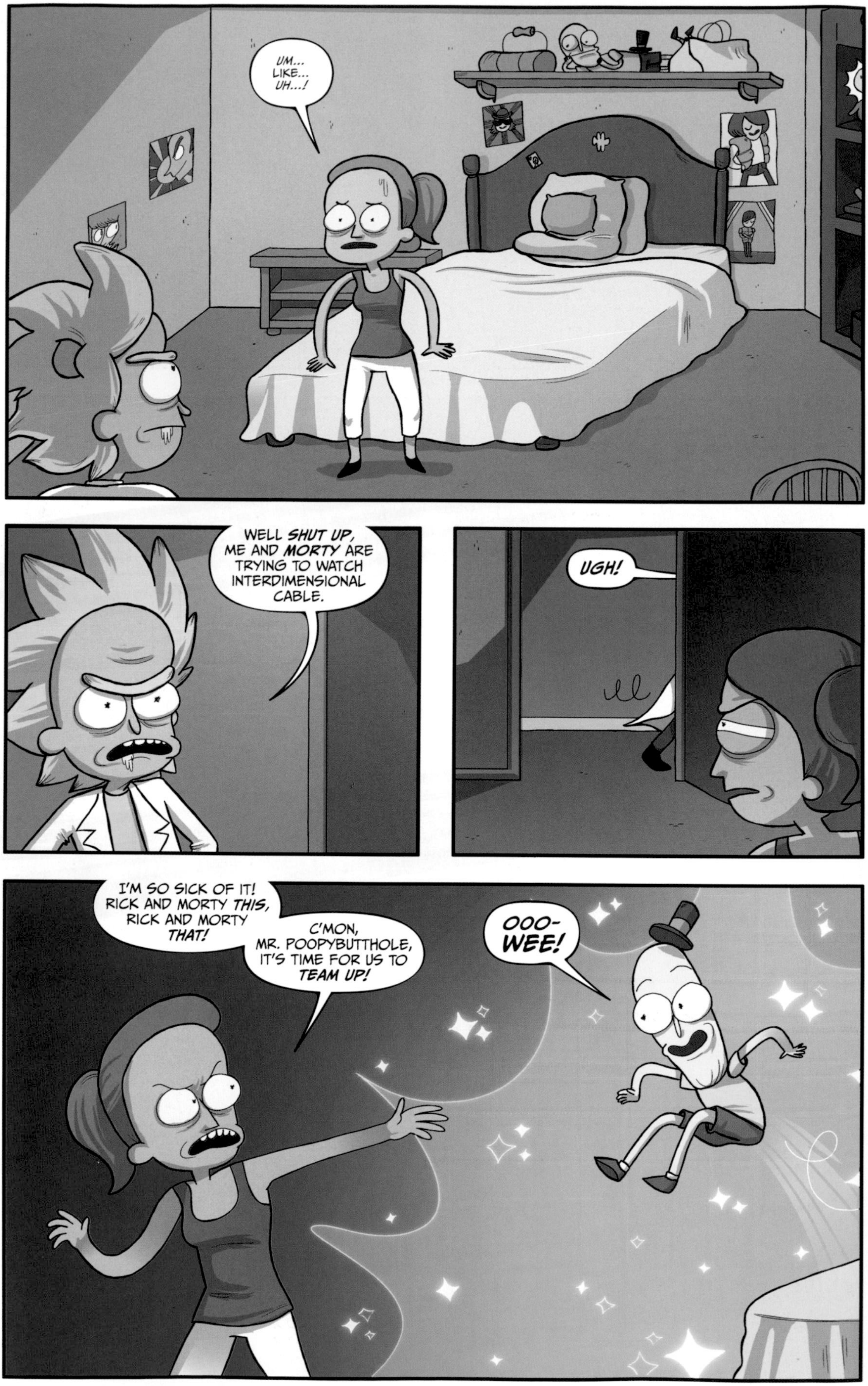
UM... LIKE... UH...!
WELL *SHUT UP*, ME AND *MORTY* ARE TRYING TO WATCH INTERDIMENSIONAL CABLE.
UGH!
I'M SO SICK OF IT! RICK AND MORTY *THIS*, RICK AND MORTY *THAT!*
C'MON, MR. POOPYBUTTHOLE, IT'S TIME FOR US TO *TEAM UP!*
OOO-WEE!

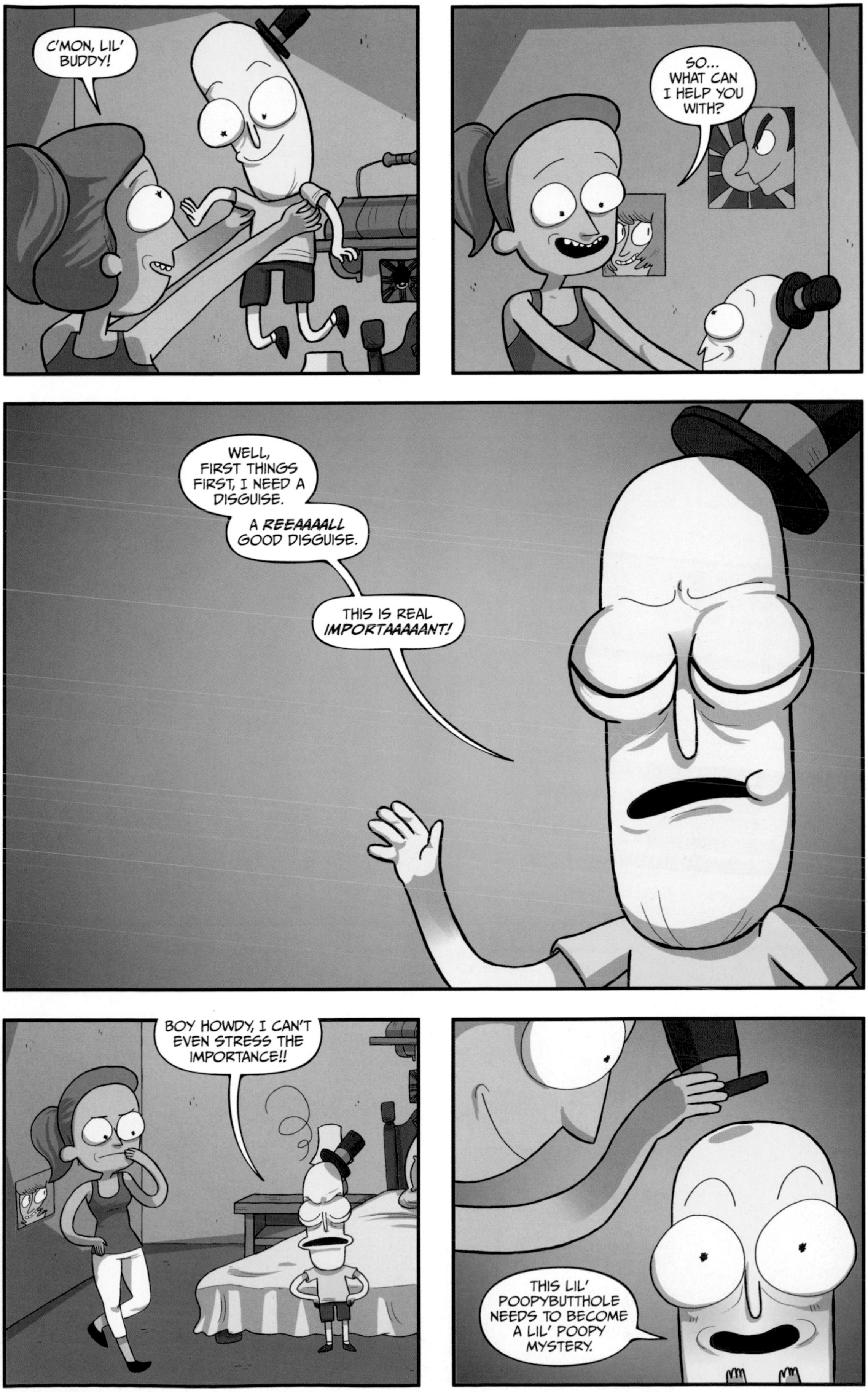
C'MON, LIL' BUDDY!
SO... WHAT CAN I HELP YOU WITH?
WELL, FIRST THINGS FIRST, I NEED A DISGUISE.
A REEAAAALL GOOD DISGUISE.
THIS IS REAL IMPORTAAAAANT!
BOY HOWDY, I CAN'T EVEN STRESS THE IMPORTANCE!!
THIS LIL' POOPYBUTTHOLE NEEDS TO BECOME A LIL' POOPY MYSTERY.

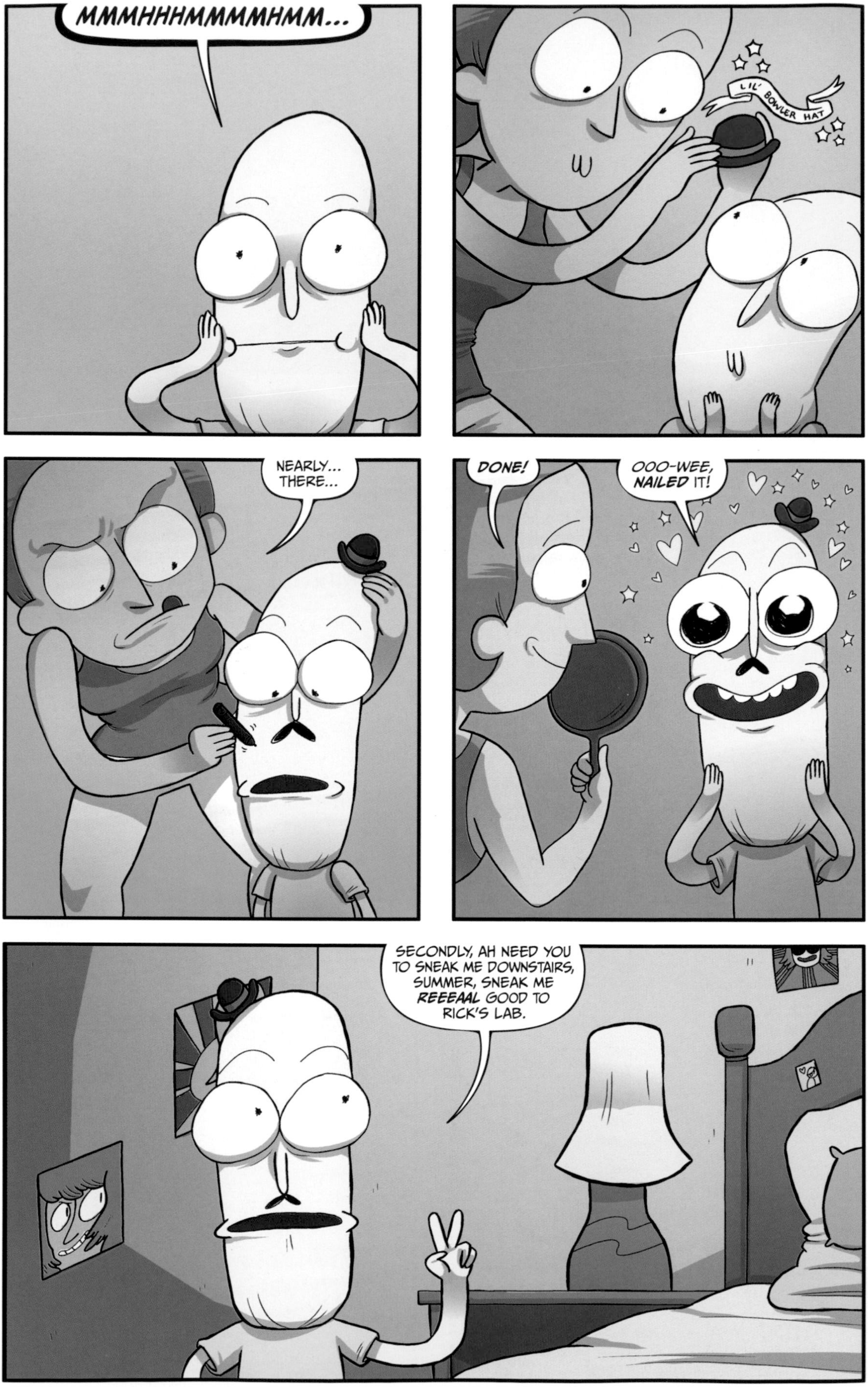
MMMHHHMMMMHMM...
LIL' BOWLER HAT
NEARLY... THERE...
DONE!
OOO-WEE, NAILED IT!
SECONDLY, AH NEED YOU TO SNEAK ME DOWNSTAIRS, SUMMER, SNEAK ME REEEAAL GOOD TO RICK'S LAB.

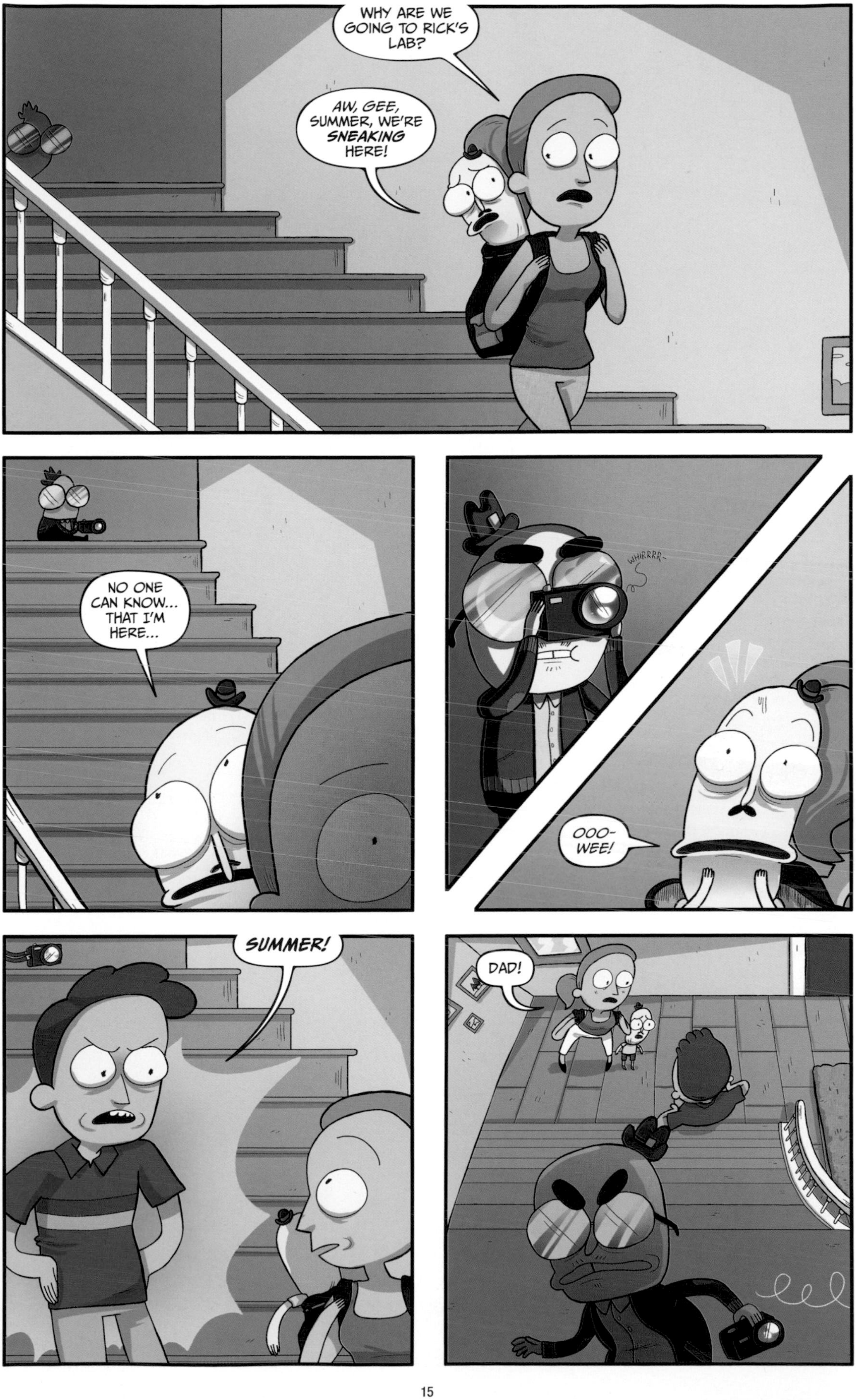
WHY ARE WE GOING TO RICK'S LAB?
AW, GEE, SUMMER, WE'RE SNEAKING HERE!
NO ONE CAN KNOW... THAT I'M HERE...
WHIRRRR-
OOO-WEE!
SUMMER!
DAD!

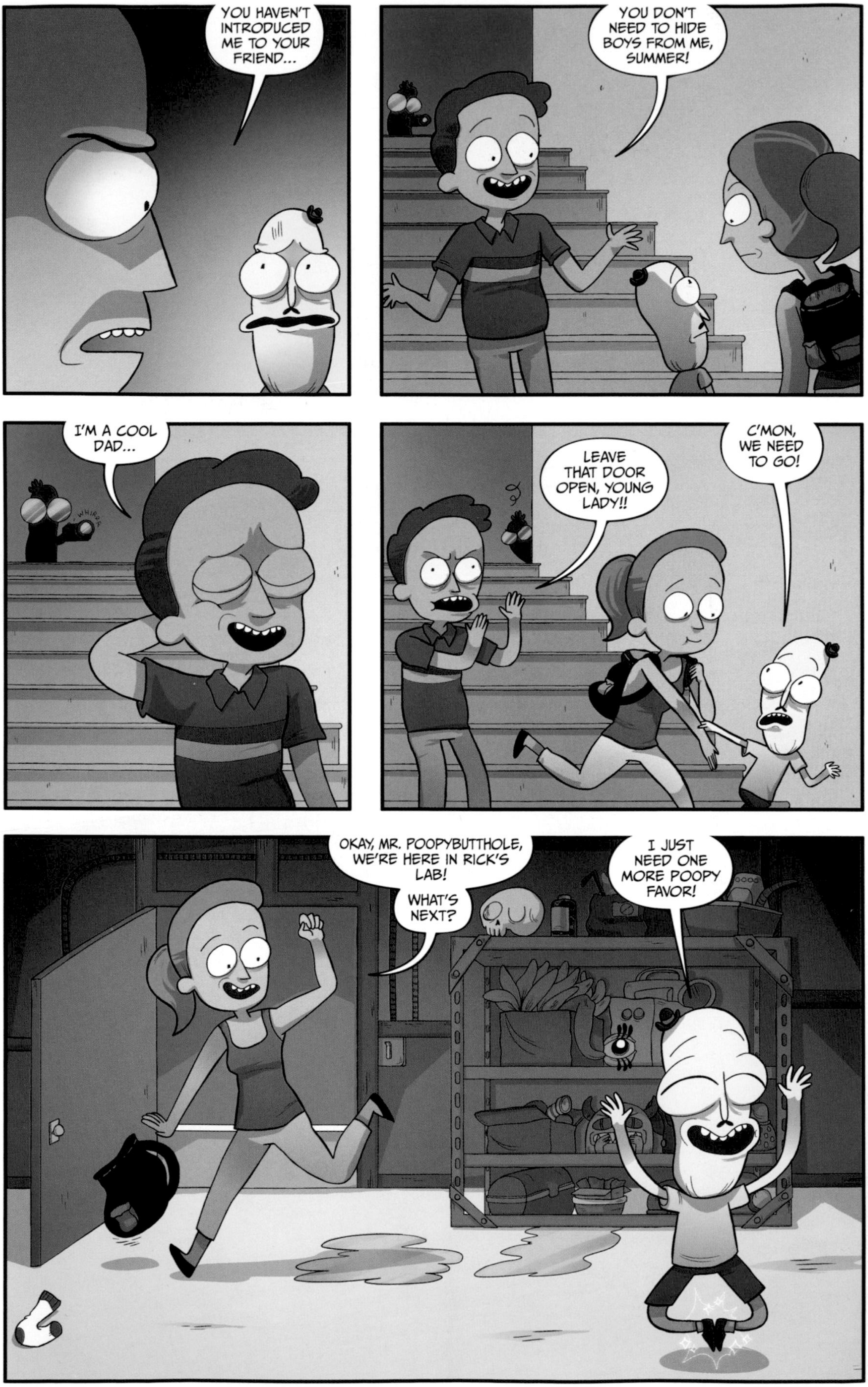
YOU HAVEN'T INTRODUCED ME TO YOUR FRIEND...
YOU DON'T NEED TO HIDE BOYS FROM ME, SUMMER!
I'M A COOL DAD...
LEAVE THAT DOOR OPEN, YOUNG LADY!!
C'MON, WE NEED TO GO!
OKAY, MR. POOPYBUTTHOLE, WE'RE HERE IN RICK'S LAB!
WHAT'S NEXT?
I JUST NEED ONE MORE POOPY FAVOR!

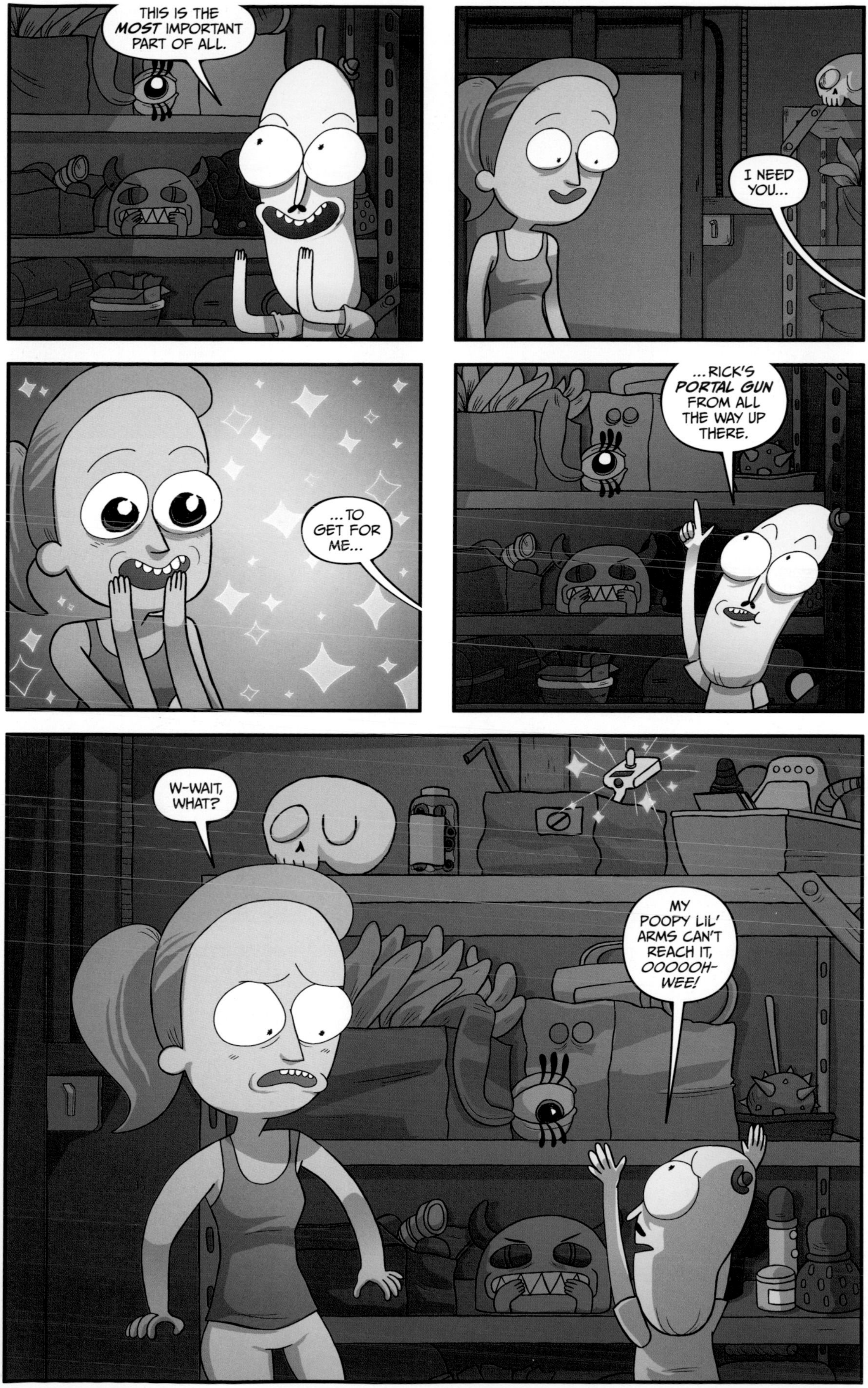
THIS IS THE MOST IMPORTANT PART OF ALL.
I NEED YOU...
...TO GET FOR ME...
...RICK'S PORTAL GUN FROM ALL THE WAY UP THERE.
W-WAIT, WHAT?
MY POOPY LIL' ARMS CAN'T REACH IT, OOOOOH-WEE!

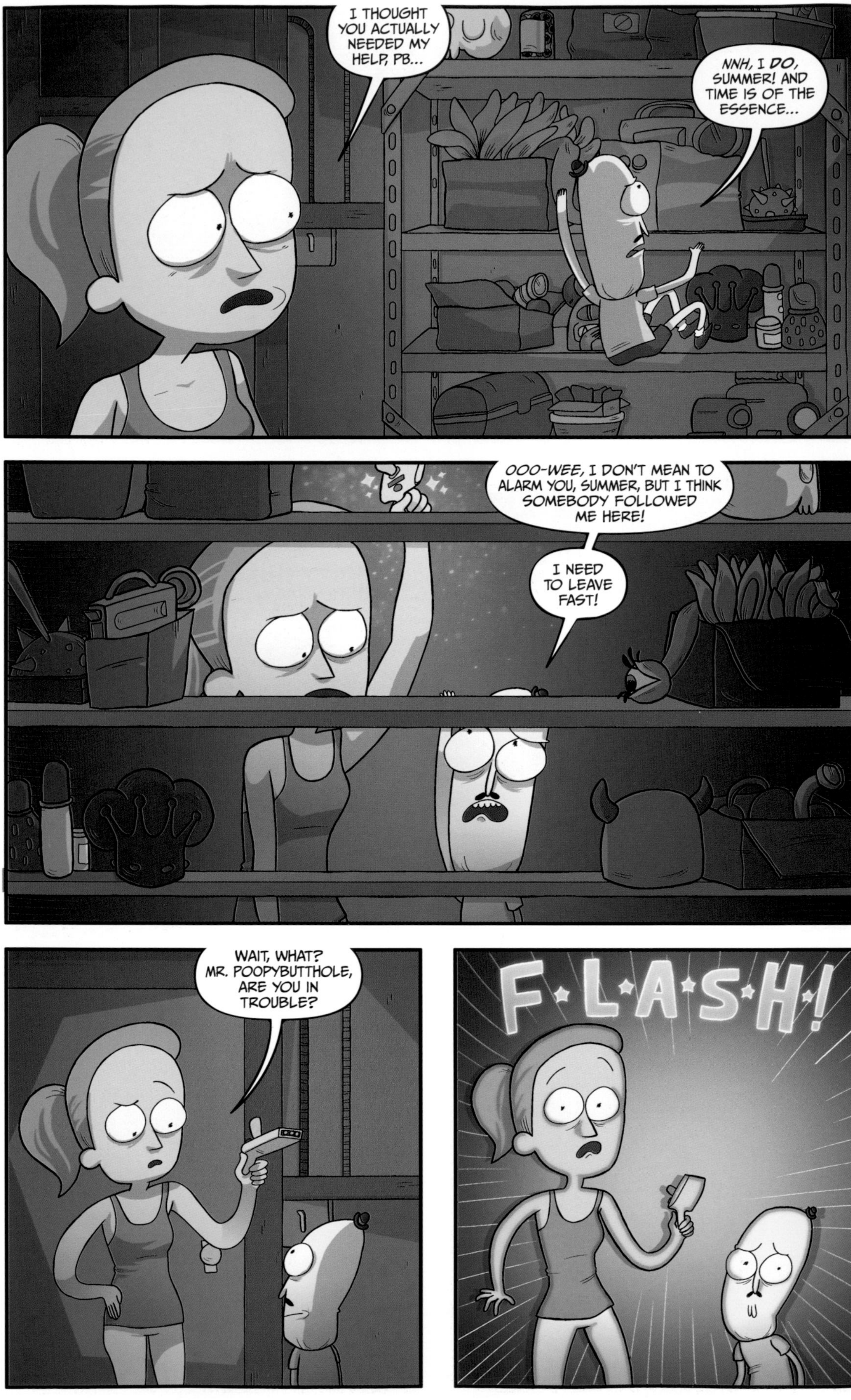
I THOUGHT YOU ACTUALLY NEEDED MY HELP, PB...
NNH, I DO, SUMMER! AND TIME IS OF THE ESSENCE...
OOO-WEE, I DON'T MEAN TO ALARM YOU, SUMMER, BUT I THINK SOMEBODY FOLLOWED ME HERE!
I NEED TO LEAVE FAST!
WAIT, WHAT? MR. POOPYBUTTHOLE, ARE YOU IN TROUBLE?
F•L•A•S•H!

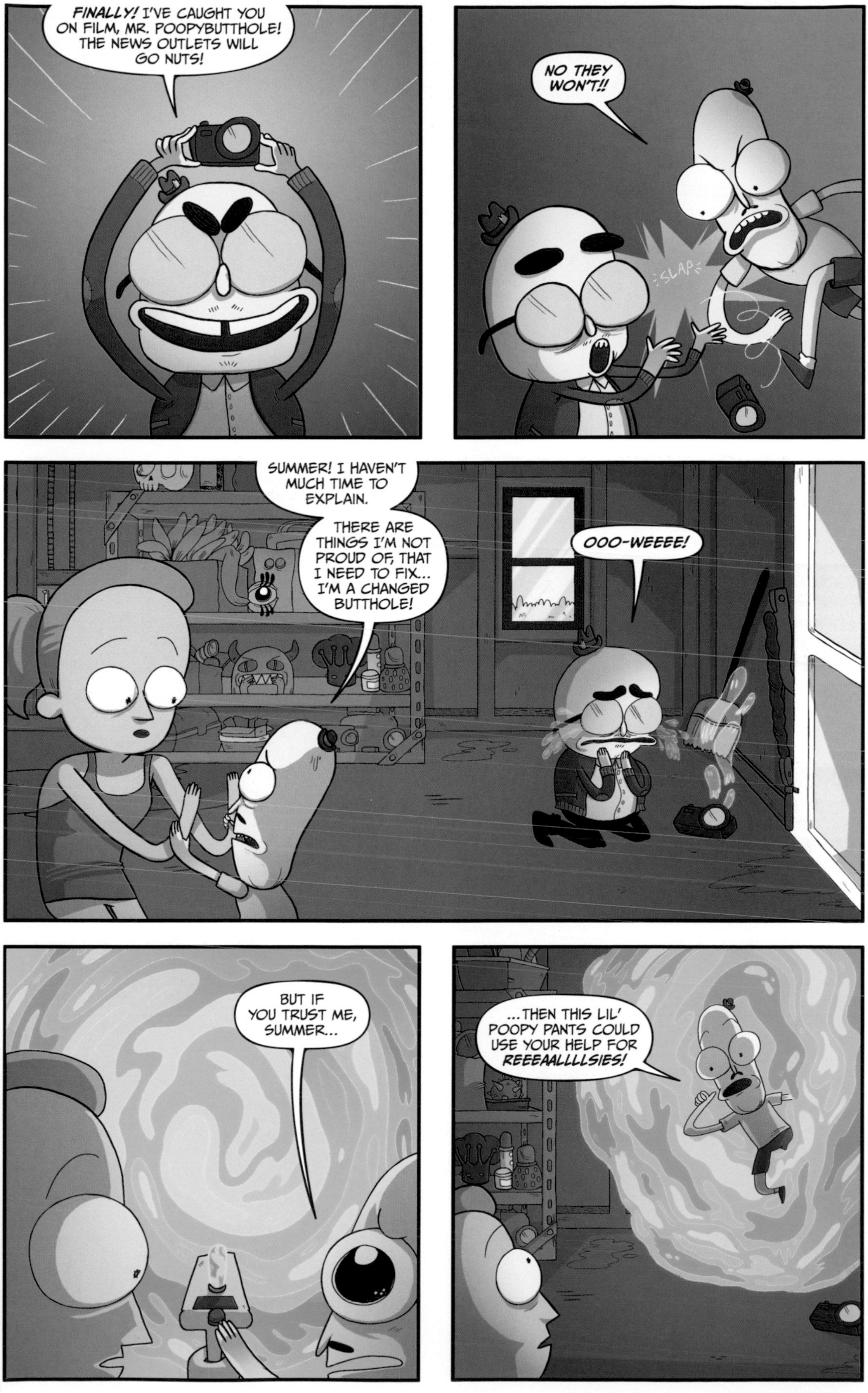
FINALLY! I'VE CAUGHT YOU ON FILM, MR. POOPYBUTTHOLE! THE NEWS OUTLETS WILL GO NUTS!
NO THEY WON'T!!
SLAP
SUMMER! I HAVEN'T MUCH TIME TO EXPLAIN.
THERE ARE THINGS I'M NOT PROUD OF, THAT I NEED TO FIX... I'M A CHANGED BUTTHOLE!
OOO-WEEEE!
BUT IF YOU TRUST ME, SUMMER...
...THEN THIS LIL' POOPY PANTS COULD USE YOUR HELP FOR REEEAALLLLSIES!

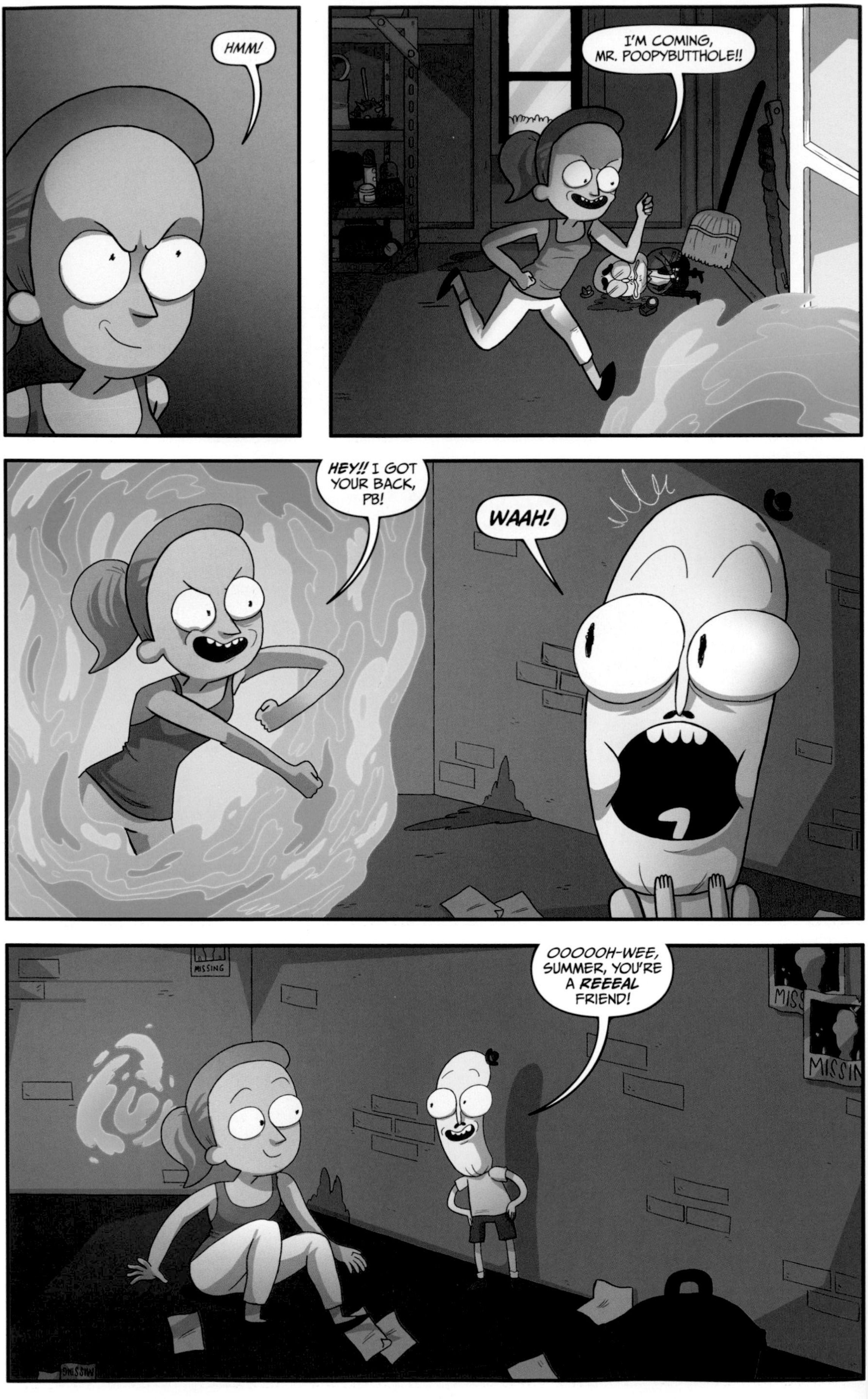
HMM!
I'M COMING, MR. POOPYBUTTHOLE!!
HEY!! I GOT YOUR BACK, PB!
WAAH!
MISSING
OOOOOH-WEE, SUMMER, YOU'RE A REEEAL FRIEND!
MISSIN

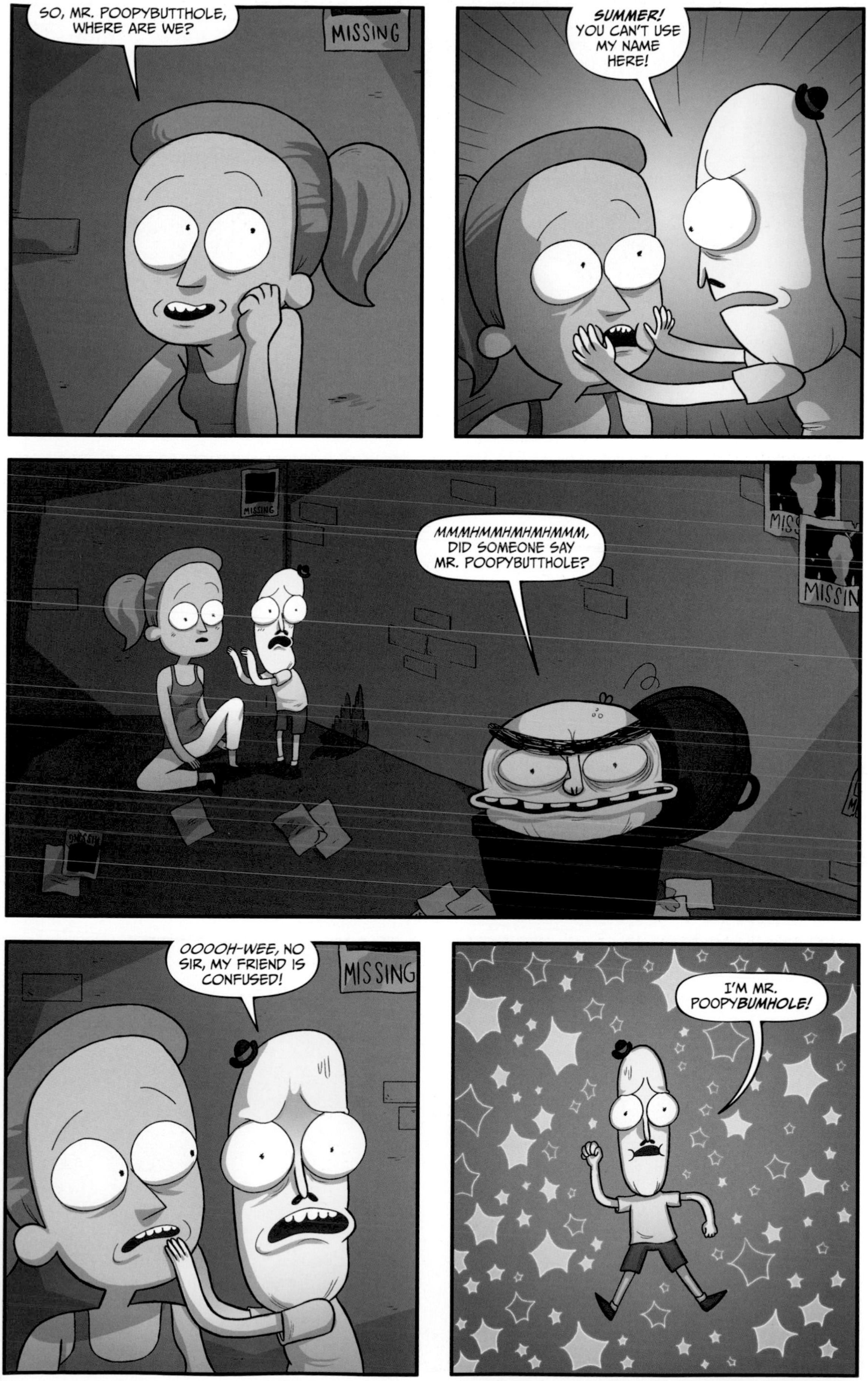
SO, MR. POOPYBUTTHOLE, WHERE ARE WE?
MISSING
SUMMER! YOU CAN'T USE MY NAME HERE!
MISSING
MMMHMMHMHMHMMM, DID SOMEONE SAY MR. POOPYBUTTHOLE?
MISSIN
OOOOH-WEE, NO SIR, MY FRIEND IS CONFUSED!
MISSING
I'M MR. POOPYBUMHOLE!

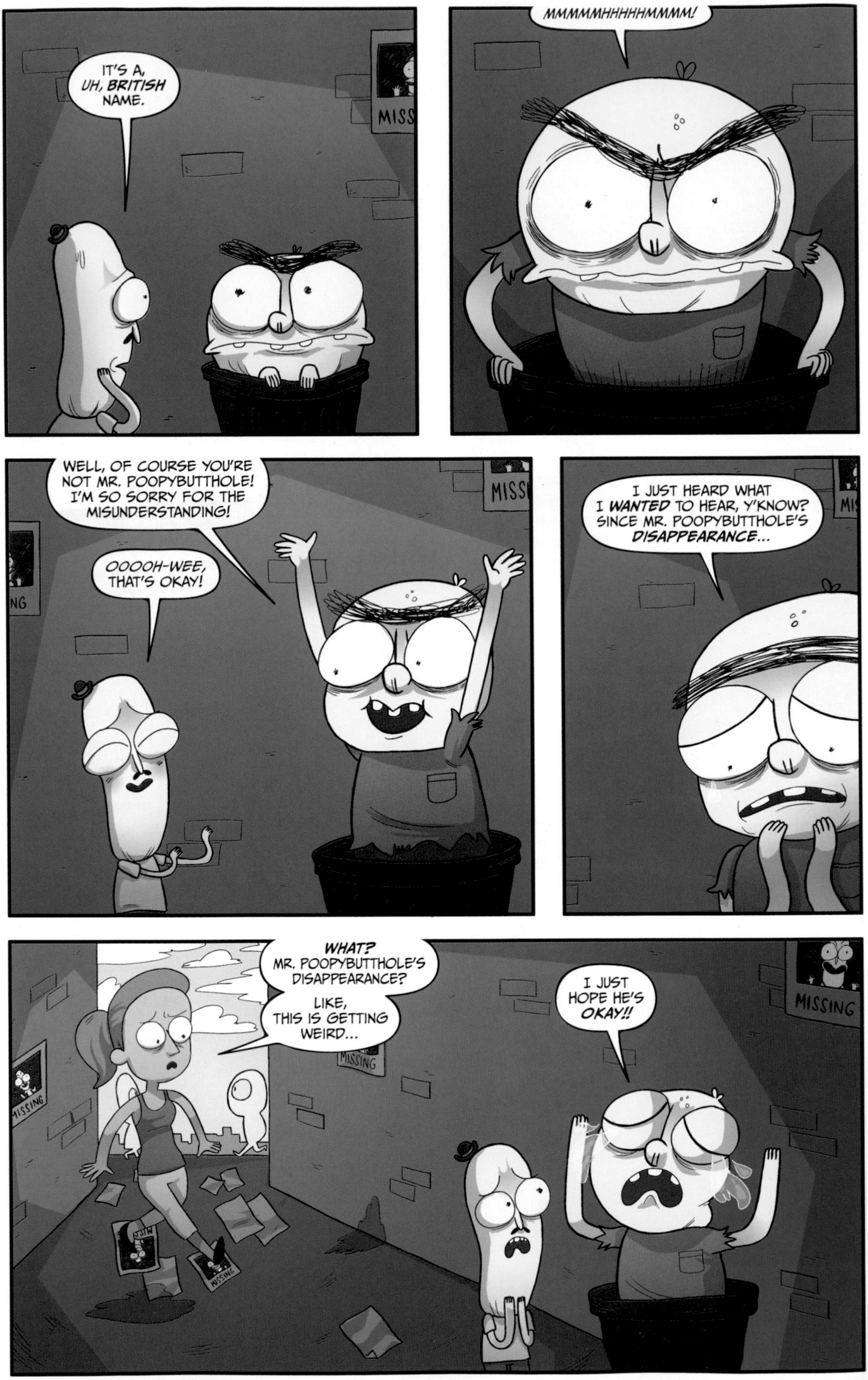
IT'S A, UH, BRITISH NAME.
MISS
MMMMMHHHHHMMMM!
MISS
WELL, OF COURSE YOU'RE NOT MR. POOPYBUTTHOLE! I'M SO SORRY FOR THE MISUNDERSTANDING!
OOOOH-WEE, THAT'S OKAY!
MISS
I JUST HEARD WHAT I WANTED TO HEAR, Y'KNOW? SINCE MR. POOPYBUTTHOLE'S DISAPPEARANCE...
WHAT? MR. POOPYBUTTHOLE'S DISAPPEARANCE?
LIKE, THIS IS GETTING WEIRD...
MISSING
I JUST HOPE HE'S OKAY!!
MISSING
MISSING
MISSING

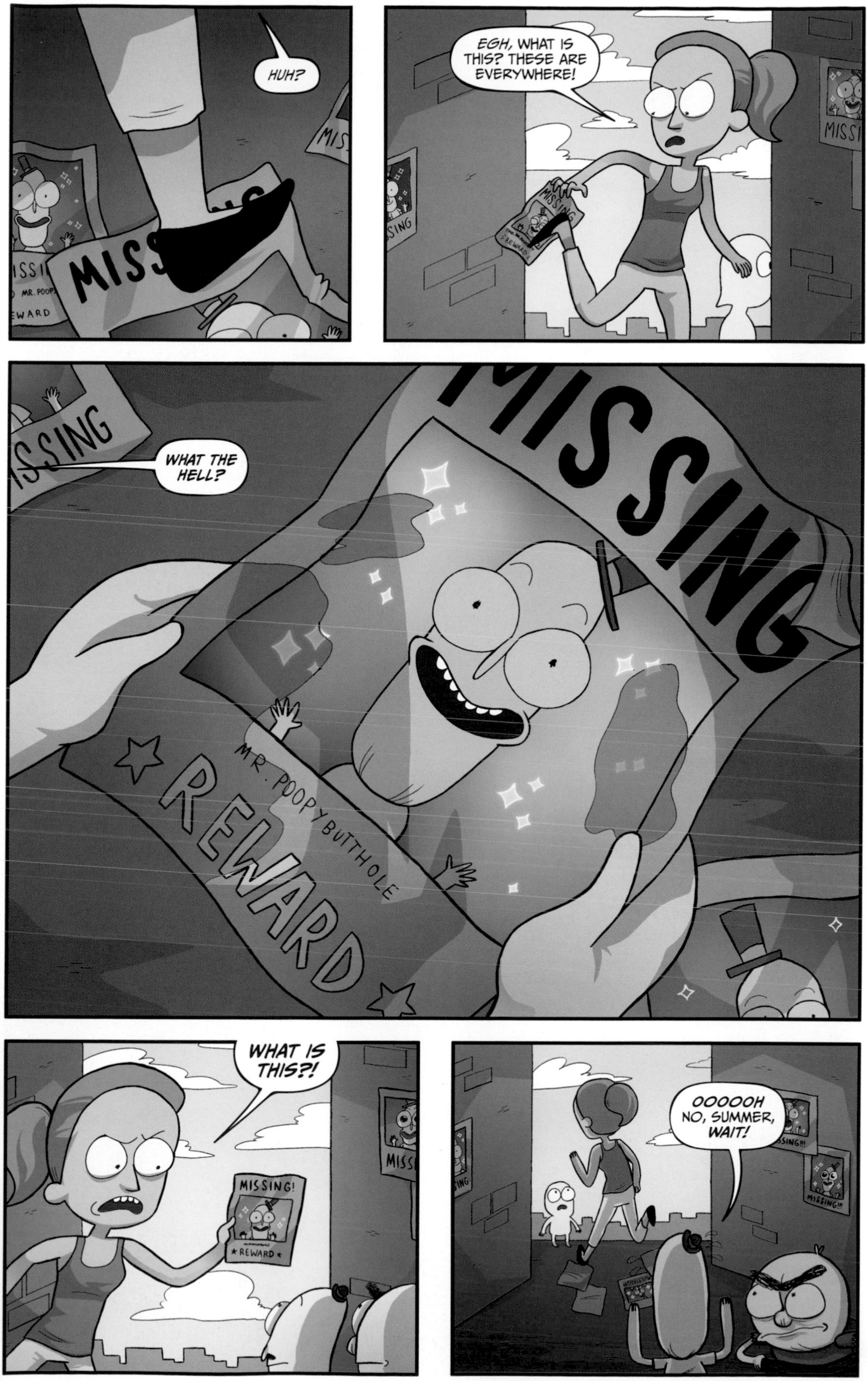
HUH?
MISS
MISSING
MR. POOPY
REWARD
EGH, WHAT IS THIS? THESE ARE EVERYWHERE!
MISSING
WHAT THE HELL?
MISSING
MR. POOPYBUTTHOLE
REWARD
WHAT IS THIS?!
MISSING!
REWARD
OOOOOH NO, SUMMER, WAIT!

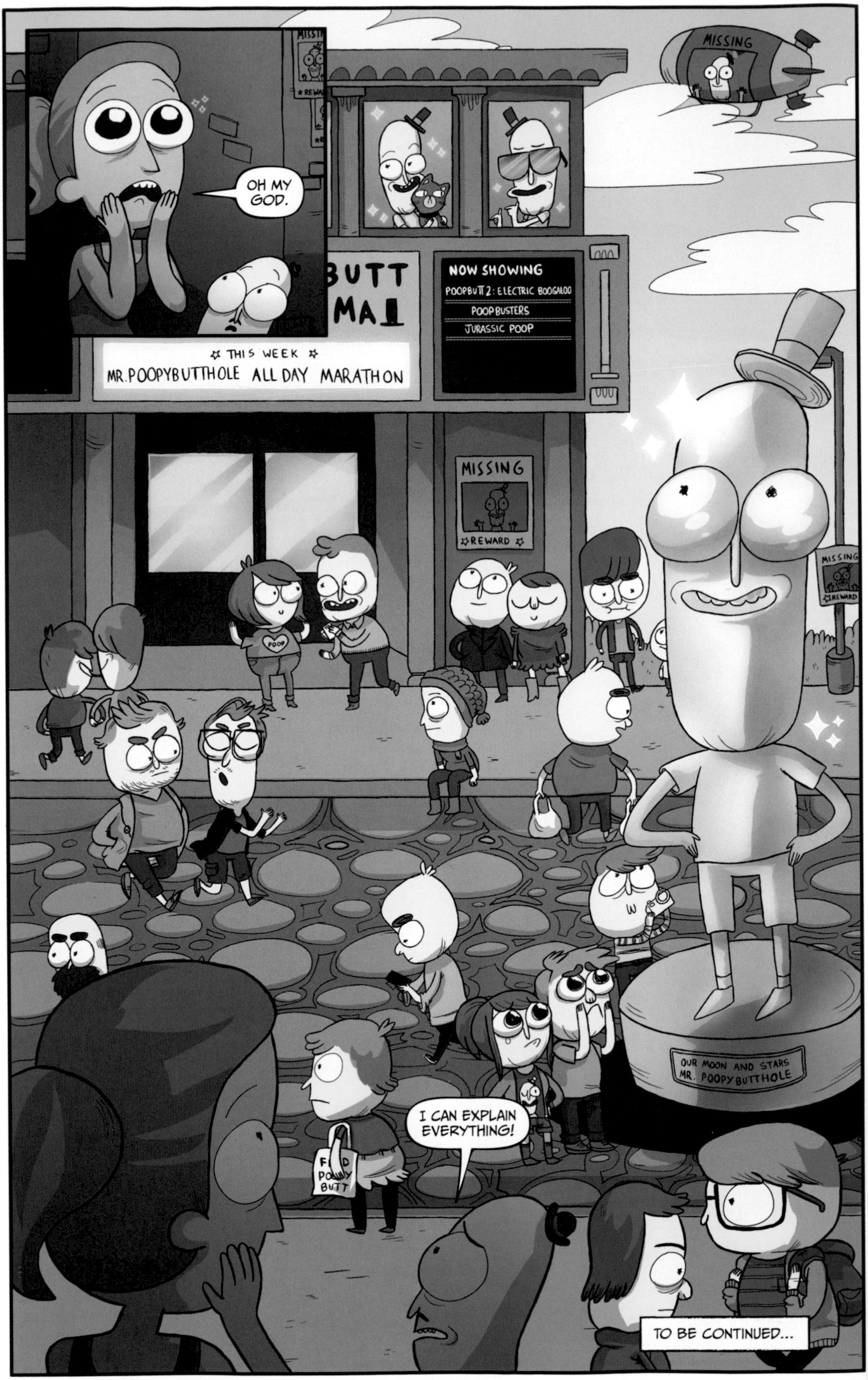

OH MY GOD.
NOW SHOWING
POOPBUTT 2: ELECTRIC BOOGALOO
POOPBUSTERS
JURASSIC POOP
THIS WEEK
MR. POOPYBUTTHOLE ALL DAY MARATHON
MISSING
REWARD
OUR MOON AND STARS MR. POOPYBUTTHOLE
I CAN EXPLAIN EVERYTHING!
TO BE CONTINUED...

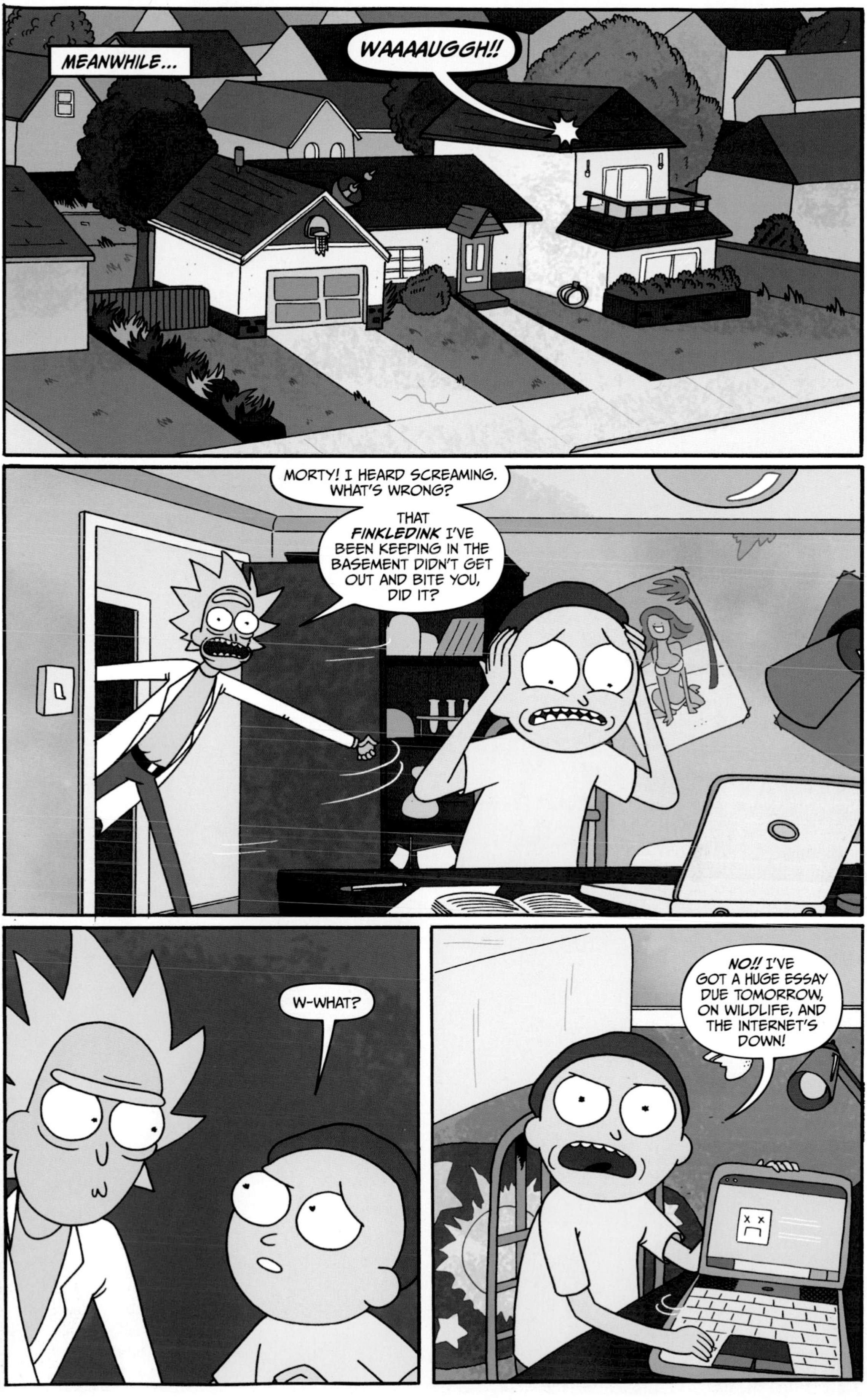
MEANWHILE...
WAAAAUGGH!!
MORTY! I HEARD SCREAMING. WHAT'S WRONG?
THAT FINKLEDINK I'VE BEEN KEEPING IN THE BASEMENT DIDN'T GET OUT AND BITE YOU, DID IT?
W-WHAT?
NO!! I'VE GOT A HUGE ESSAY DUE TOMORROW, ON WILDLIFE, AND THE INTERNET'S DOWN!

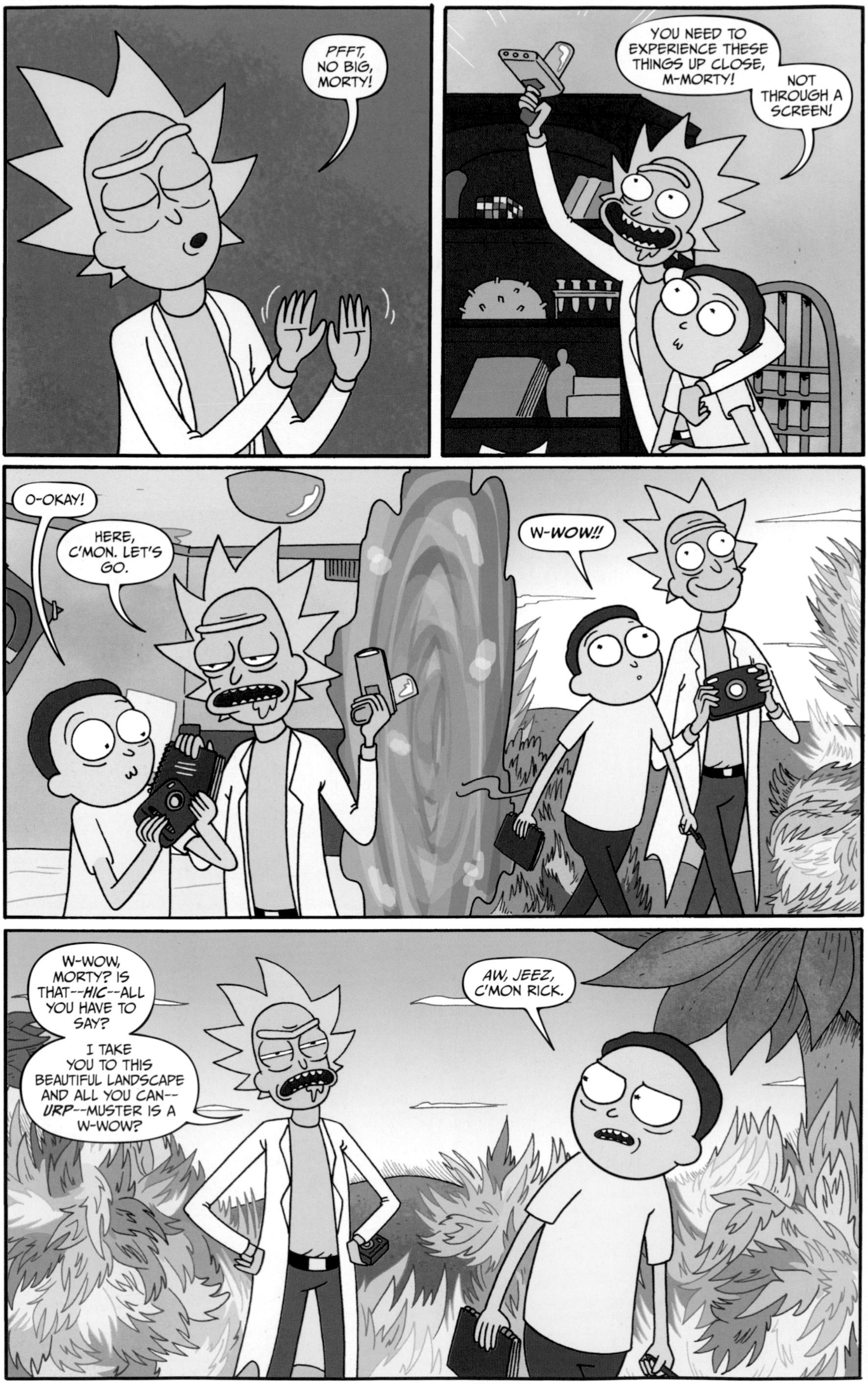
PFFT, NO BIG, MORTY!
YOU NEED TO EXPERIENCE THESE THINGS UP CLOSE, M-MORTY!
NOT THROUGH A SCREEN!
O-OKAY!
HERE, C'MON. LET'S GO.
W-WOW!!
W-WOW, MORTY? IS THAT--HIC--ALL YOU HAVE TO SAY?
I TAKE YOU TO THIS BEAUTIFUL LANDSCAPE AND ALL YOU CAN--URP--MUSTER IS A W-WOW?
AW, JEEZ, C'MON RICK.

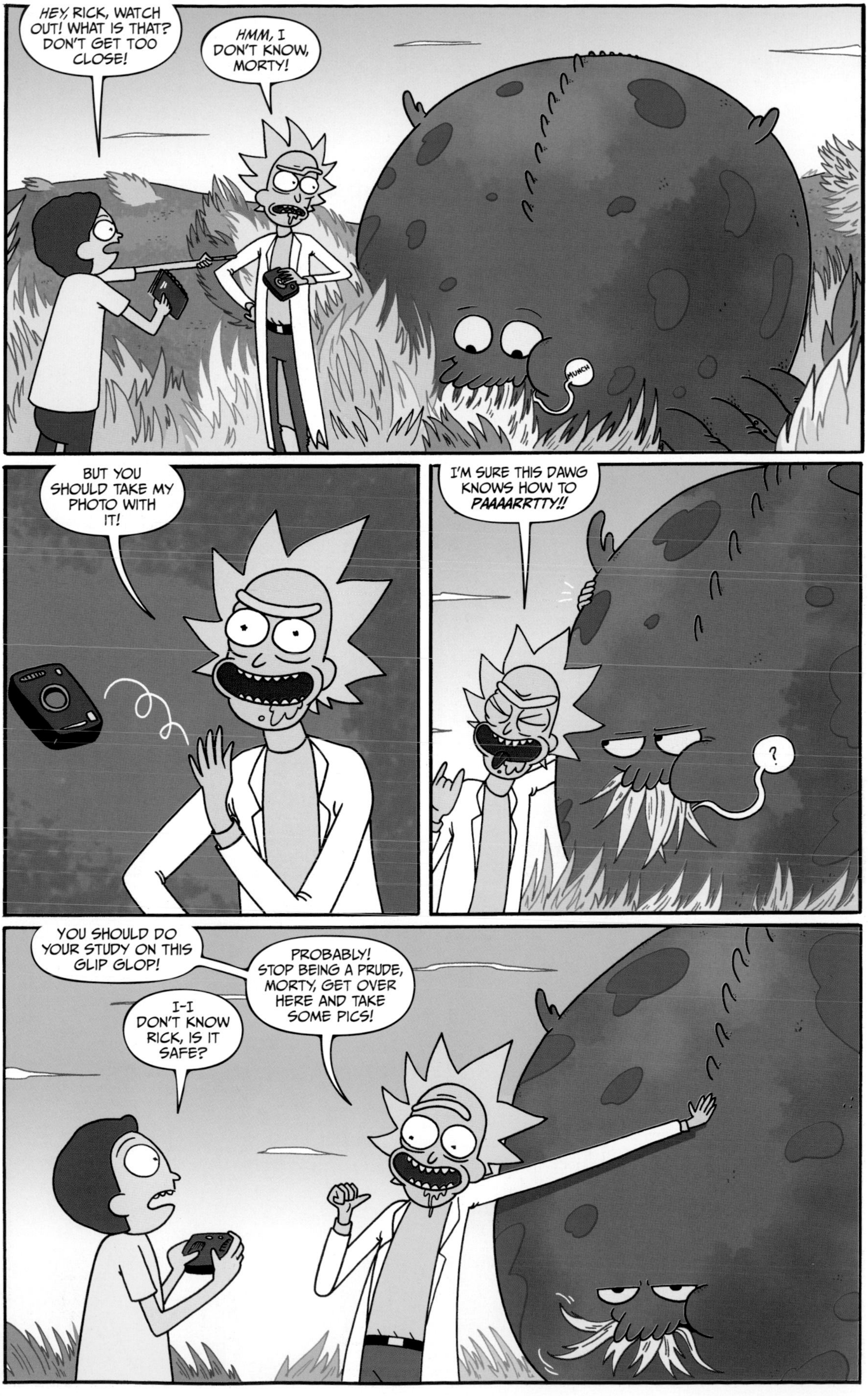
HEY, RICK, WATCH OUT! WHAT IS THAT? DON'T GET TOO CLOSE!
HMM, I DON'T KNOW, MORTY!
MUNCH
BUT YOU SHOULD TAKE MY PHOTO WITH IT!
I'M SURE THIS DAWG KNOWS HOW TO PAAAARRTTY!!
?
YOU SHOULD DO YOUR STUDY ON THIS GLIP GLOP!
I-I DON'T KNOW RICK, IS IT SAFE?
PROBABLY! STOP BEING A PRUDE, MORTY, GET OVER HERE AND TAKE SOME PICS!

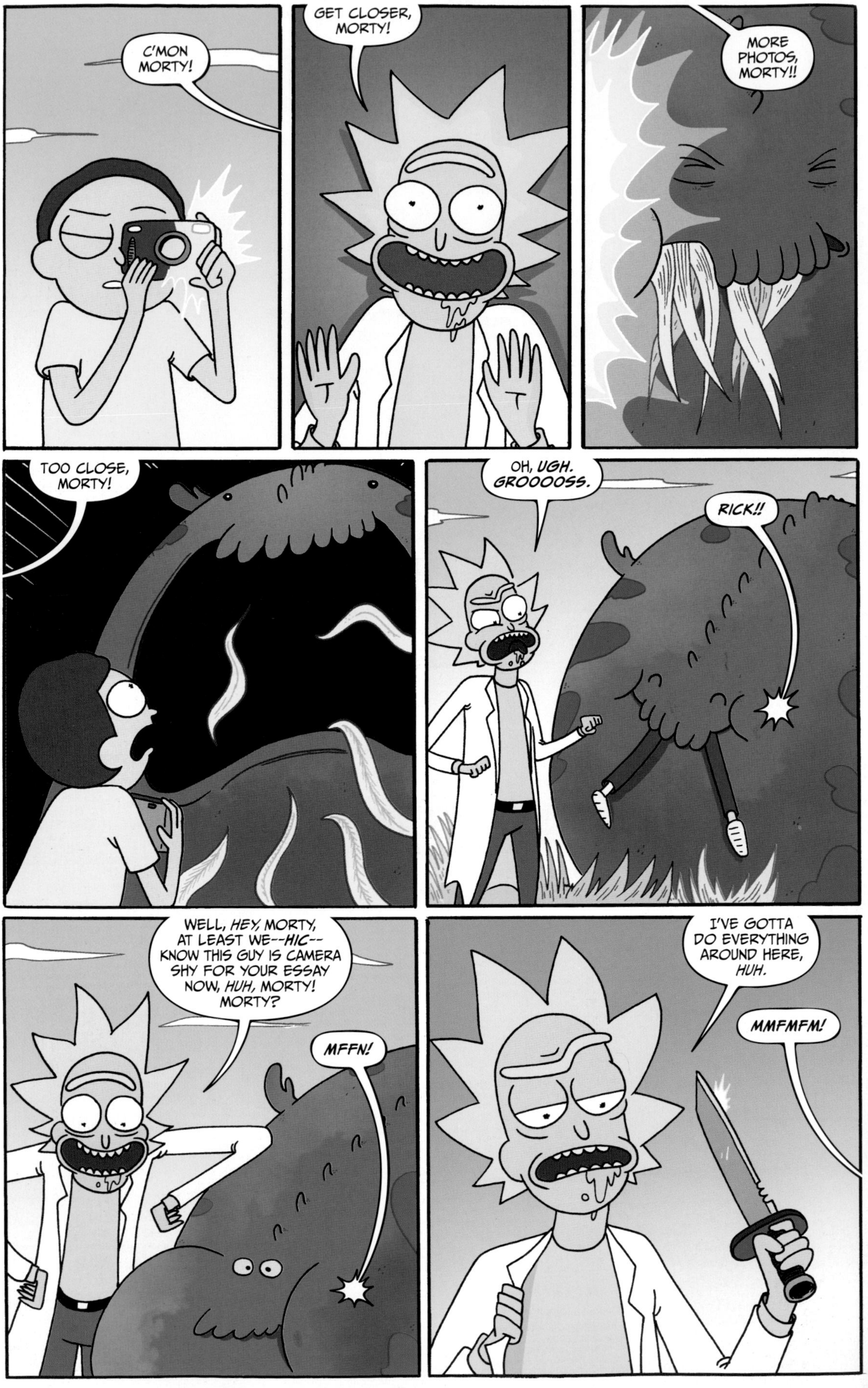
C'MON MORTY!
GET CLOSER, MORTY!
MORE PHOTOS, MORTY!!
TOO CLOSE, MORTY!
OH, UGH. GROOOOSS.
RICK!!
WELL, HEY, MORTY, AT LEAST WE--HIC--KNOW THIS GUY IS CAMERA SHY FOR YOUR ESSAY NOW, HUH, MORTY! MORTY?
MFFN!
I'VE GOTTA DO EVERYTHING AROUND HERE, HUH.
MMFMFM!

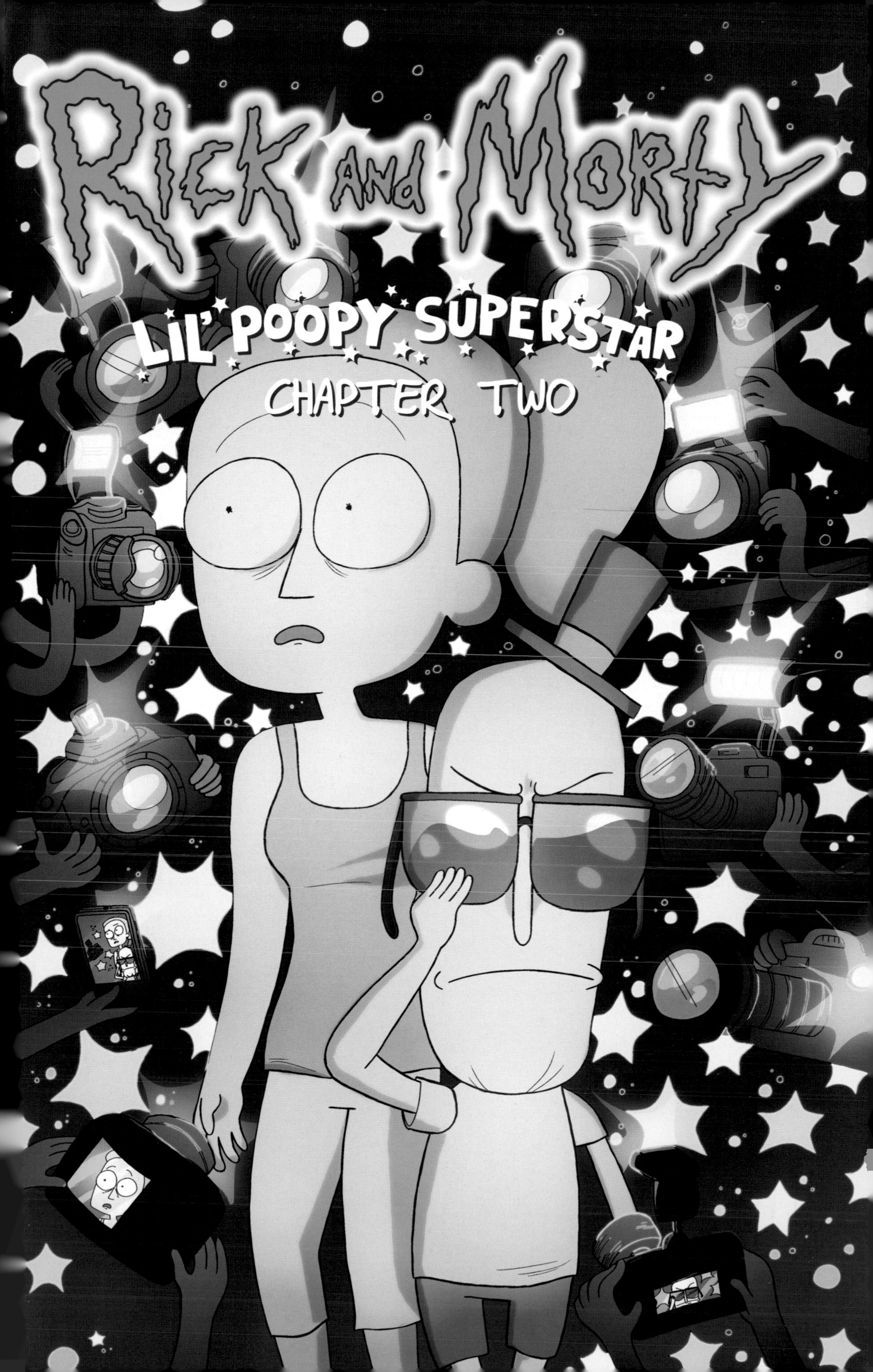
Rick and Morty
LIL' POOPY SUPERSTAR
CHAPTER TWO

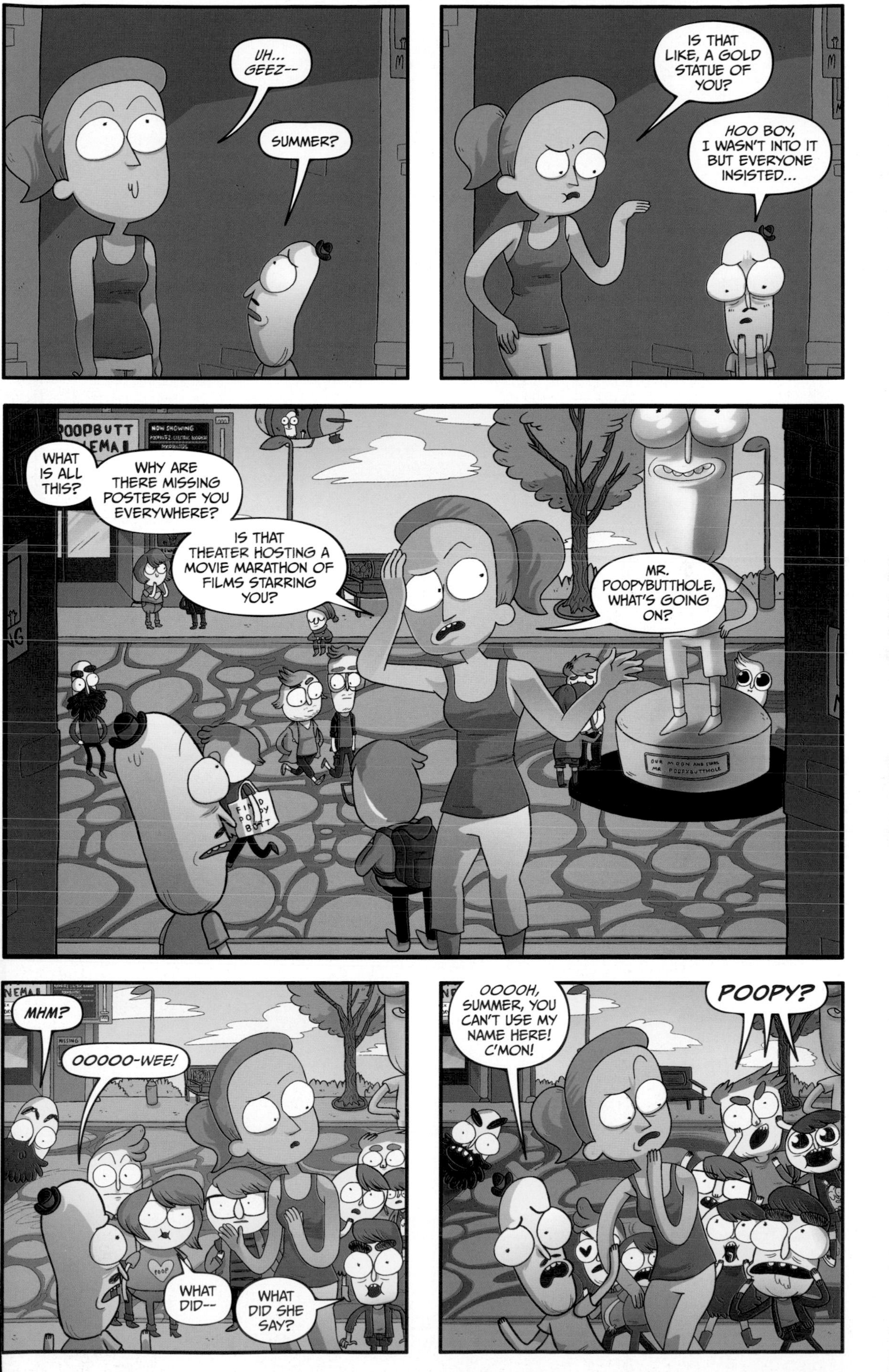

UH... GEEZ--
SUMMER?
IS THAT LIKE, A GOLD STATUE OF YOU?
HOO BOY, I WASN'T INTO IT BUT EVERYONE INSISTED...
NOW SHOWING
WHAT IS ALL THIS?
WHY ARE THERE MISSING POSTERS OF YOU EVERYWHERE?
IS THAT THEATER HOSTING A MOVIE MARATHON OF FILMS STARRING YOU?
MR. POOPYBUTTHOLE, WHAT'S GOING ON?
FIND POOPY BUTT
OUR MOON AND STARS MR. POOPYBUTTHOLE
MHM?
OOOOO-WEE!
MISSING
POOP
WHAT DID--
WHAT DID SHE SAY?
OOOOH, SUMMER, YOU CAN'T USE MY NAME HERE! C'MON!
POOPY?

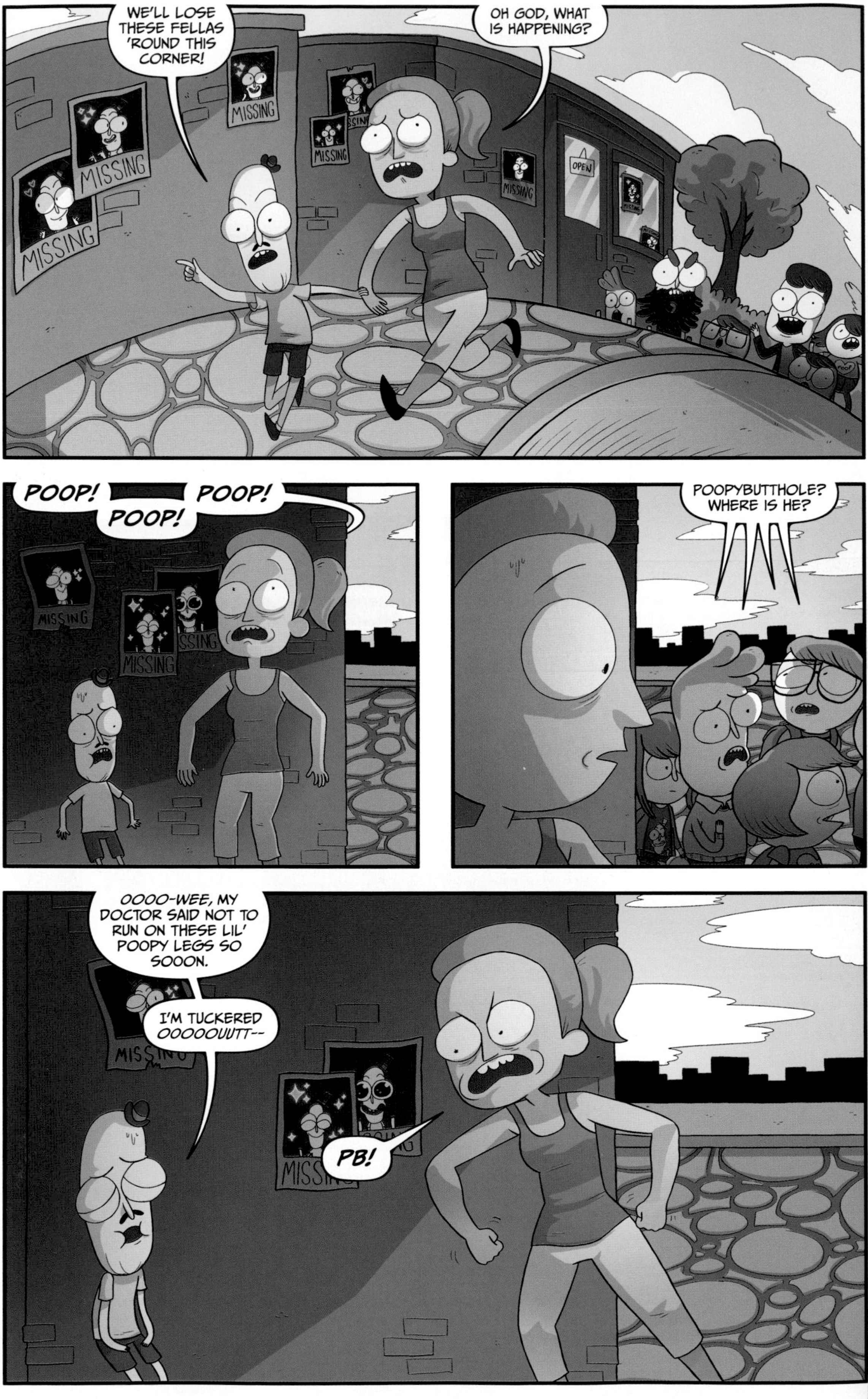
WE'LL LOSE THESE FELLAS 'ROUND THIS CORNER!
OH GOD, WHAT IS HAPPENING?
MISSING
MISSING
MISSING
MISSING
MISSING
OPEN
POOP!
POOP!
POOP!
MISSING
MISSING
POOPYBUTTHOLE? WHERE IS HE?
OOOO-WEE, MY DOCTOR SAID NOT TO RUN ON THESE LIL' POOPY LEGS SO SOOON.
I'M TUCKERED OOOOOUUTT--
PB!

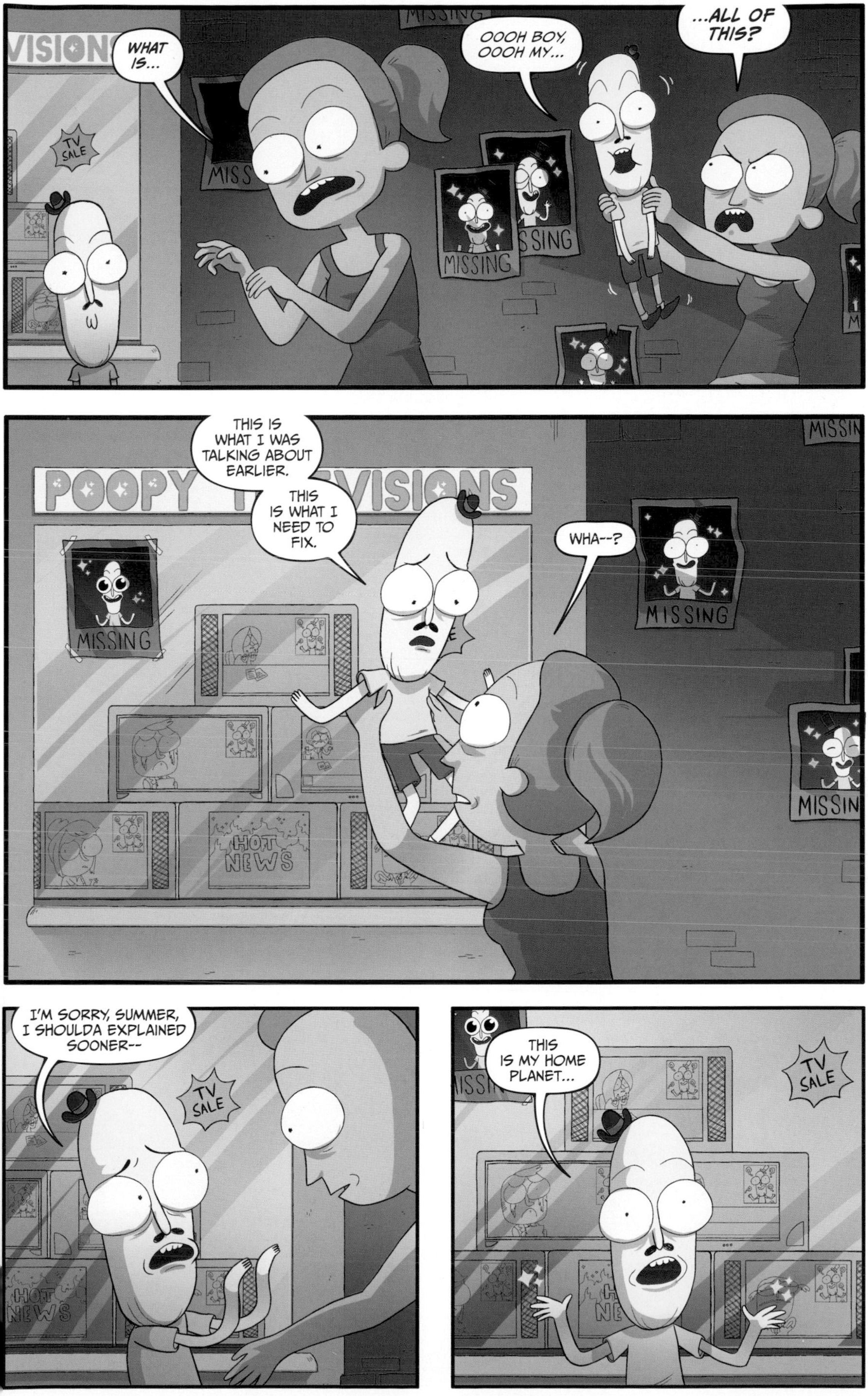
VISIONS
TV SALE
WHAT IS...
MISSING
OOOH BOY, OOOH MY...
MISSING
MISSING
...ALL OF THIS?
THIS IS WHAT I WAS TALKING ABOUT EARLIER.
THIS IS WHAT I NEED TO FIX.
POOPY VISIONS
MISSING
WHA--?
MISSING
HOT NEWS
MISSING
I'M SORRY, SUMMER, I SHOULDA EXPLAINED SOONER--
TV SALE
HOT NEWS
THIS IS MY HOME PLANET...
TV SALE

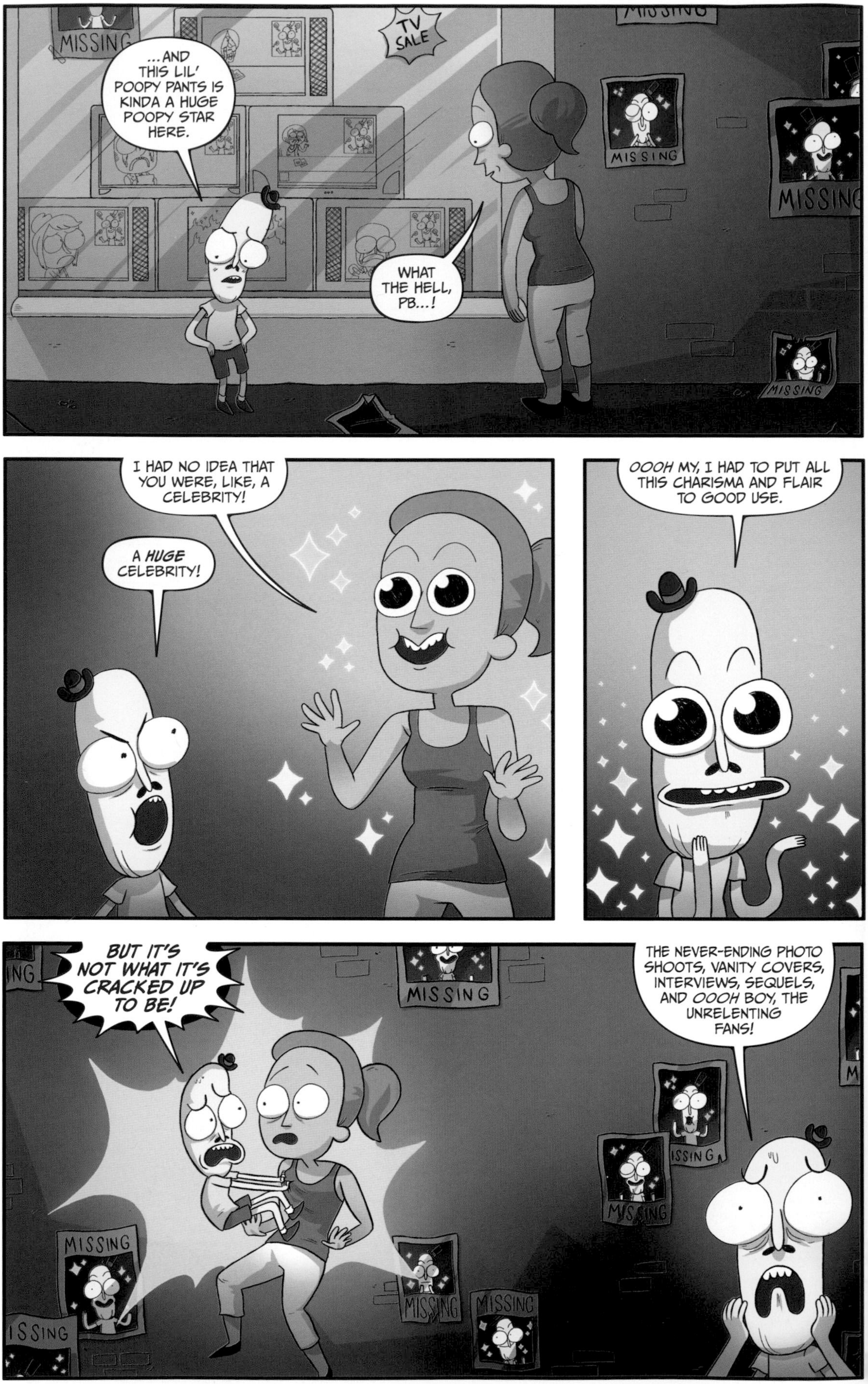
MISSING
...AND THIS LIL' POOPY PANTS IS KINDA A HUGE POOPY STAR HERE.
TV SALE
MISSING
MISSING
MISSING
WHAT THE HELL, PB...!
MISSING
I HAD NO IDEA THAT YOU WERE, LIKE, A CELEBRITY!
A *HUGE* CELEBRITY!
OOOH MY, I HAD TO PUT ALL THIS CHARISMA AND FLAIR TO GOOD USE.
MISSING
BUT IT'S NOT WHAT IT'S CRACKED UP TO BE!
THE NEVER-ENDING PHOTO SHOOTS, VANITY COVERS, INTERVIEWS, SEQUELS, AND *OOOH* BOY, THE UNRELENTING FANS!
MISSING
MISSING
MISSING
MISSING
MISSING

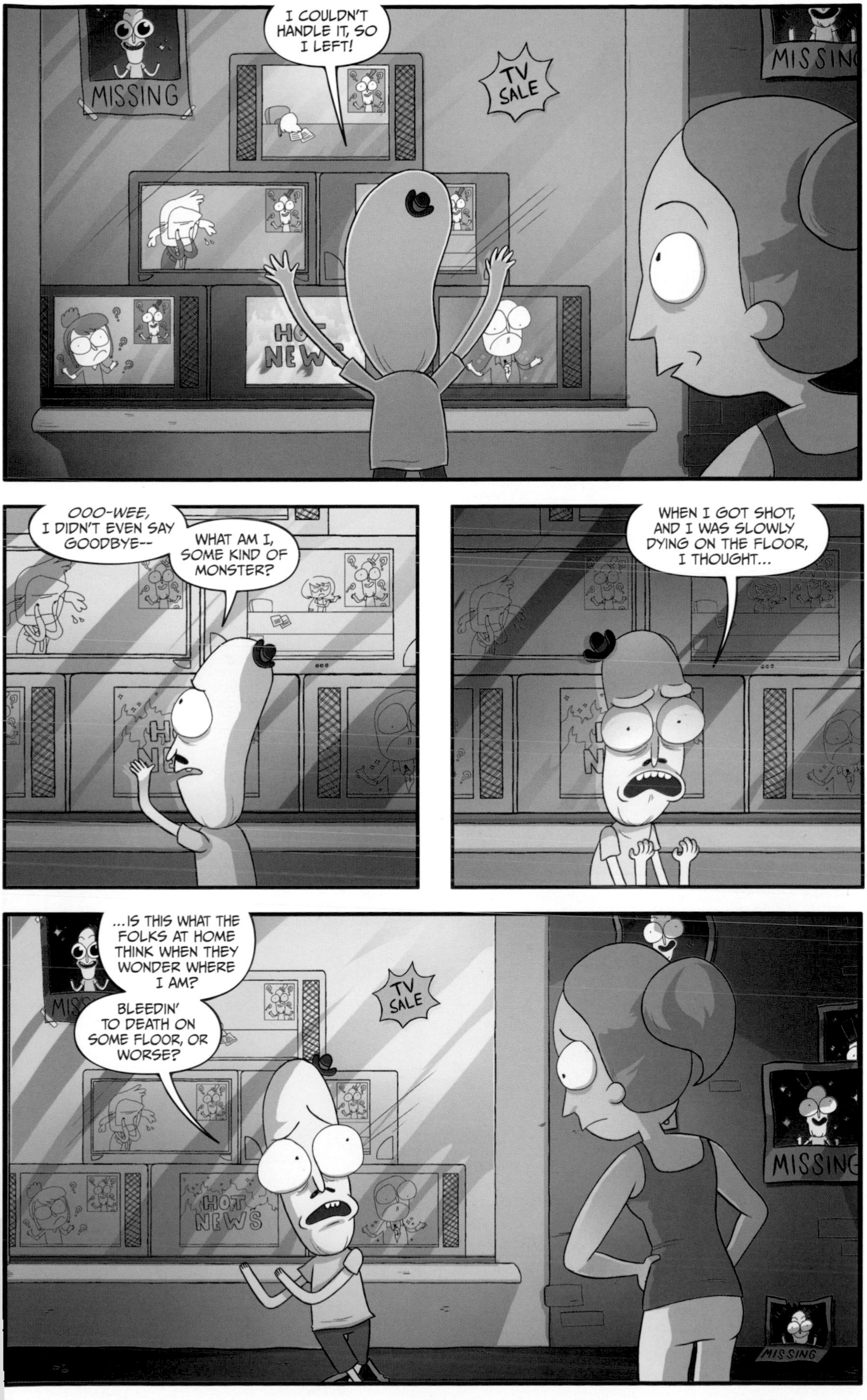
MISSING
I COULDN'T HANDLE IT, SO I LEFT!
TV SALE
MISSING
HOT NEWS
OOO-WEE, I DIDN'T EVEN SAY GOODBYE--
WHAT AM I, SOME KIND OF MONSTER?
WHEN I GOT SHOT, AND I WAS SLOWLY DYING ON THE FLOOR, I THOUGHT...
...IS THIS WHAT THE FOLKS AT HOME THINK WHEN THEY WONDER WHERE I AM?
BLEEDIN' TO DEATH ON SOME FLOOR, OR WORSE?
TV SALE
HOT NEWS
MISSING
MISSING

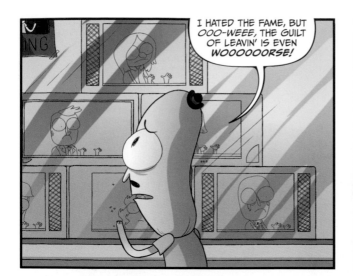

I HATED THE FAME, BUT *OOO-WEEE,* THE GUILT OF LEAVIN' IS EVEN *WOOOOOORSE!*

I'M NOT COMING BACK, BUT THEY NEED TO KNOW I'M ALIVE AND WELL.

WELL OKAY!

LET'S GO TELL THIS PLANET THAT YOU'RE ALRIGHT, PB!

YOU'RE GONNA HELP THIS LIL' POOPY PANTS?

MISSING

TV SALE

MISSING

MISSING

MISSING

OF COURSE, WE'RE A TEAM! AND TEAMS LET PLANETS KNOW THEIR FAVORITE CELEBS ARE NOT DEAD.

team high five

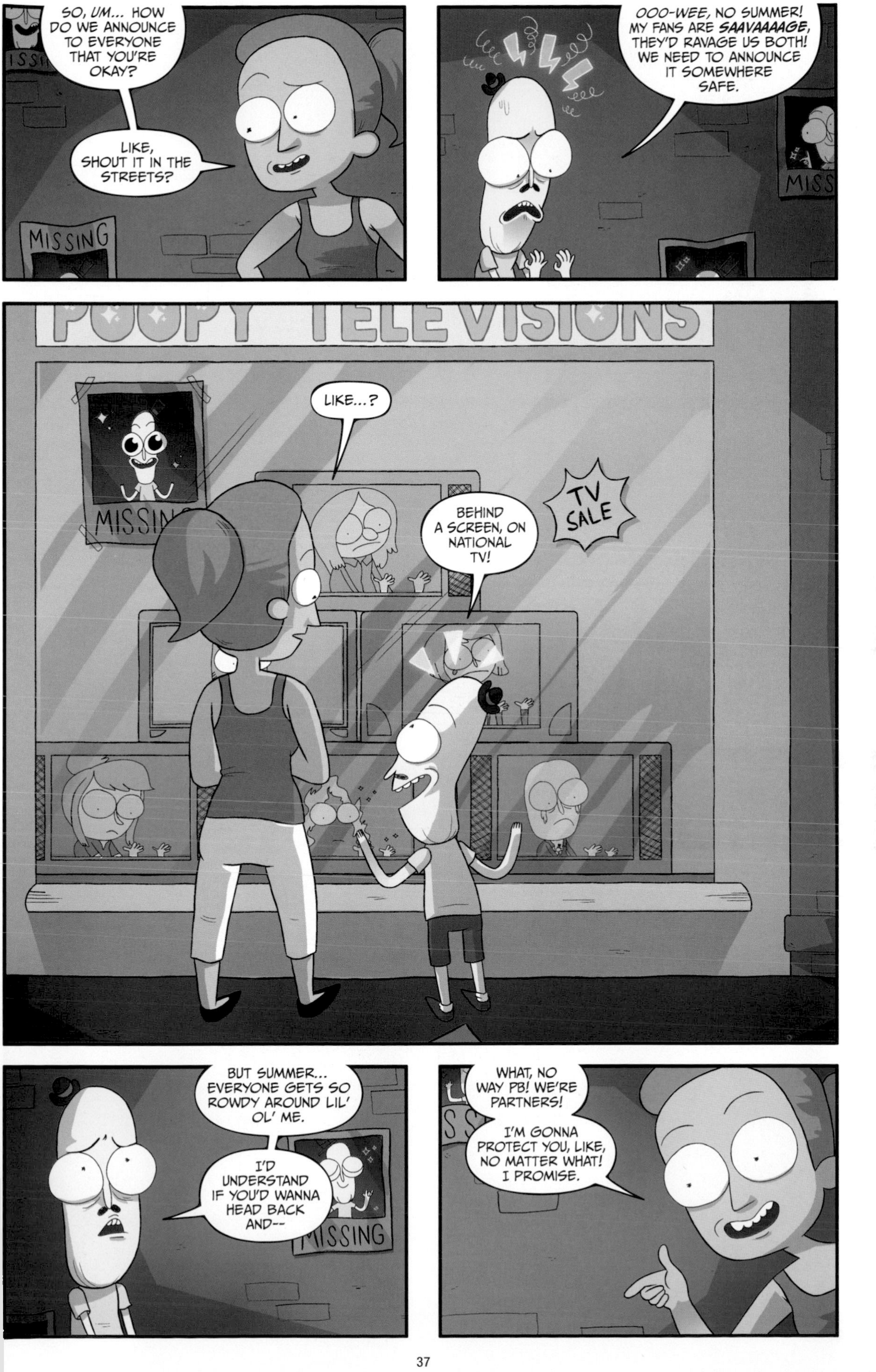
SO, UM... HOW DO WE ANNOUNCE TO EVERYONE THAT YOU'RE OKAY?
LIKE, SHOUT IT IN THE STREETS?
MISSING
OOO-WEE, NO SUMMER! MY FANS ARE SAAVAAAAGE, THEY'D RAVAGE US BOTH! WE NEED TO ANNOUNCE IT SOMEWHERE SAFE.
POOPY TELEVISIONS
LIKE...?
MISSING
BEHIND A SCREEN, ON NATIONAL TV!
TV SALE
BUT SUMMER... EVERYONE GETS SO ROWDY AROUND LIL' OL' ME.
I'D UNDERSTAND IF YOU'D WANNA HEAD BACK AND--
MISSING
WHAT, NO WAY PB! WE'RE PARTNERS!
I'M GONNA PROTECT YOU, LIKE, NO MATTER WHAT! I PROMISE.

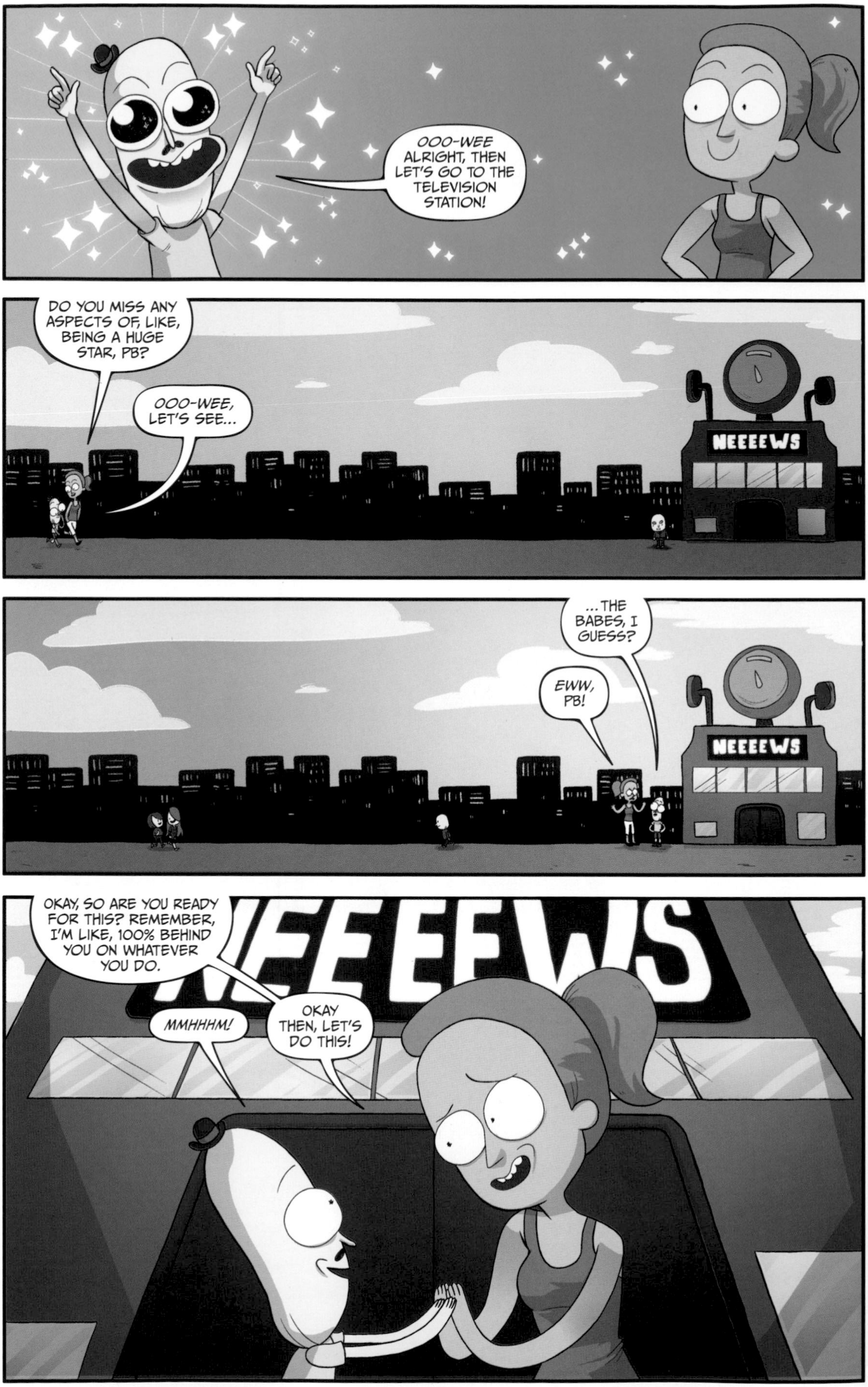
OOO-WEE ALRIGHT, THEN LET'S GO TO THE TELEVISION STATION!
DO YOU MISS ANY ASPECTS OF, LIKE, BEING A HUGE STAR, PB?
OOO-WEE, LET'S SEE...
NEEEEWS
...THE BABES, I GUESS?
EWW, PB!
NEEEEWS
OKAY, SO ARE YOU READY FOR THIS? REMEMBER, I'M LIKE, 100% BEHIND YOU ON WHATEVER YOU DO.
MMHHHM!
OKAY THEN, LET'S DO THIS!

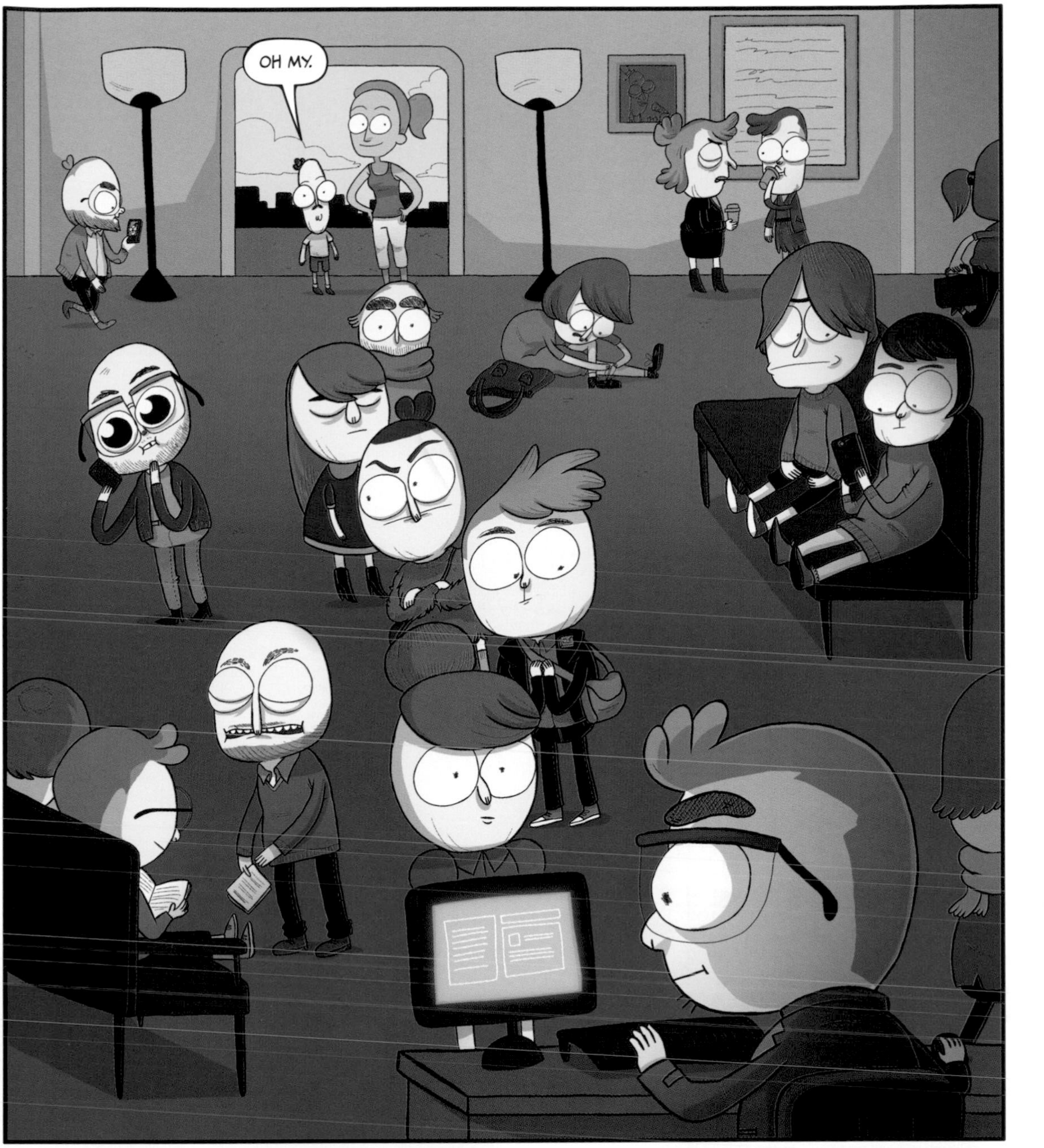
OH MY.

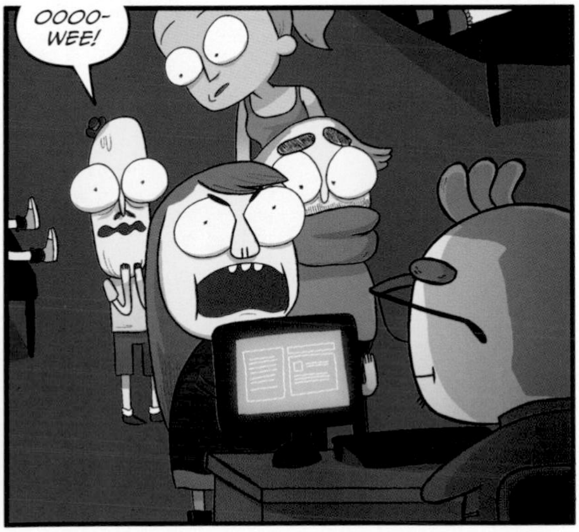
OOOO-
WEE!

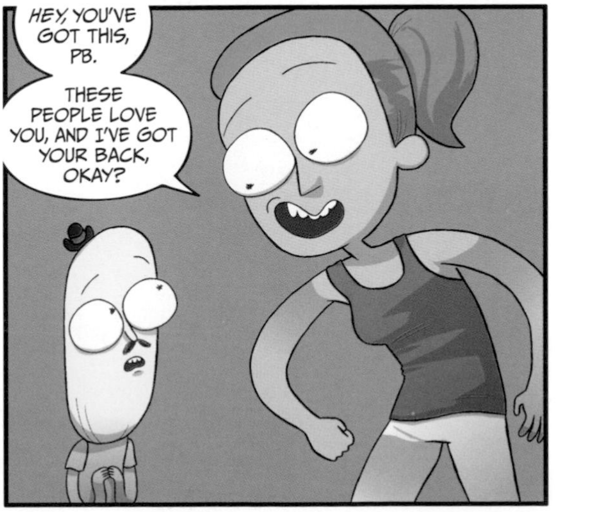
HEY, YOU'VE GOT THIS, PB.
THESE PEOPLE LOVE YOU, AND I'VE GOT YOUR BACK, OKAY?

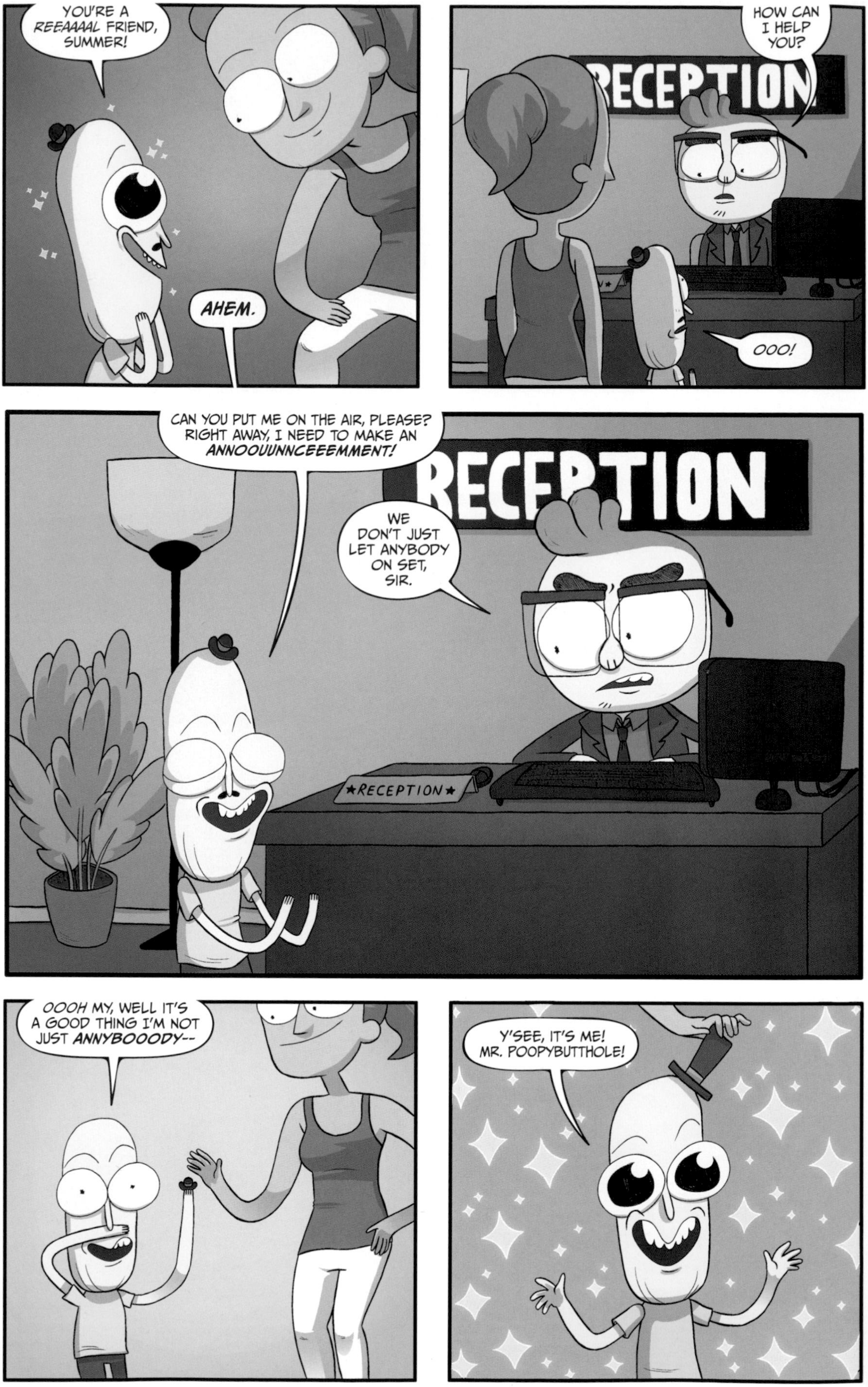
YOU'RE A REEAAAAL FRIEND, SUMMER!
AHEM.
HOW CAN I HELP YOU?
RECEPTION
OOO!
CAN YOU PUT ME ON THE AIR, PLEASE? RIGHT AWAY, I NEED TO MAKE AN ANNOOUUNNCEEEMMENT!
RECEPTION
WE DON'T JUST LET ANYBODY ON SET, SIR.
★RECEPTION★
OOOH MY, WELL IT'S A GOOD THING I'M NOT JUST ANNYBOOODY--
Y'SEE, IT'S ME! MR. POOPYBUTTHOLE!

AND AHH NEED TO TELL EVERYBODY THAT I'M ALIVE!

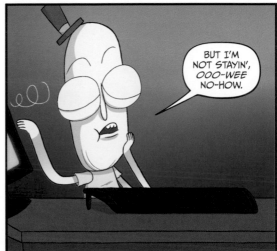

BUT I'M NOT STAYIN', OOO-WEE NO-HOW.

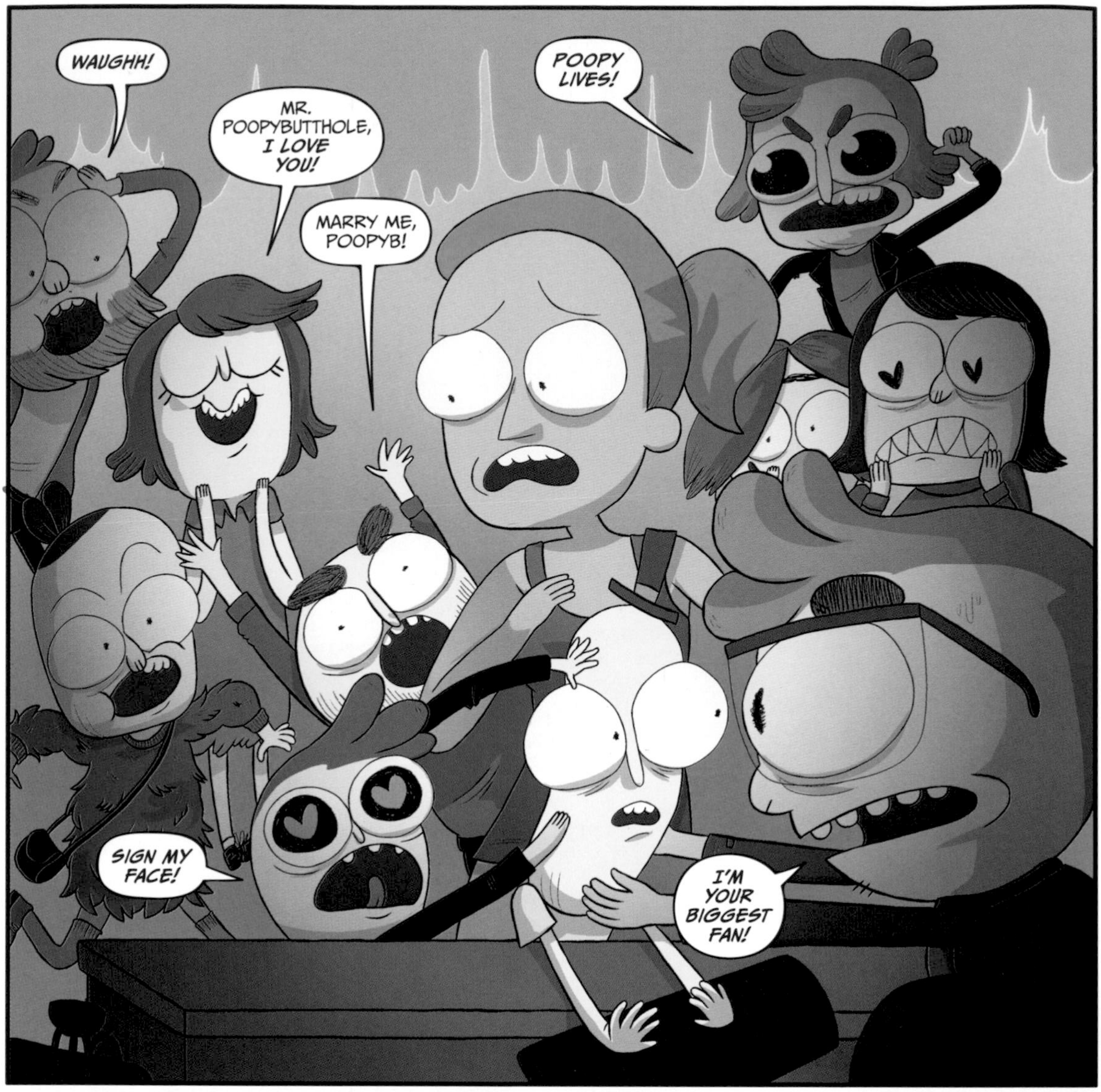
WAUGHH!
MR. POOPYBUTTHOLE, I LOVE YOU!
MARRY ME, POOPYB!
POOPY LIVES!
SIGN MY FACE!
I'M YOUR BIGGEST FAN!

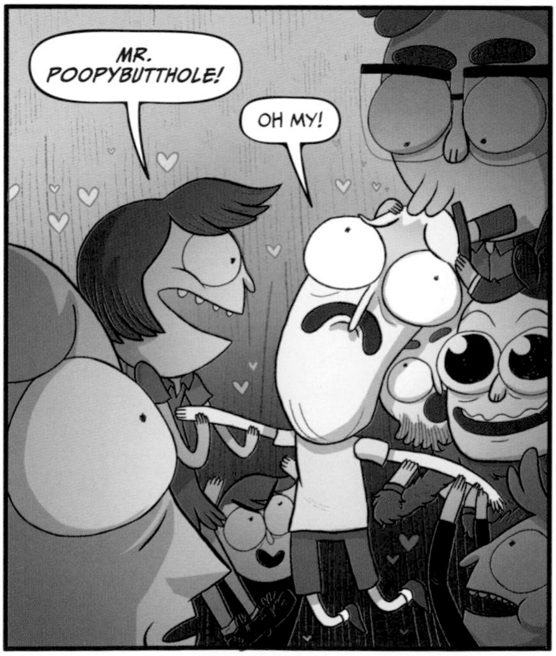
MR. POOPYBUTTHOLE!
OH MY!

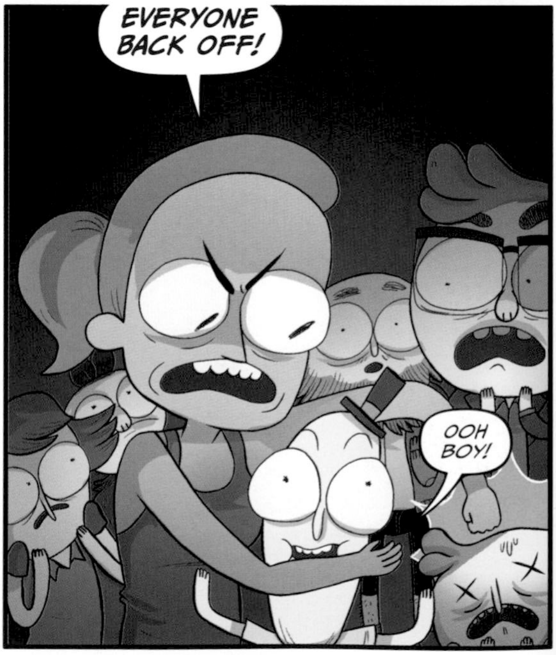
EVERYONE BACK OFF!
OOH BOY!

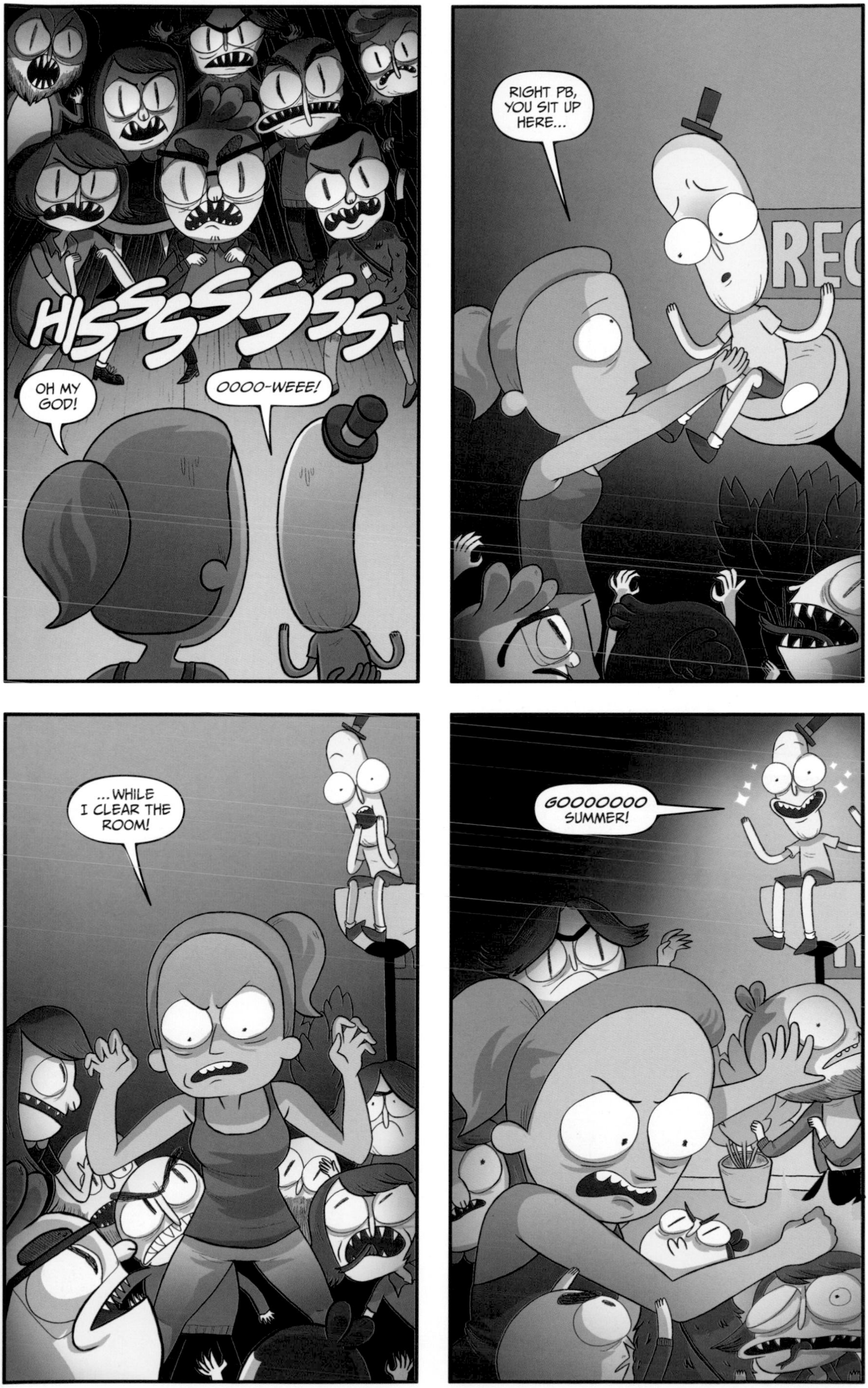
HISSSSSSS
OH MY GOD!
OOOO-WEEE!
RIGHT PB, YOU SIT UP HERE...
...WHILE I CLEAR THE ROOM!
GOOOOOOO SUMMER!

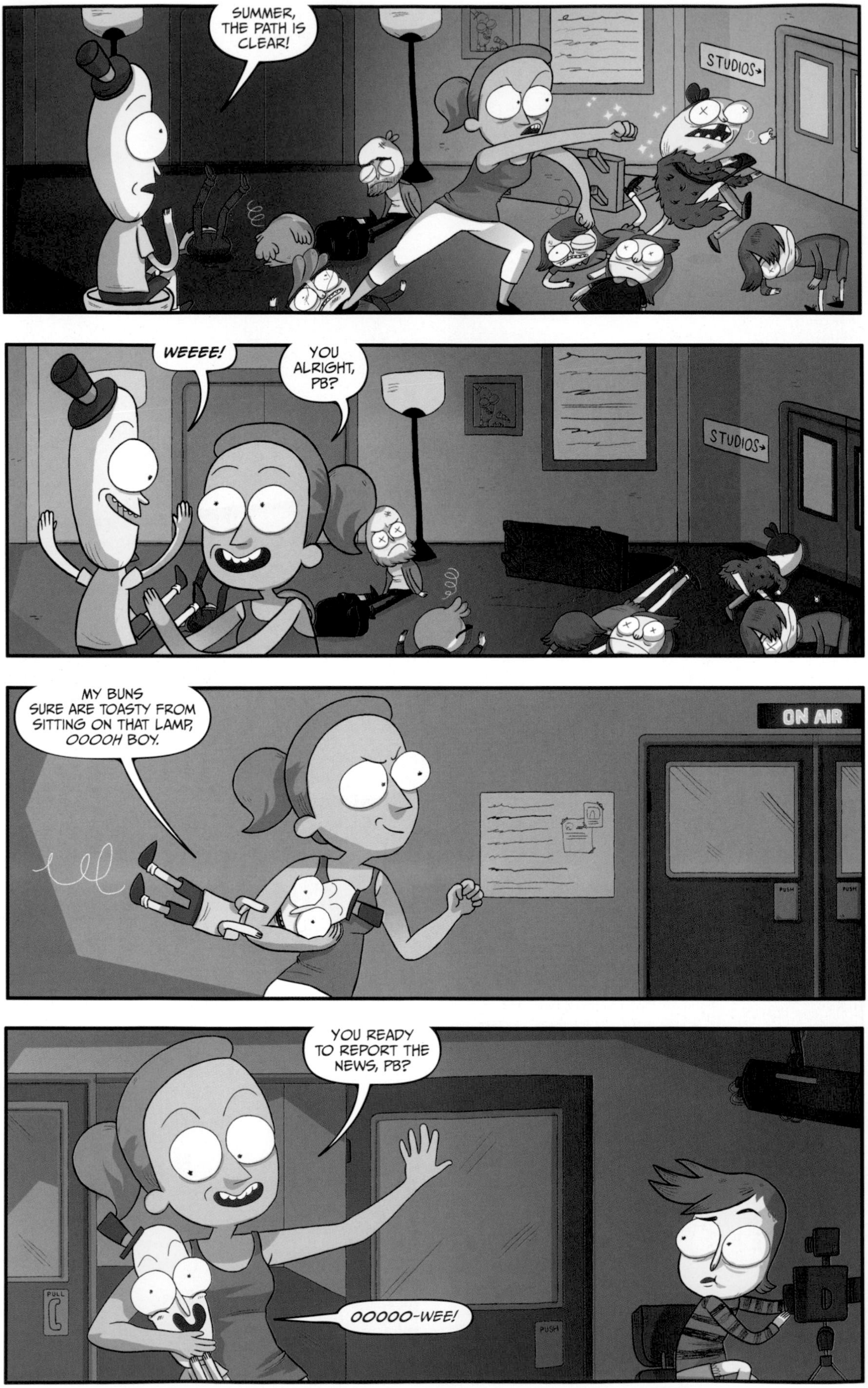
SUMMER, THE PATH IS CLEAR!
STUDIOS→
WEEEE!
YOU ALRIGHT, PB?
STUDIOS→
MY BUNS SURE ARE TOASTY FROM SITTING ON THAT LAMP, *OOOOH* BOY.
ON AIR
PUSH
PUSH
YOU READY TO REPORT THE NEWS, PB?
PULL
PUSH
OOOOO-WEE!

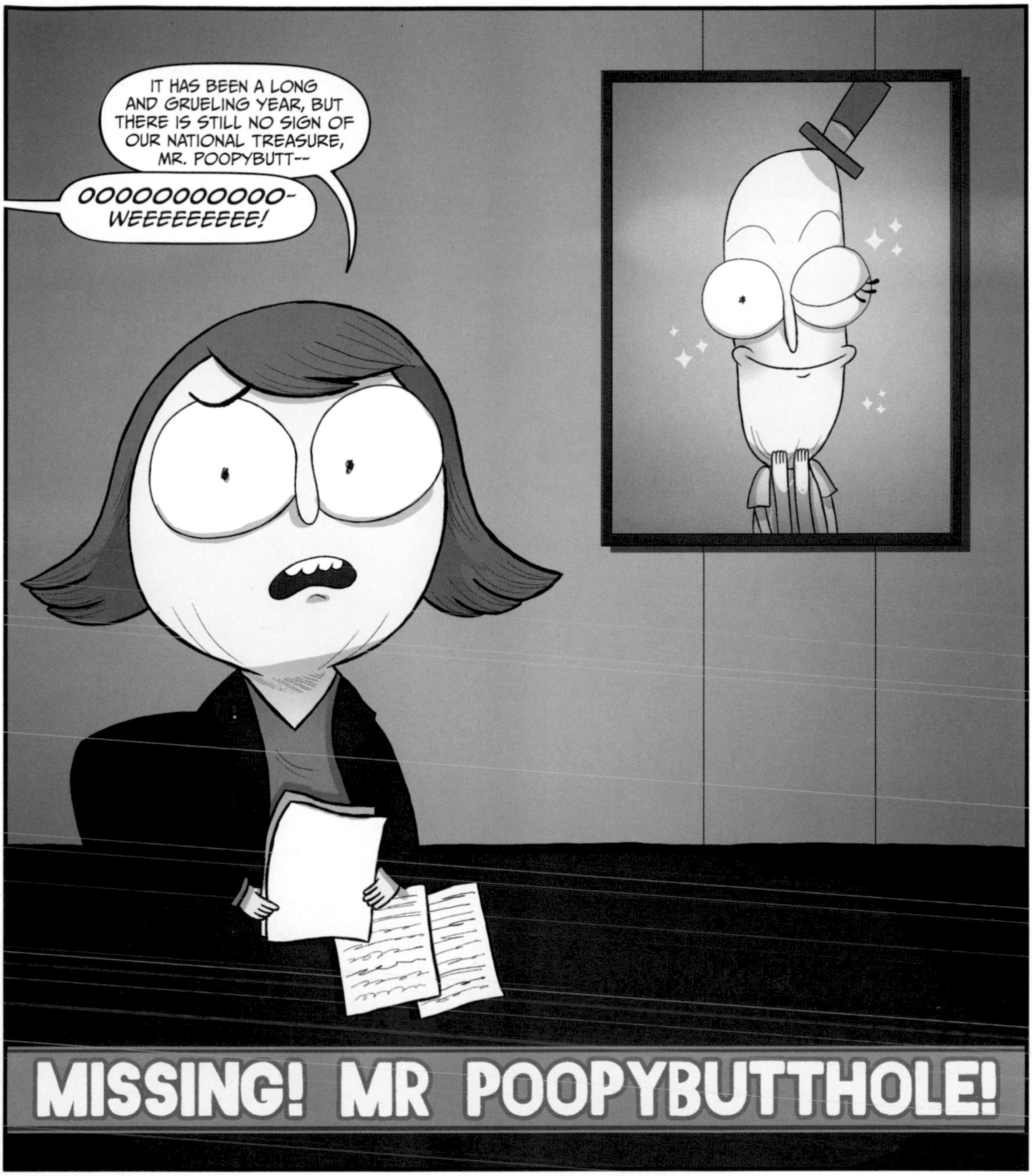
IT HAS BEEN A LONG AND GRUELING YEAR, BUT THERE IS STILL NO SIGN OF OUR NATIONAL TREASURE, MR. POOPYBUTT--
OOOOOOOOOOO-WEEEEEEEEE!
MISSING! MR POOPYBUTTHOLE!

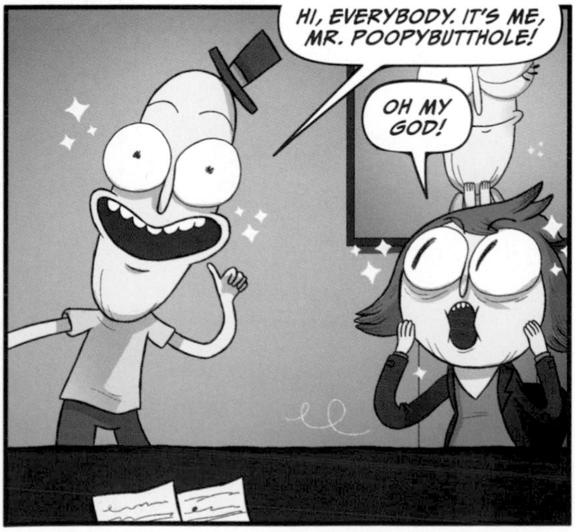
HI, EVERYBODY. IT'S ME, MR. POOPYBUTTHOLE!
OH MY GOD!

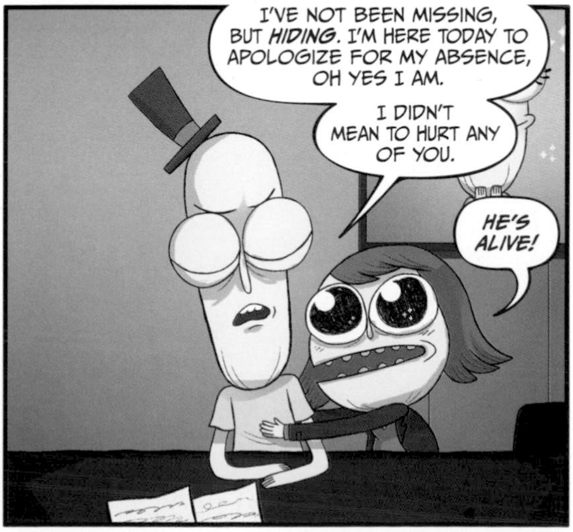
I'VE NOT BEEN MISSING, BUT HIDING. I'M HERE TODAY TO APOLOGIZE FOR MY ABSENCE, OH YES I AM.
I DIDN'T MEAN TO HURT ANY OF YOU.
HE'S ALIVE!

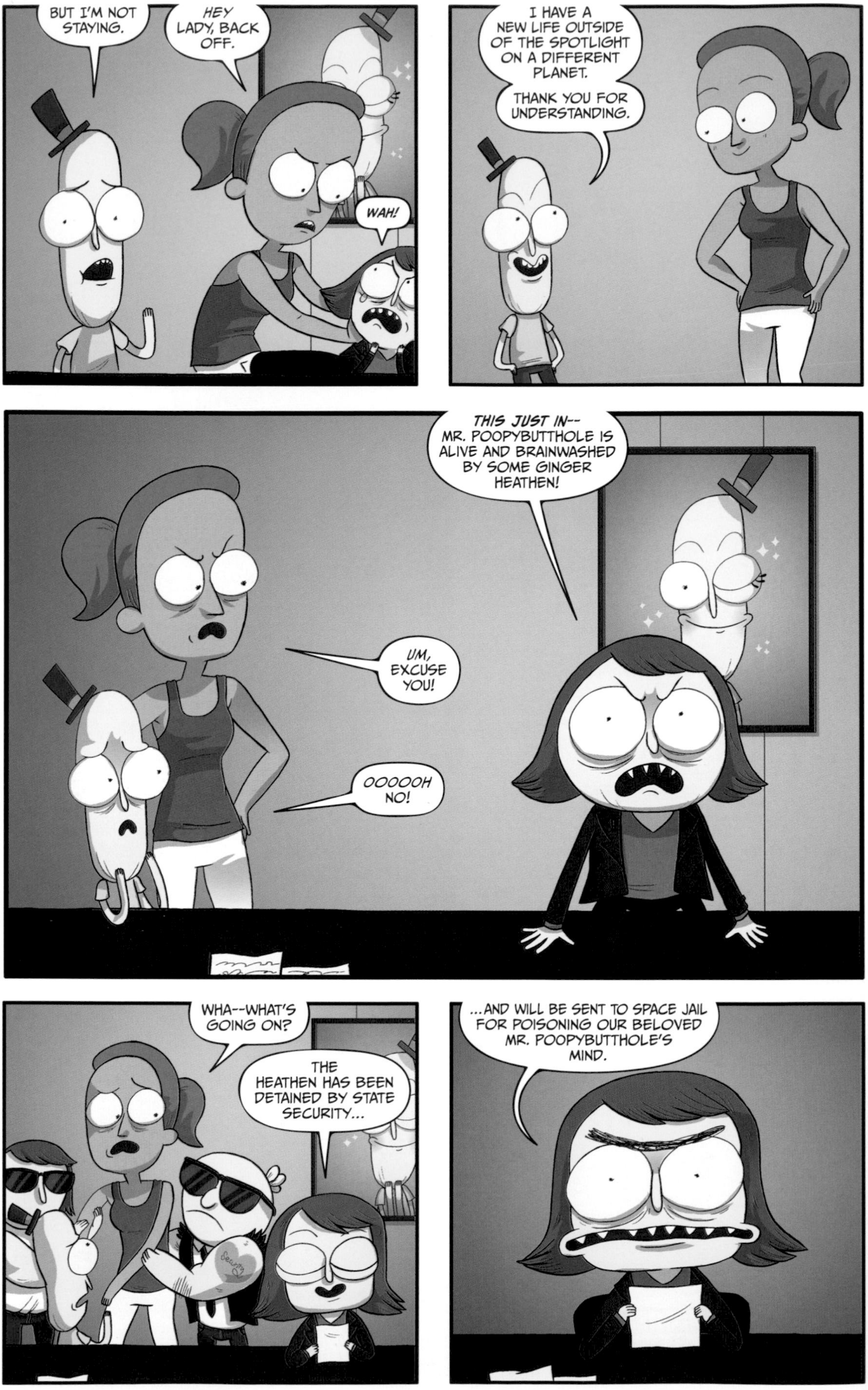
BUT I'M NOT STAYING.
HEY LADY, BACK OFF.
WAH!
I HAVE A NEW LIFE OUTSIDE OF THE SPOTLIGHT ON A DIFFERENT PLANET.
THANK YOU FOR UNDERSTANDING.
THIS JUST IN-- MR. POOPYBUTTHOLE IS ALIVE AND BRAINWASHED BY SOME GINGER HEATHEN!
UM, EXCUSE YOU!
OOOOOH NO!
WHA--WHAT'S GOING ON?
THE HEATHEN HAS BEEN DETAINED BY STATE SECURITY...
...AND WILL BE SENT TO SPACE JAIL FOR POISONING OUR BELOVED MR. POOPYBUTTHOLE'S MIND.

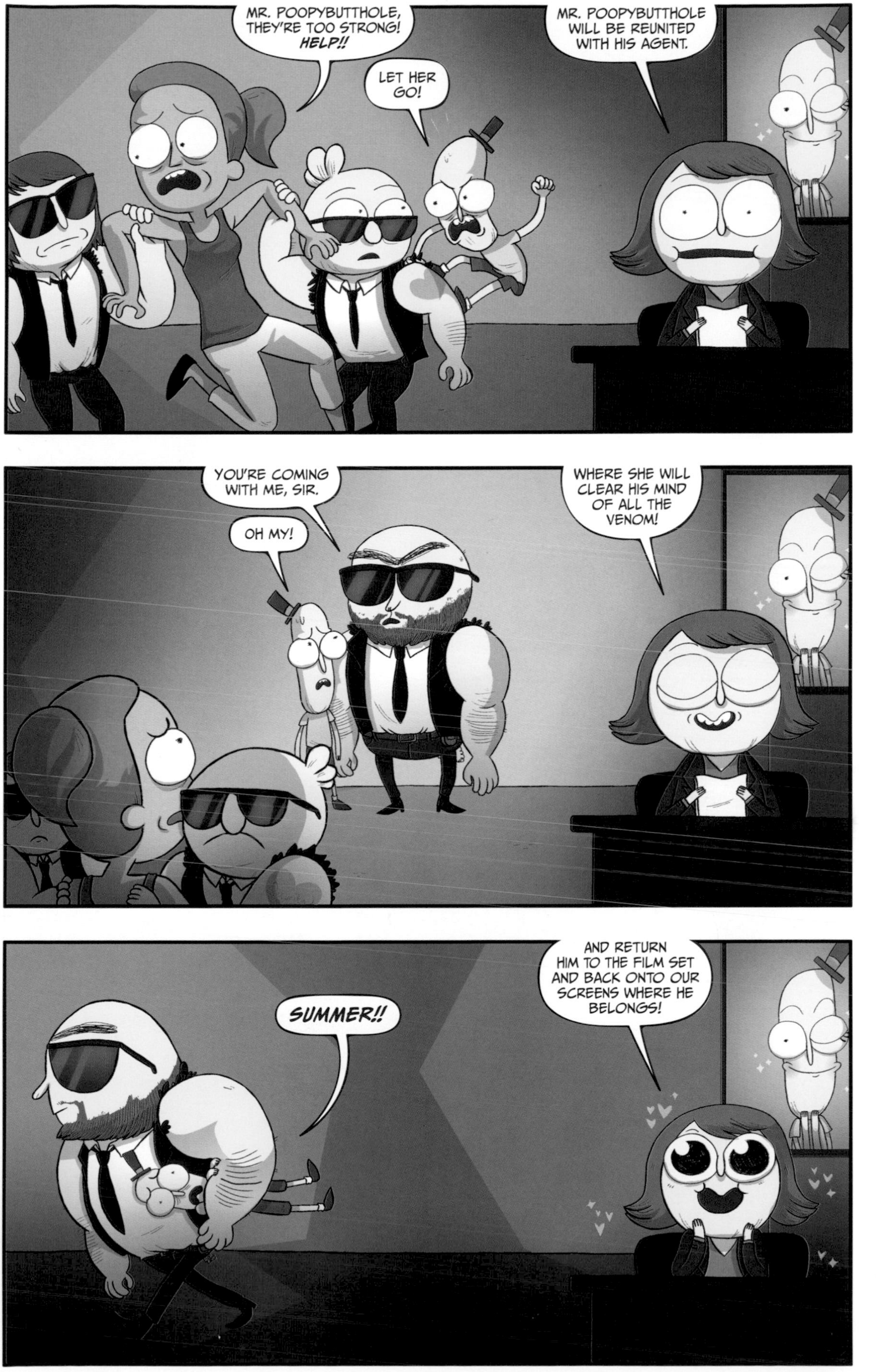
MR. POOPYBUTTHOLE, THEY'RE TOO STRONG! HELP!!
LET HER GO!
MR. POOPYBUTTHOLE WILL BE REUNITED WITH HIS AGENT.
YOU'RE COMING WITH ME, SIR.
OH MY!
WHERE SHE WILL CLEAR HIS MIND OF ALL THE VENOM!
SUMMER!!
AND RETURN HIM TO THE FILM SET AND BACK ONTO OUR SCREENS WHERE HE BELONGS!

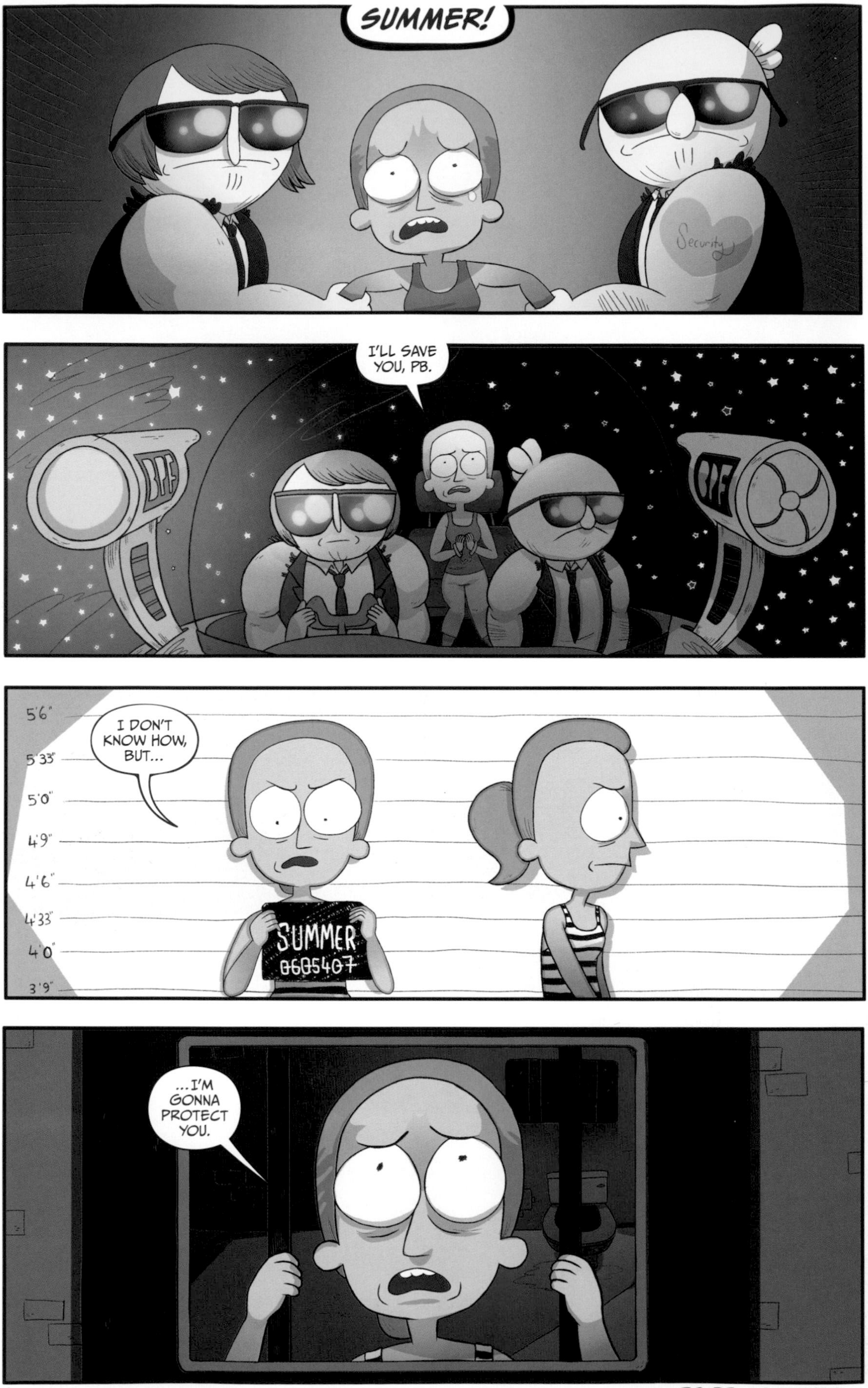
SUMMER!
Security
I'LL SAVE YOU, PB.
BPF
BPF
5'6"
5'33"
5'0"
4'9"
4'6"
4'33"
4'0"
3'9"
I DON'T KNOW HOW, BUT...
SUMMER
0605407
...I'M GONNA PROTECT YOU.

TO BE CONTINUED...

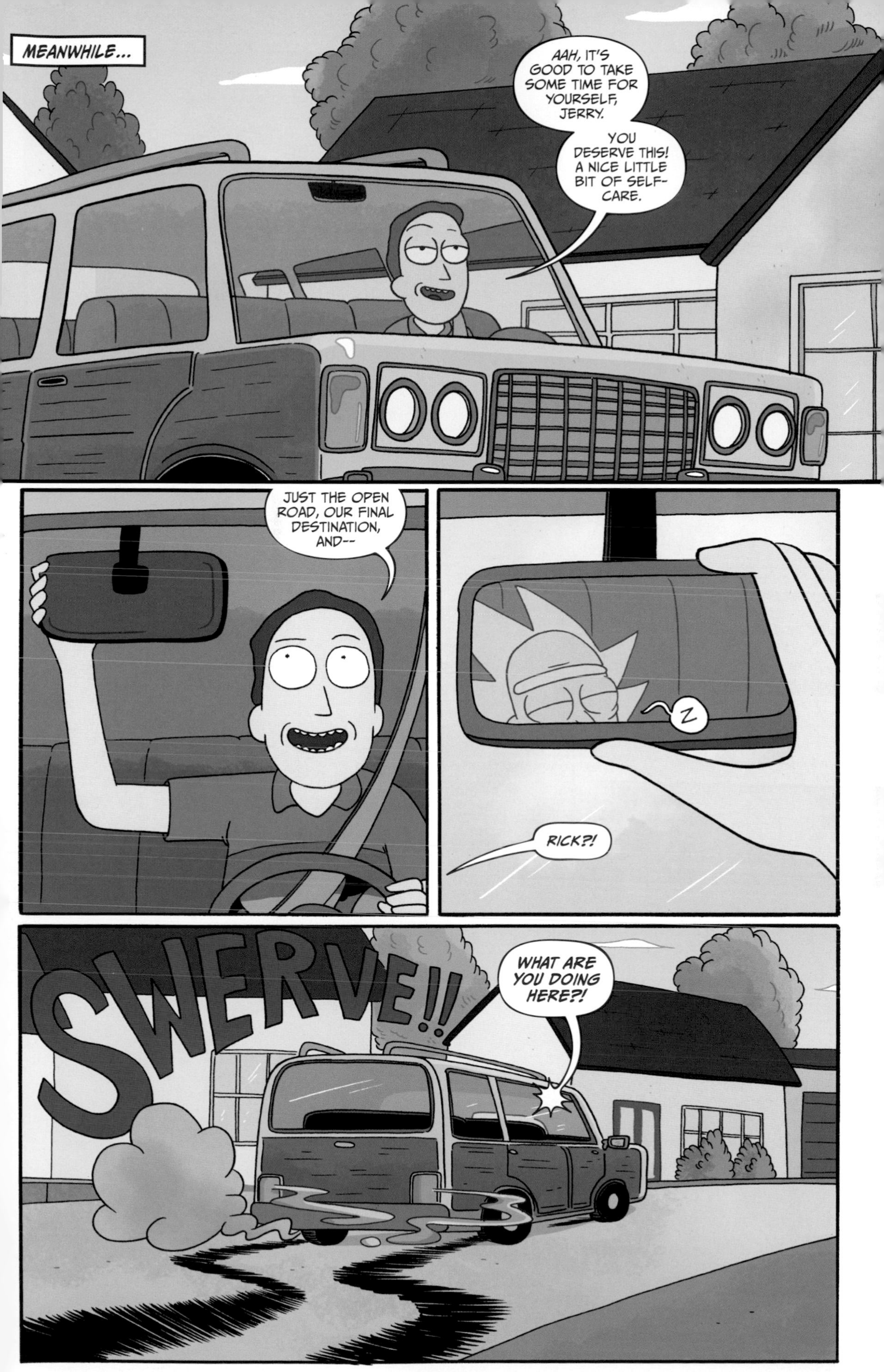
MEANWHILE...
AAH, IT'S GOOD TO TAKE SOME TIME FOR YOURSELF, JERRY.
YOU DESERVE THIS! A NICE LITTLE BIT OF SELF-CARE.
JUST THE OPEN ROAD, OUR FINAL DESTINATION, AND--
Z
RICK?!
SWERVE!!
WHAT ARE YOU DOING HERE?!

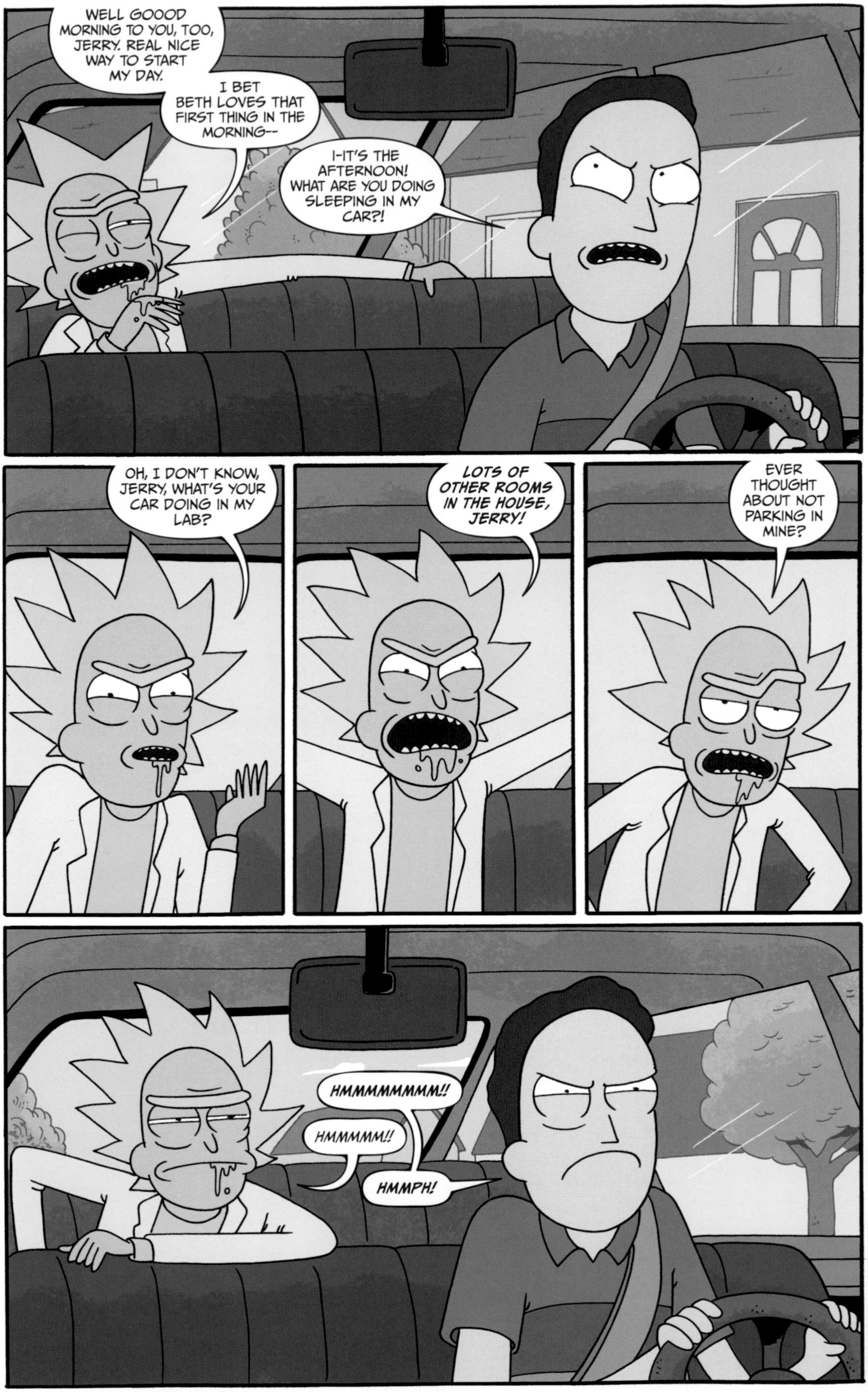
WELL GOOOD MORNING TO YOU, TOO, JERRY. REAL NICE WAY TO START MY DAY.
I BET BETH LOVES THAT FIRST THING IN THE MORNING--
I-IT'S THE AFTERNOON! WHAT ARE YOU DOING SLEEPING IN MY CAR?!
OH, I DON'T KNOW, JERRY, WHAT'S YOUR CAR DOING IN MY LAB?
LOTS OF OTHER ROOMS IN THE HOUSE, JERRY!
EVER THOUGHT ABOUT NOT PARKING IN MINE?
HMMMMMMMM!!
HMMMMM!!
HMMPH!

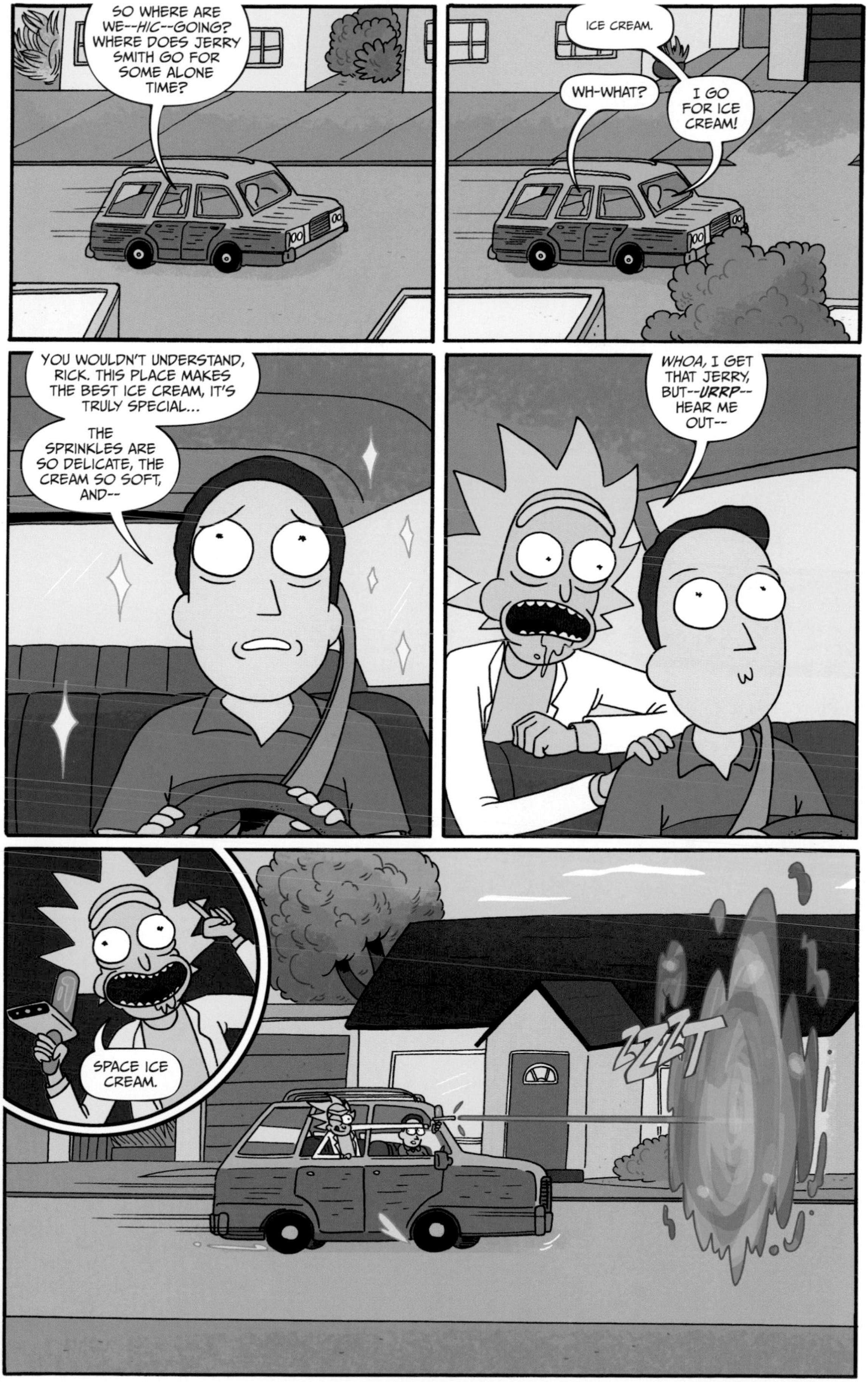
SO WHERE ARE WE--*HIC*--GOING? WHERE DOES JERRY SMITH GO FOR SOME ALONE TIME?
ICE CREAM.
WH-WHAT?
I GO FOR ICE CREAM!
YOU WOULDN'T UNDERSTAND, RICK. THIS PLACE MAKES THE BEST ICE CREAM, IT'S TRULY SPECIAL...
THE SPRINKLES ARE SO DELICATE, THE CREAM SO SOFT, AND--
WHOA, I GET THAT JERRY, BUT--***URRP***--HEAR ME OUT--
SPACE ICE CREAM.
ZZZT

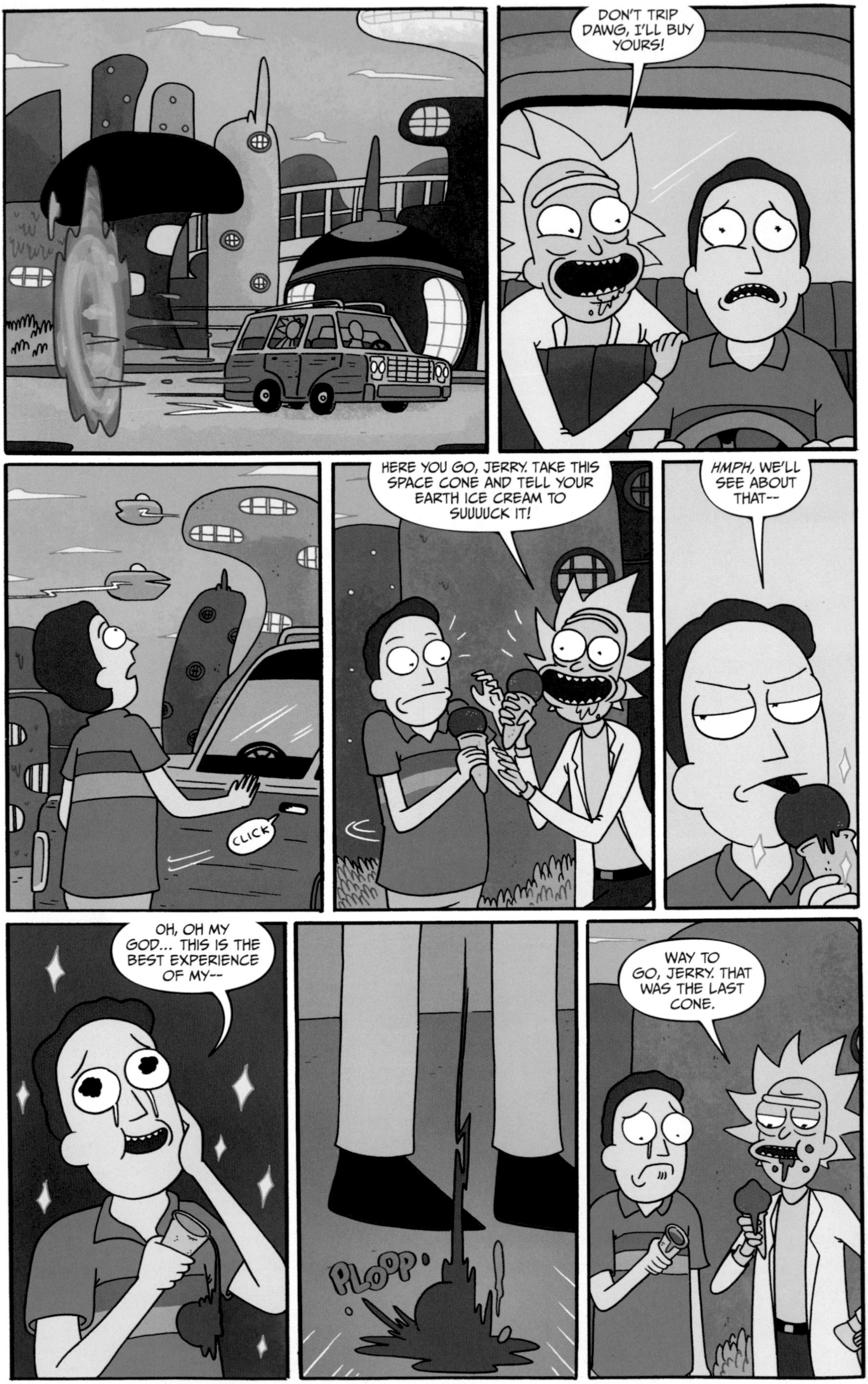
DON'T TRIP DAWG, I'LL BUY YOURS!
CLICK
HERE YOU GO, JERRY. TAKE THIS SPACE CONE AND TELL YOUR EARTH ICE CREAM TO SUUUUCK IT!
HMPH, WE'LL SEE ABOUT THAT--
OH, OH MY GOD... THIS IS THE BEST EXPERIENCE OF MY--
PLOOP!
WAY TO GO, JERRY. THAT WAS THE LAST CONE.

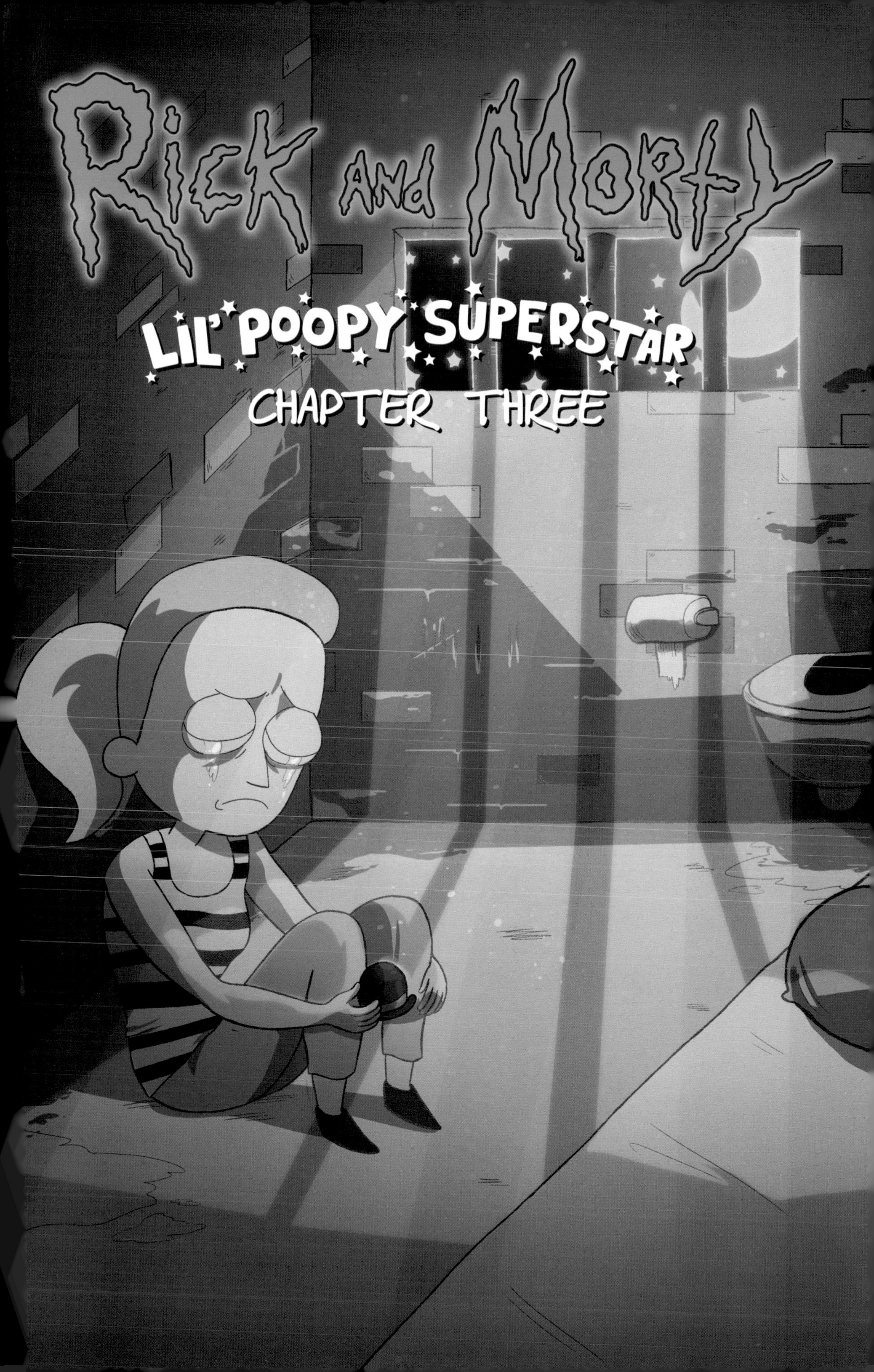
Rick and Morty
LIL' POOPY SUPERSTAR
CHAPTER THREE

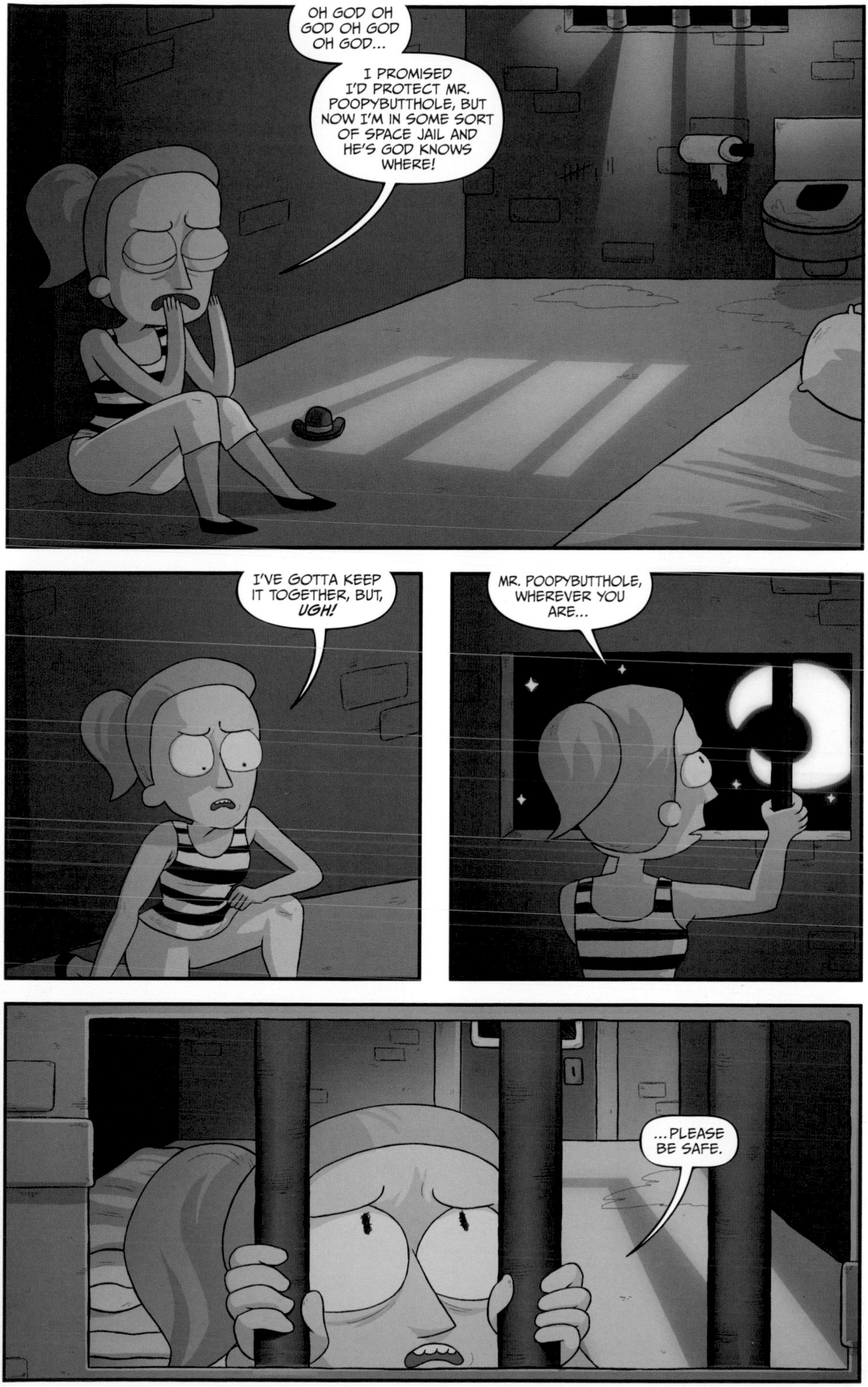
OH GOD OH GOD OH GOD OH GOD...
I PROMISED I'D PROTECT MR. POOPYBUTTHOLE, BUT NOW I'M IN SOME SORT OF SPACE JAIL AND HE'S GOD KNOWS WHERE!
I'VE GOTTA KEEP IT TOGETHER, BUT, *UGH!*
MR. POOPYBUTTHOLE, WHEREVER YOU ARE...
...PLEASE BE SAFE.

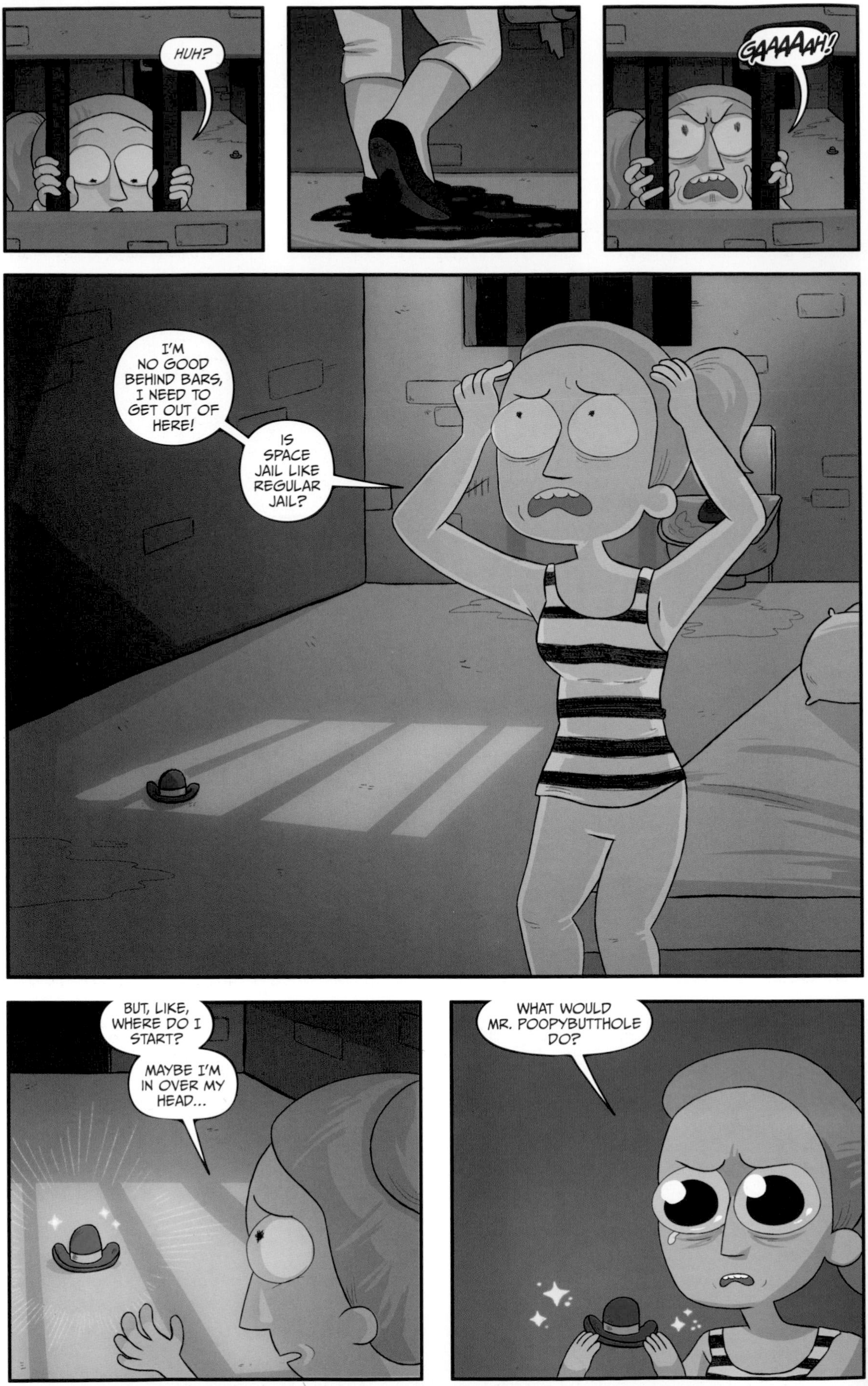
HUH?
GAAAAAH!
I'M NO GOOD BEHIND BARS, I NEED TO GET OUT OF HERE!
IS SPACE JAIL LIKE REGULAR JAIL?
BUT, LIKE, WHERE DO I START?
MAYBE I'M IN OVER MY HEAD...
WHAT WOULD MR. POOPYBUTTHOLE DO?

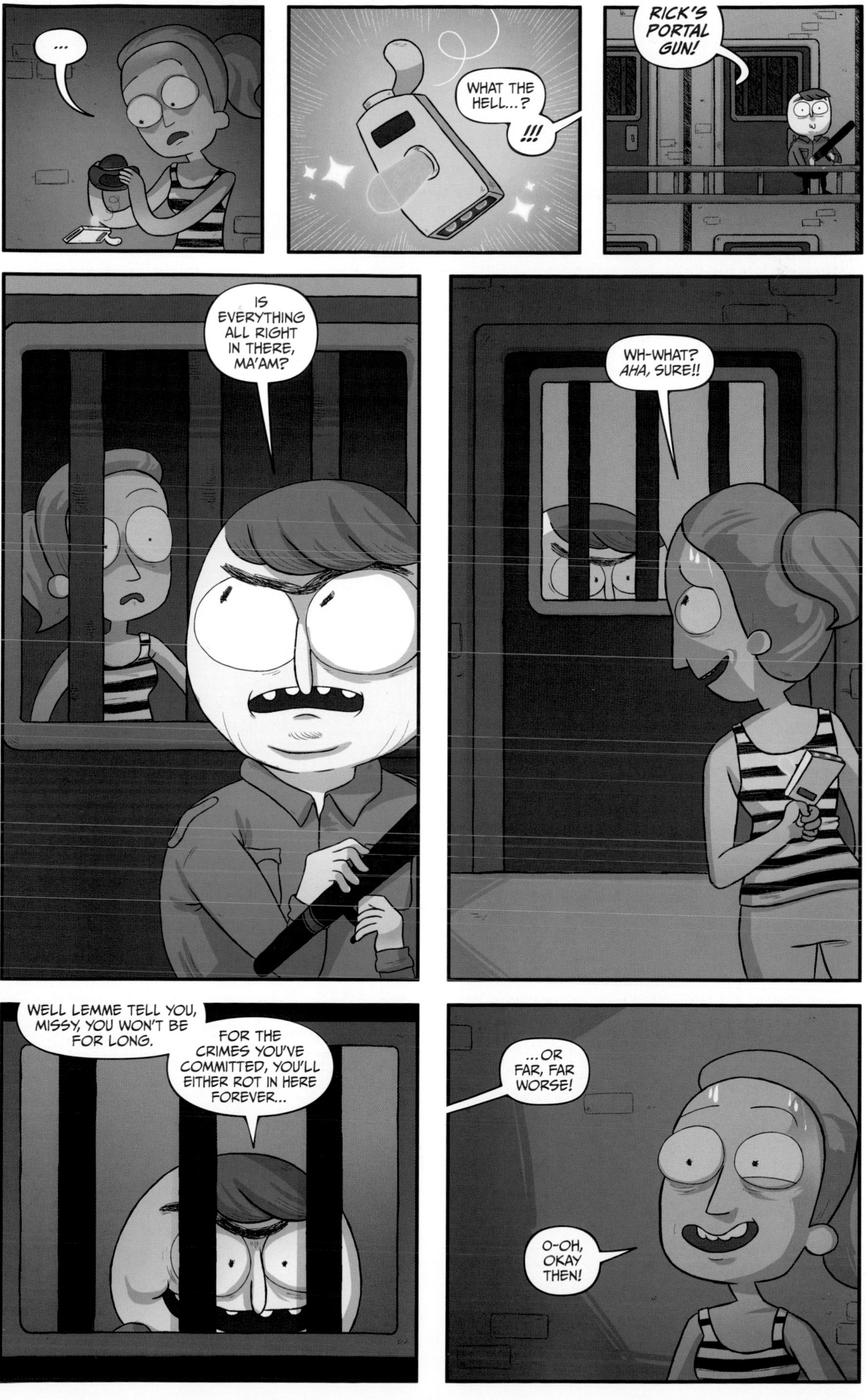
...
WHAT THE HELL...?
!!!
RICK'S PORTAL GUN!
IS EVERYTHING ALL RIGHT IN THERE, MA'AM?
WH-WHAT? *AHA,* SURE!!
WELL LEMME TELL YOU, MISSY, YOU WON'T BE FOR LONG.
FOR THE CRIMES YOU'VE COMMITTED, YOU'LL EITHER ROT IN HERE FOREVER...
...OR FAR, FAR WORSE!
O-OH, OKAY THEN!

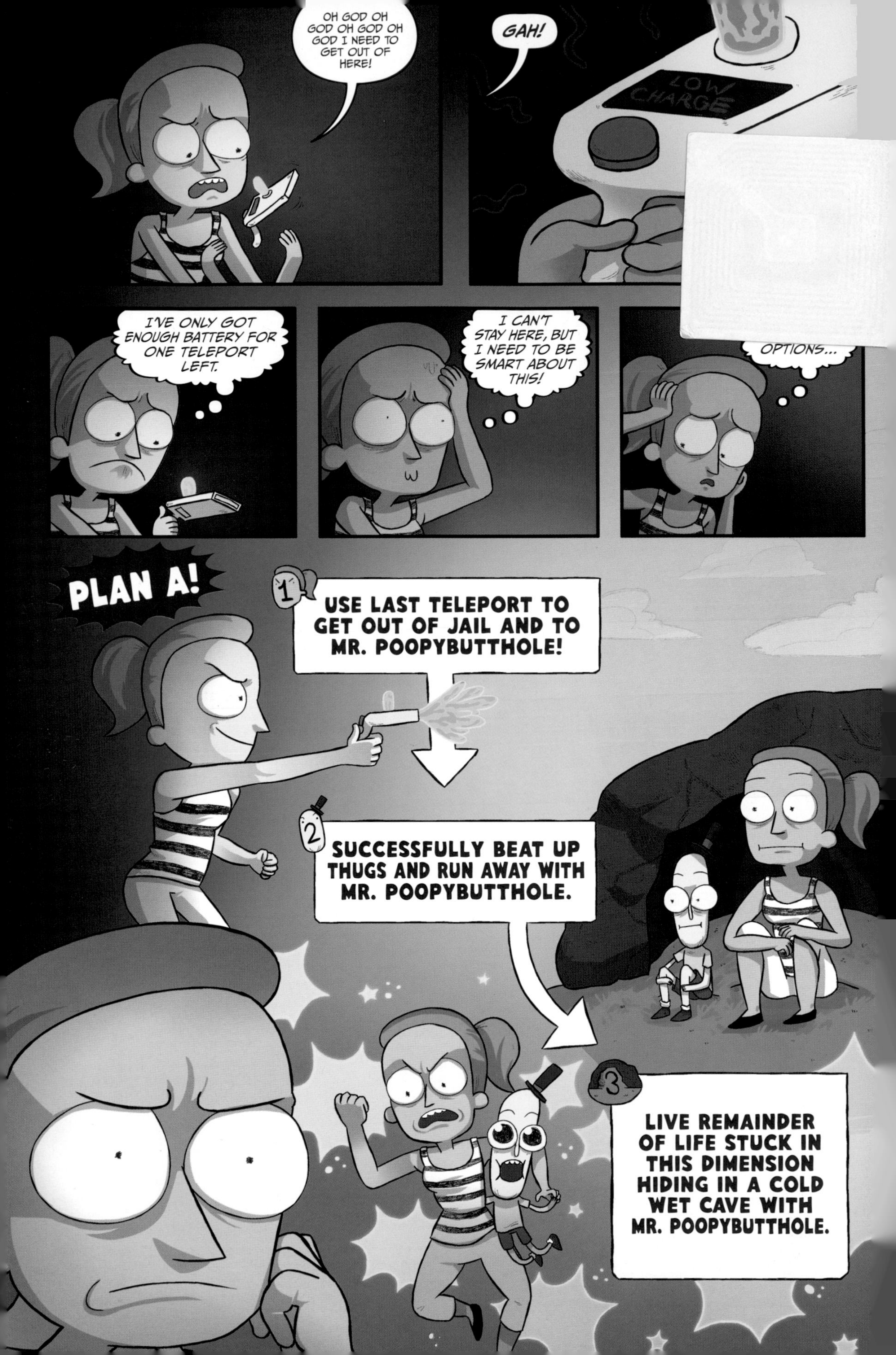
OH GOD OH GOD OH GOD OH GOD I NEED TO GET OUT OF HERE!
GAH!
LOW CHARGE
I'VE ONLY GOT ENOUGH BATTERY FOR ONE TELEPORT LEFT.
I CAN'T STAY HERE, BUT I NEED TO BE SMART ABOUT THIS!
OPTIONS...
PLAN A!
1
USE LAST TELEPORT TO GET OUT OF JAIL AND TO MR. POOPYBUTTHOLE!
2
SUCCESSFULLY BEAT UP THUGS AND RUN AWAY WITH MR. POOPYBUTTHOLE.
3
LIVE REMAINDER OF LIFE STUCK IN THIS DIMENSION HIDING IN A COLD WET CAVE WITH MR. POOPYBUTTHOLE.

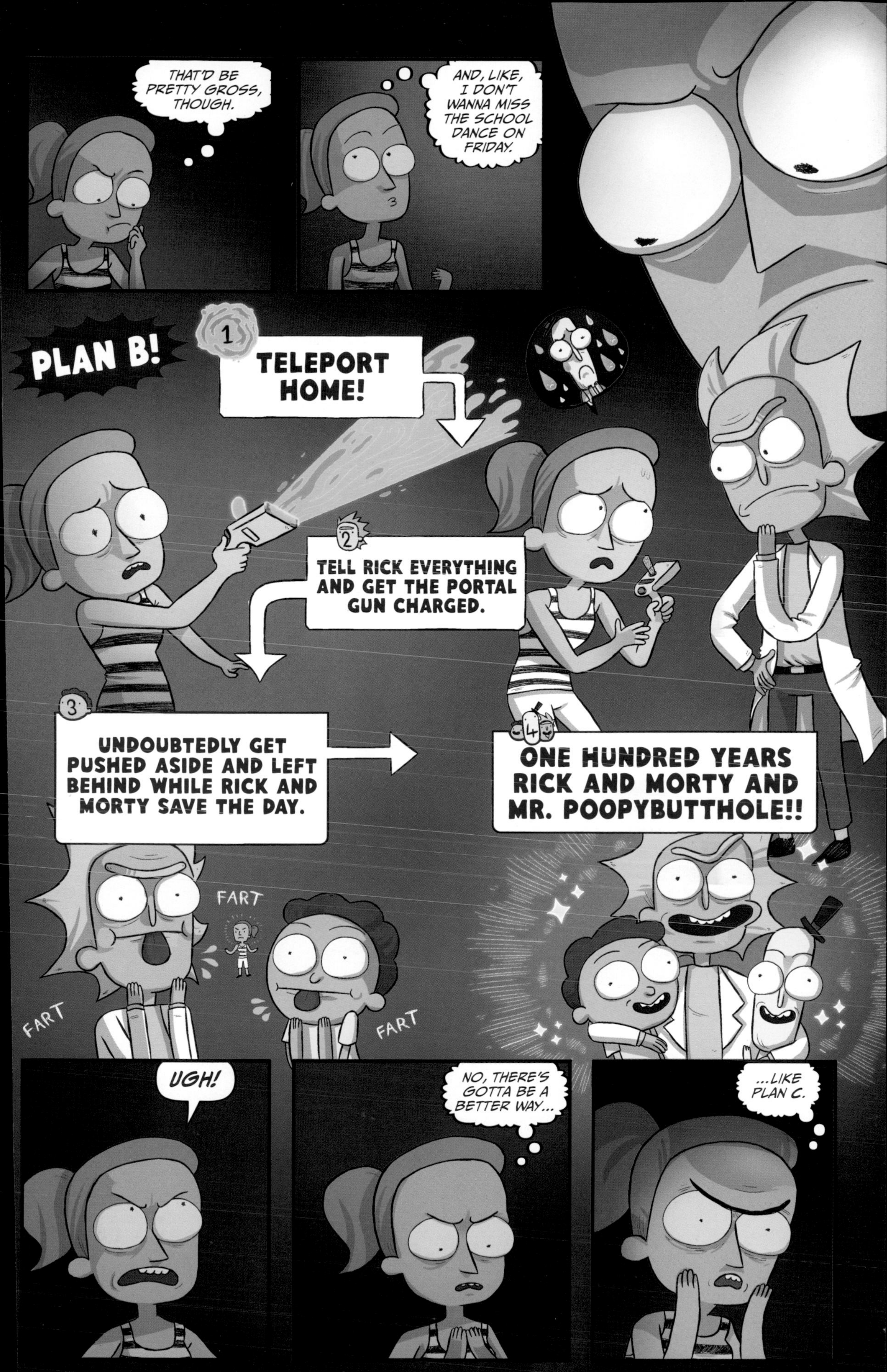

THAT'D BE PRETTY GROSS, THOUGH.
AND, LIKE, I DON'T WANNA MISS THE SCHOOL DANCE ON FRIDAY.
PLAN B!
1
TELEPORT HOME!
2
TELL RICK EVERYTHING AND GET THE PORTAL GUN CHARGED.
3
UNDOUBTEDLY GET PUSHED ASIDE AND LEFT BEHIND WHILE RICK AND MORTY SAVE THE DAY.
4
ONE HUNDRED YEARS RICK AND MORTY AND MR. POOPYBUTTHOLE!!
FART
FART
FART
UGH!
NO, THERE'S GOTTA BE A BETTER WAY...
...LIKE PLAN C.

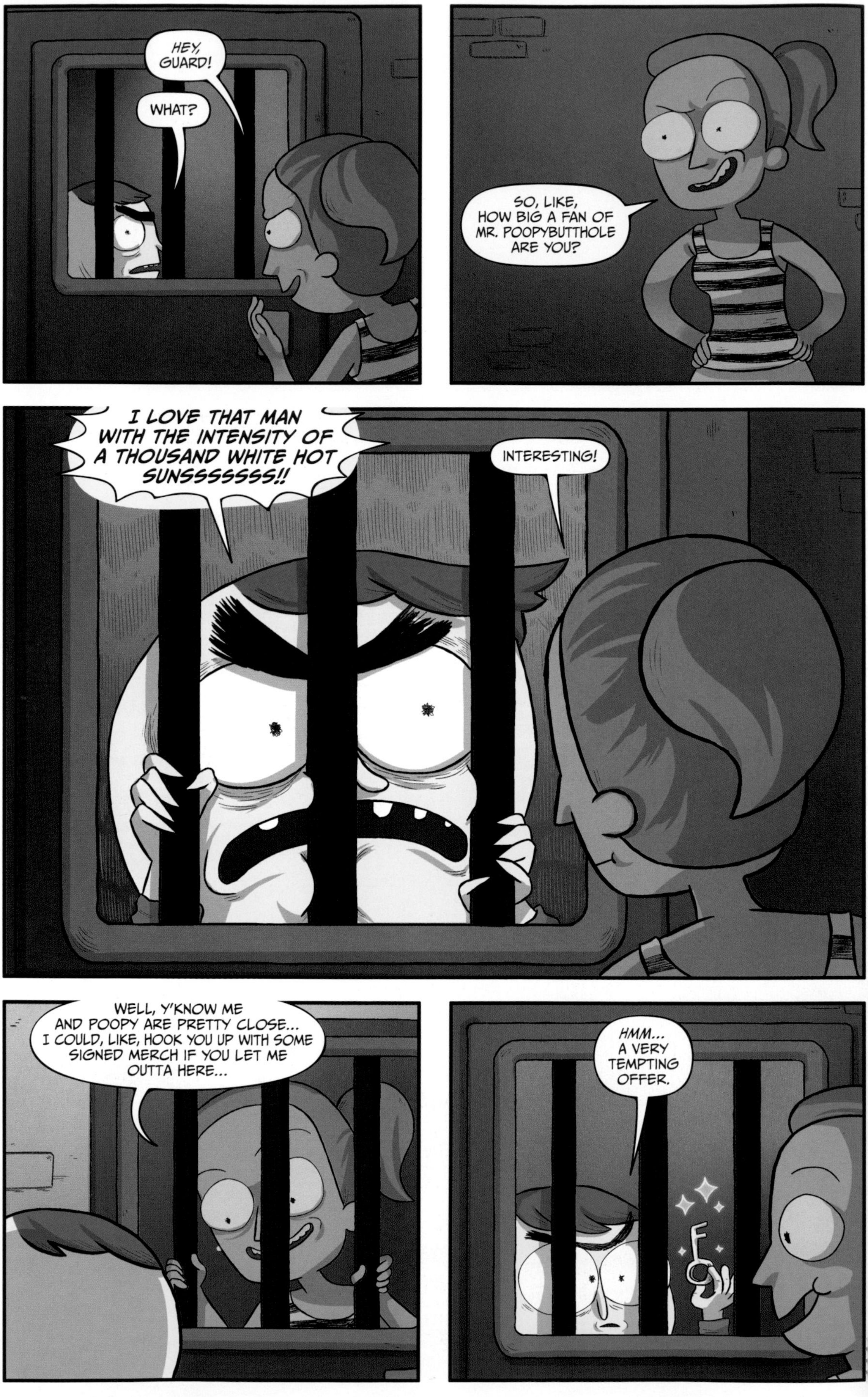
HEY, GUARD!
WHAT?
SO, LIKE, HOW BIG A FAN OF MR. POOPYBUTTHOLE ARE YOU?
I LOVE THAT MAN WITH THE INTENSITY OF A THOUSAND WHITE HOT SUNSSSSSSS!!
INTERESTING!
WELL, Y'KNOW ME AND POOPY ARE PRETTY CLOSE... I COULD, LIKE, HOOK YOU UP WITH SOME SIGNED MERCH IF YOU LET ME OUTTA HERE...
HMM... A VERY TEMPTING OFFER.

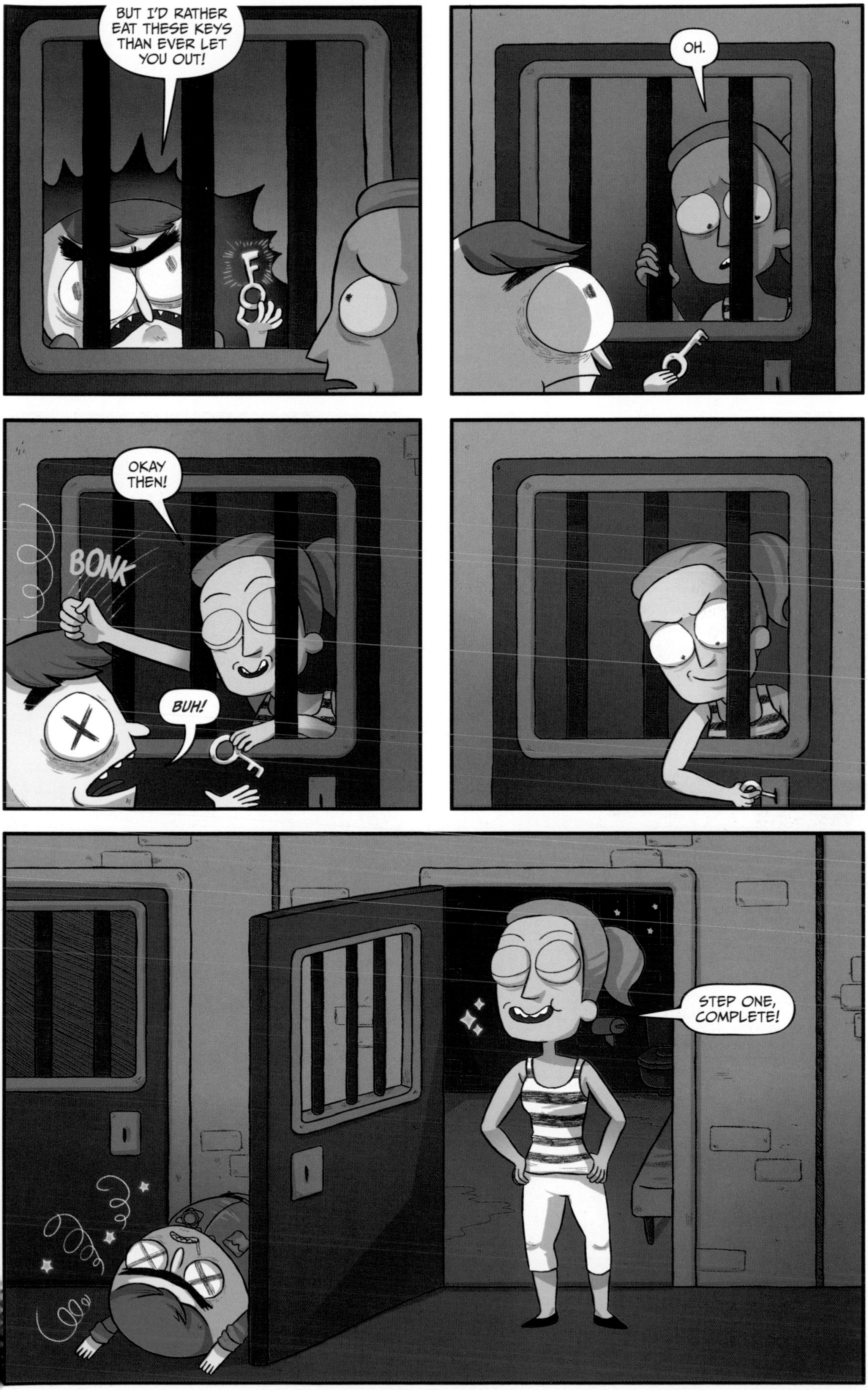
BUT I'D RATHER EAT THESE KEYS THAN EVER LET YOU OUT!
OH.
OKAY THEN!
BONK
BUH!
STEP ONE, COMPLETE!

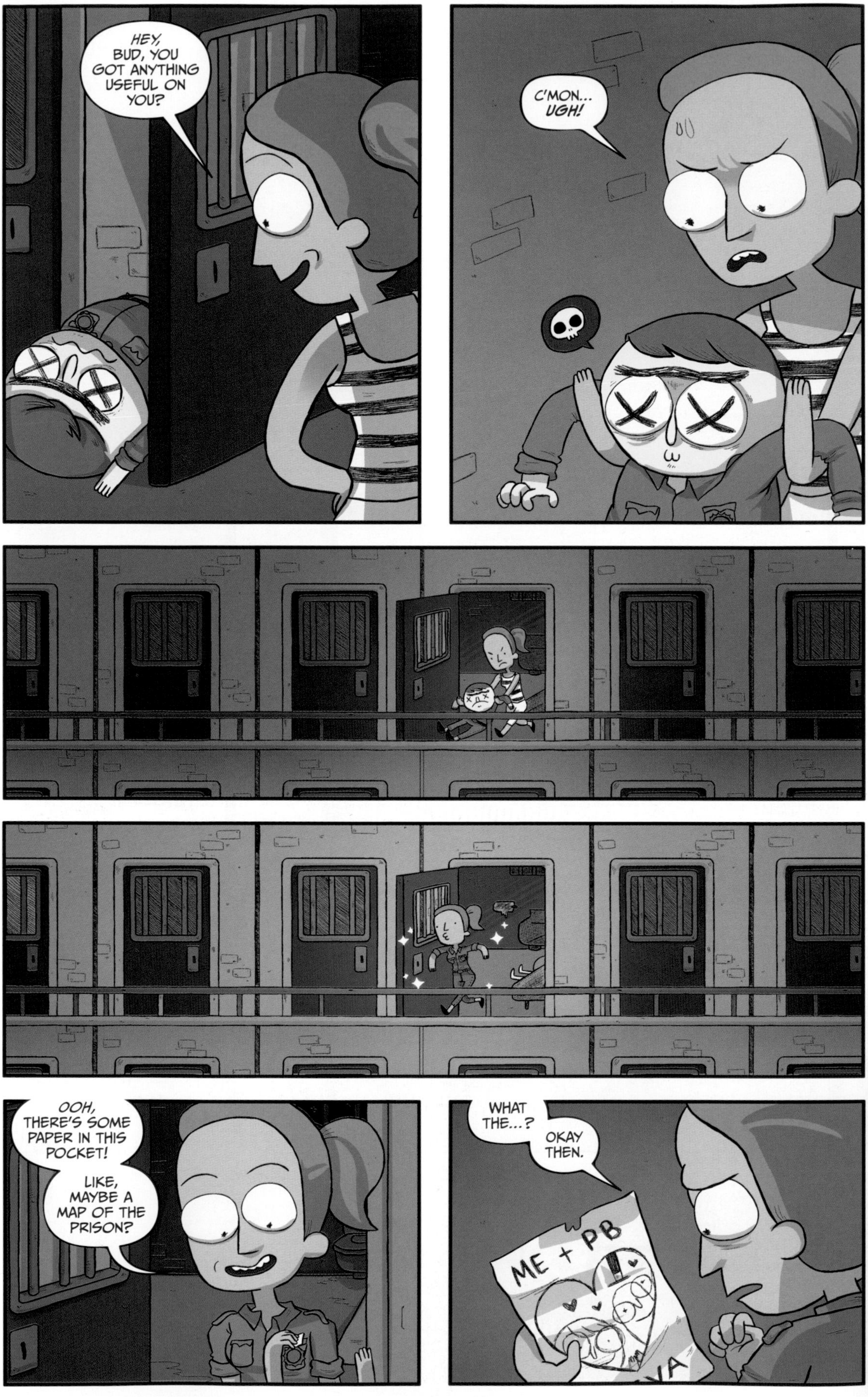
HEY, BUD, YOU GOT ANYTHING USEFUL ON YOU?
C'MON... UGH!
OOH, THERE'S SOME PAPER IN THIS POCKET!
LIKE, MAYBE A MAP OF THE PRISON?
WHAT THE...?
OKAY THEN.
ME + PB

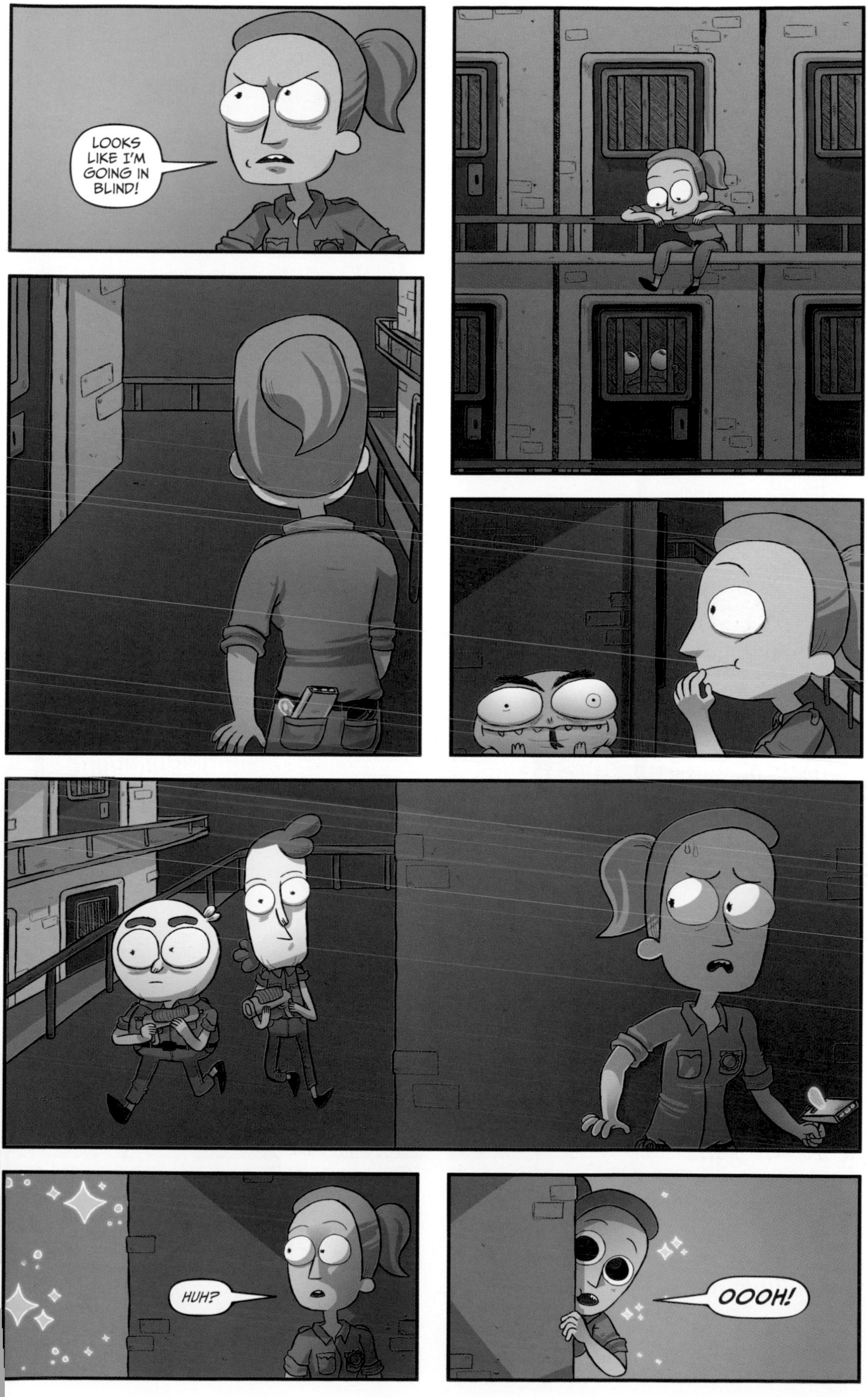
LOOKS LIKE I'M GOING IN BLIND!
HUH?
OOOH!

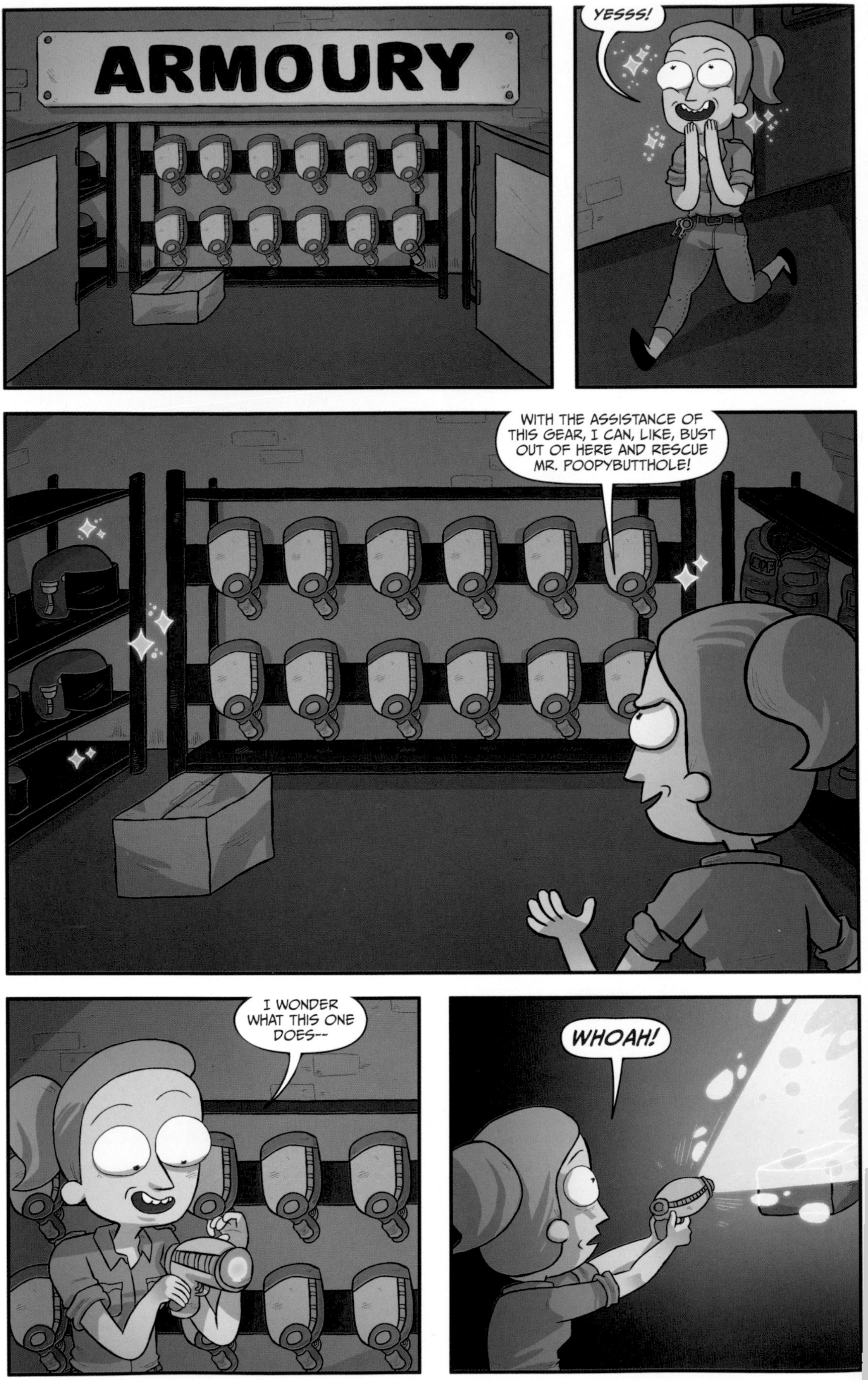
ARMOURY
YESSS!
WITH THE ASSISTANCE OF THIS GEAR, I CAN, LIKE, BUST OUT OF HERE AND RESCUE MR. POOPYBUTTHOLE!
I WONDER WHAT THIS ONE DOES--
WHOAH!

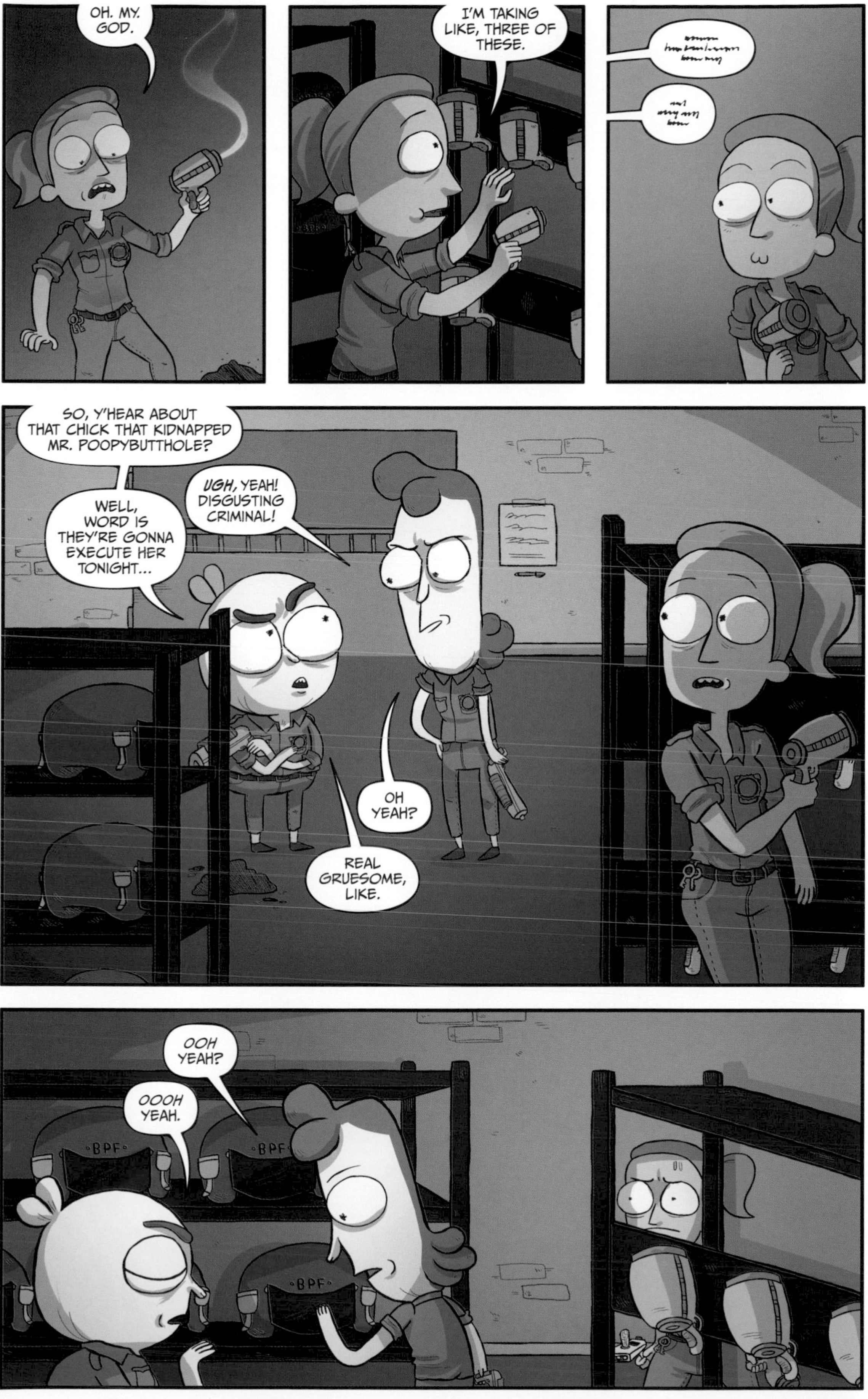
OH. MY. GOD.
I'M TAKING LIKE, THREE OF THESE.
SO, Y'HEAR ABOUT THAT CHICK THAT KIDNAPPED MR. POOPYBUTTHOLE?
UGH, YEAH! DISGUSTING CRIMINAL!
WELL, WORD IS THEY'RE GONNA EXECUTE HER TONIGHT...
OH YEAH?
REAL GRUESOME, LIKE.
OOH YEAH?
OOOH YEAH.

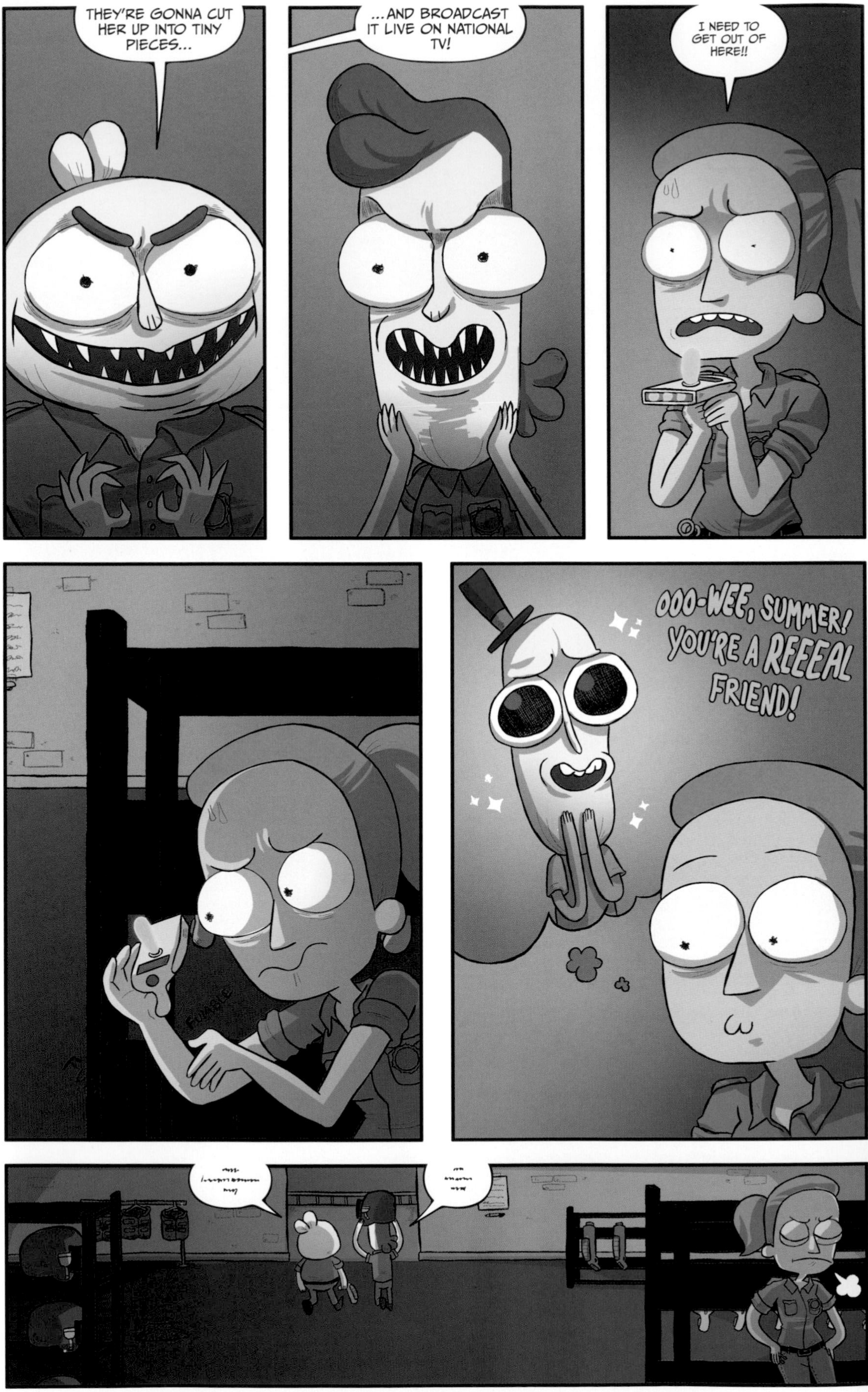
THEY'RE GONNA CUT HER UP INTO TINY PIECES...
...AND BROADCAST IT LIVE ON NATIONAL TV!
I NEED TO GET OUT OF HERE!!
FUMBLE
OOO-WEE, SUMMER! YOU'RE A REEEAL FRIEND!

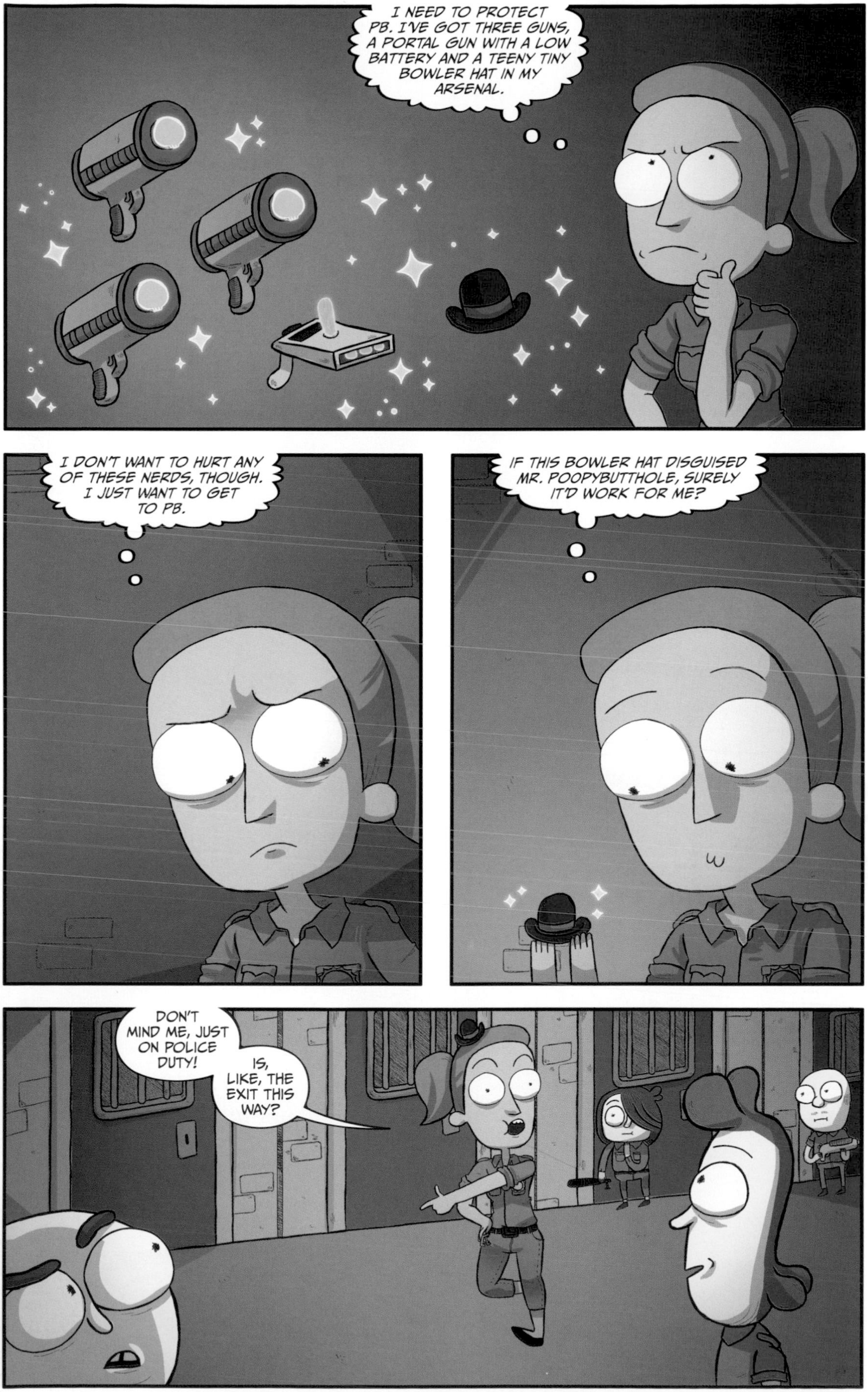

I NEED TO PROTECT PB. I'VE GOT THREE GUNS, A PORTAL GUN WITH A LOW BATTERY AND A TEENY TINY BOWLER HAT IN MY ARSENAL.
I DON'T WANT TO HURT ANY OF THESE NERDS, THOUGH. I JUST WANT TO GET TO PB.
IF THIS BOWLER HAT DISGUISED MR. POOPYBUTTHOLE, SURELY IT'D WORK FOR ME?
DON'T MIND ME, JUST ON POLICE DUTY!
IS, LIKE, THE EXIT THIS WAY?

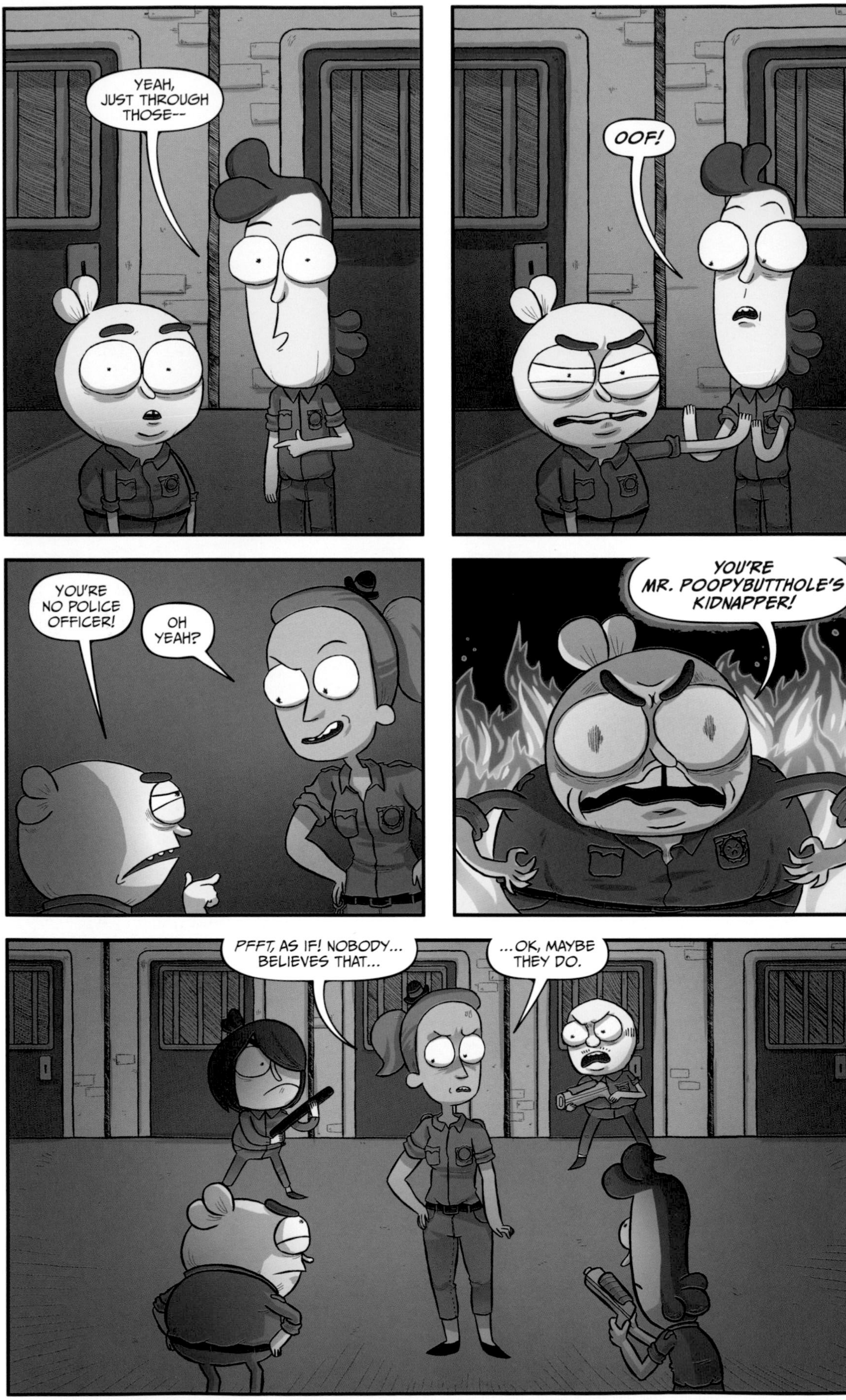
YEAH, JUST THROUGH THOSE--
OOF!
YOU'RE NO POLICE OFFICER!
OH YEAH?
YOU'RE MR. POOPYBUTTHOLE'S KIDNAPPER!
PFFT, AS IF! NOBODY... BELIEVES THAT...
...OK, MAYBE THEY DO.

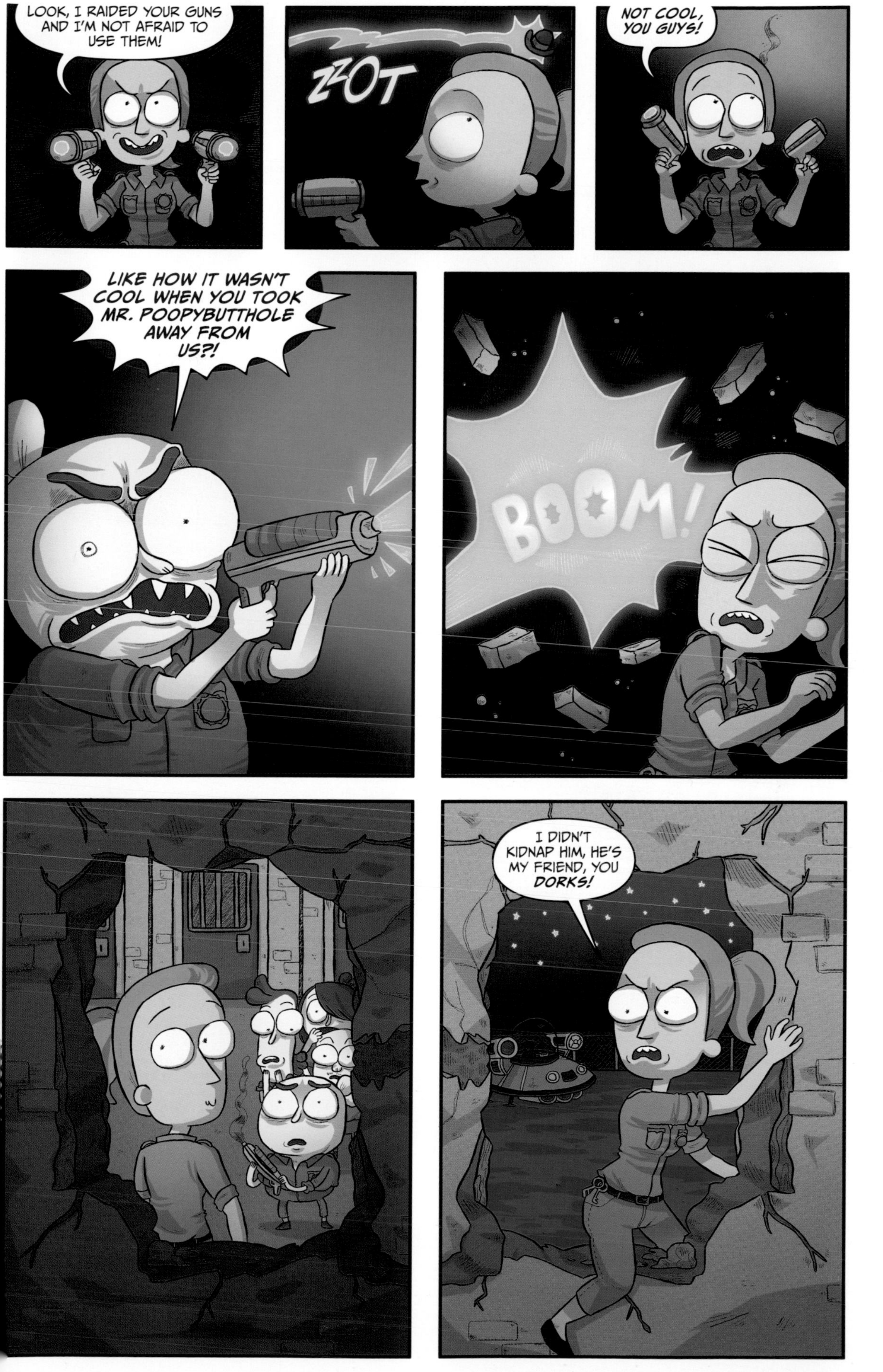
LOOK, I RAIDED YOUR GUNS AND I'M NOT AFRAID TO USE THEM!
ZZOT
NOT COOL, YOU GUYS!
LIKE HOW IT WASN'T COOL WHEN YOU TOOK MR. POOPYBUTTHOLE AWAY FROM US?!
BOOM!
I DIDN'T KIDNAP HIM, HE'S MY FRIEND, YOU DORKS!

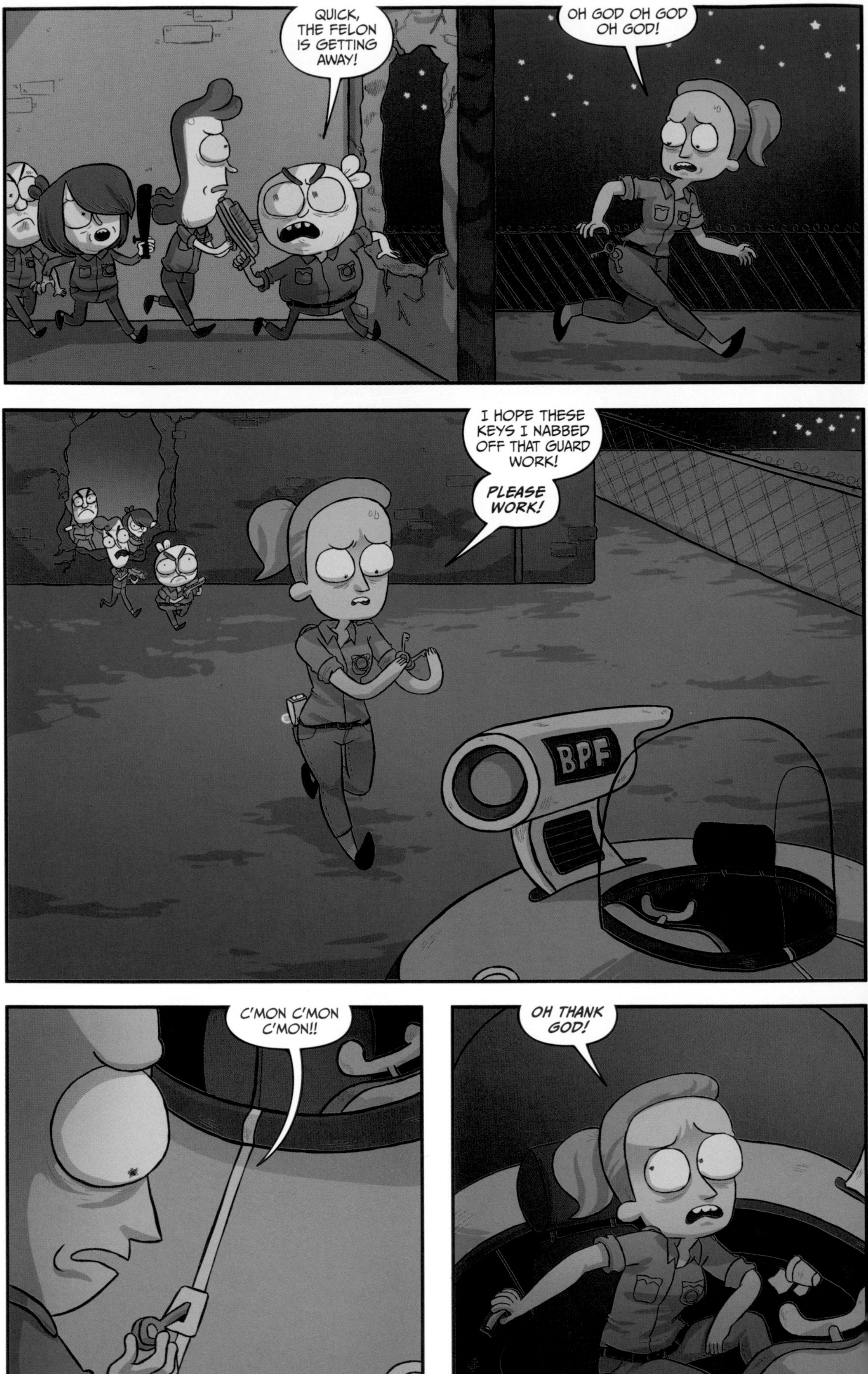
QUICK, THE FELON IS GETTING AWAY!
OH GOD OH GOD OH GOD!
I HOPE THESE KEYS I NABBED OFF THAT GUARD WORK!
PLEASE WORK!
BPF
C'MON C'MON C'MON!!
OH THANK GOD!

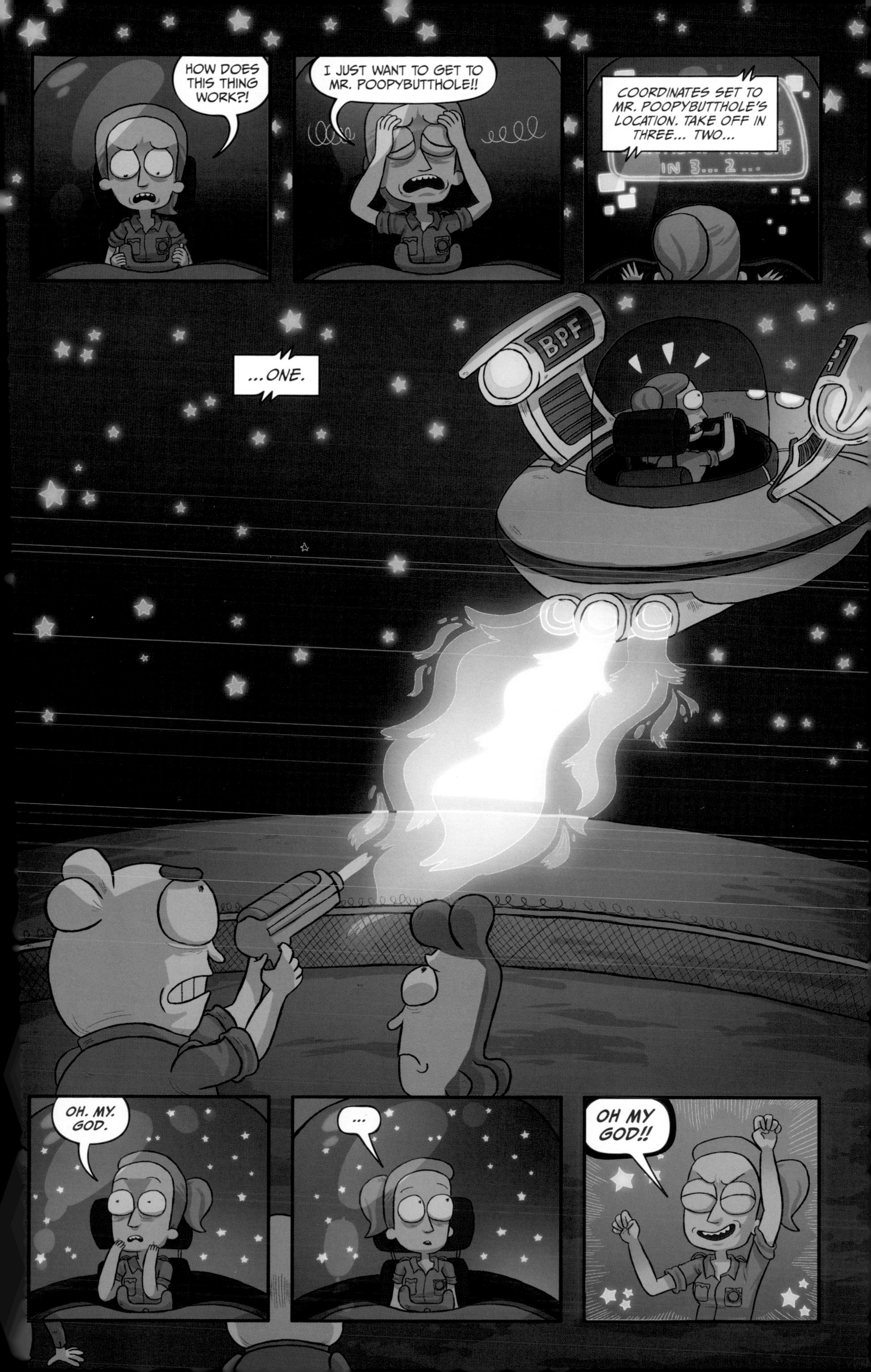
HOW DOES THIS THING WORK?!
I JUST WANT TO GET TO MR. POOPYBUTTHOLE!!
COORDINATES SET TO MR. POOPYBUTTHOLE'S LOCATION. TAKE OFF IN THREE... TWO...
IN 3... 2...
...ONE.
BPF
OH. MY. GOD.
...
OH MY GOD!!

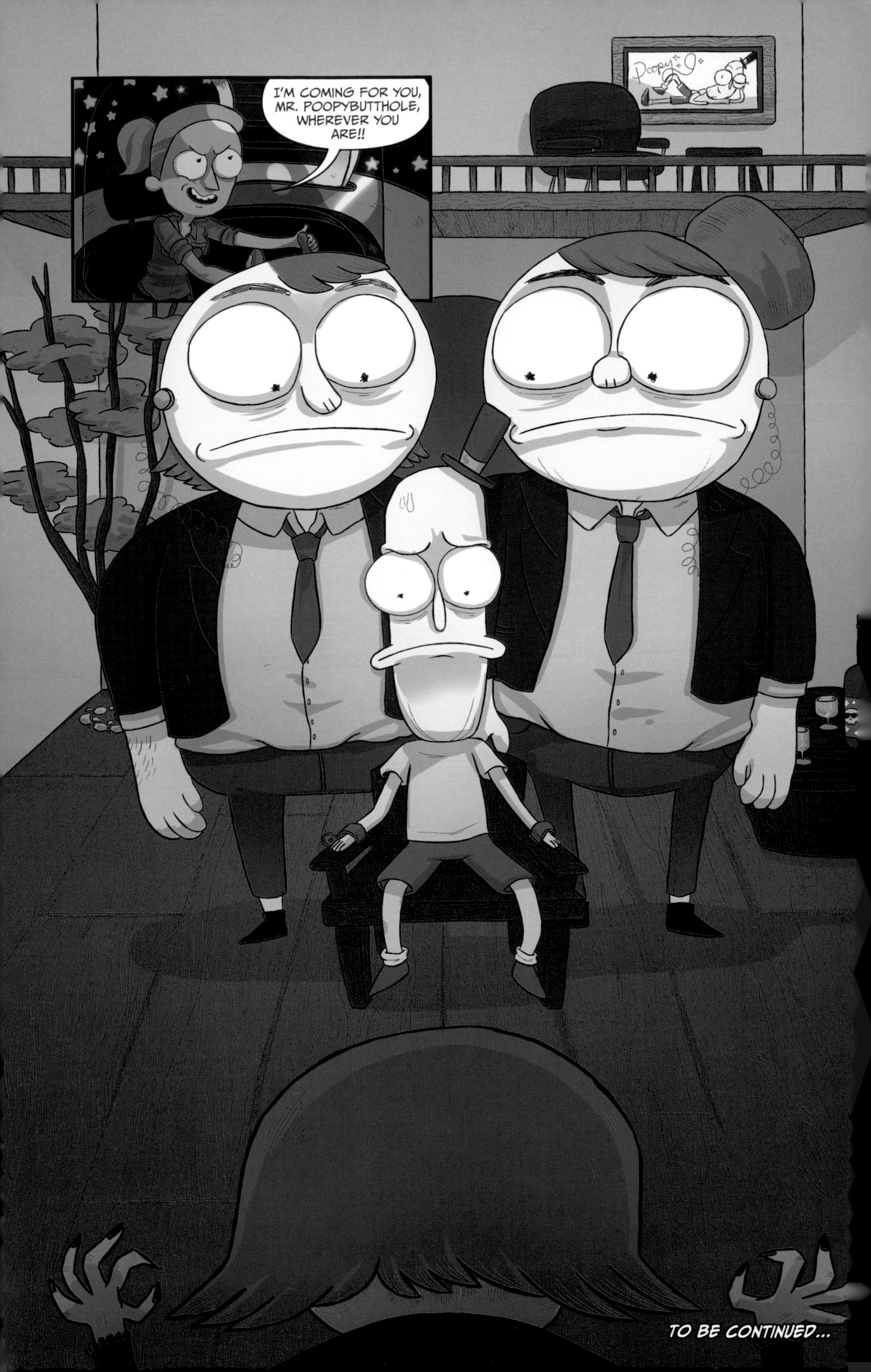
I'M COMING FOR YOU, MR. POOPYBUTTHOLE, WHEREVER YOU ARE!!
Poopy
TO BE CONTINUED...

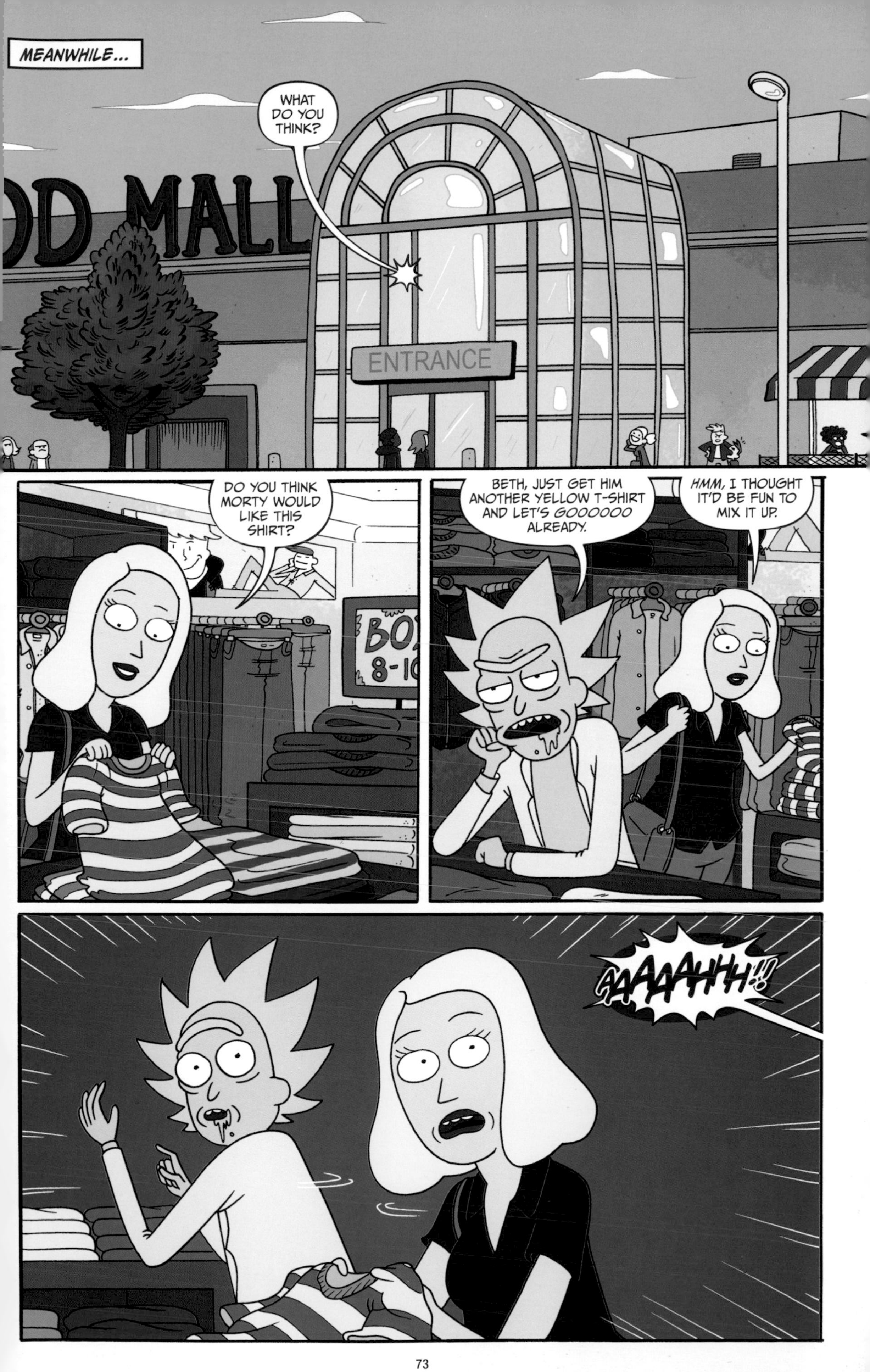
MEANWHILE...
WHAT DO YOU THINK?
OD MALL
ENTRANCE
DO YOU THINK MORTY WOULD LIKE THIS SHIRT?
BETH, JUST GET HIM ANOTHER YELLOW T-SHIRT AND LET'S GOOOOOO ALREADY.
HMM, I THOUGHT IT'D BE FUN TO MIX IT UP.
AAAAAHHH!!

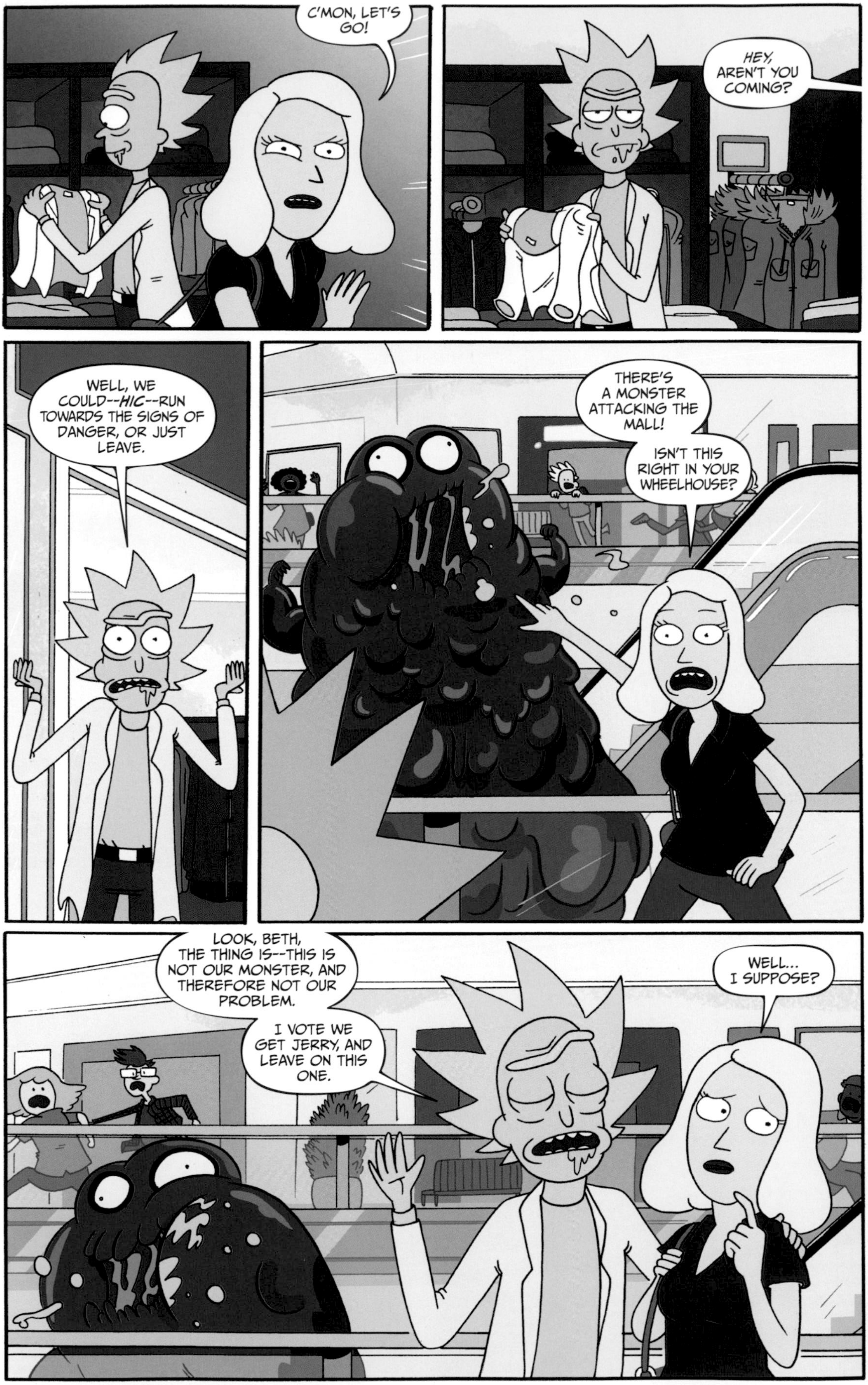
C'MON, LET'S GO!
HEY, AREN'T YOU COMING?
WELL, WE COULD--HIC--RUN TOWARDS THE SIGNS OF DANGER, OR JUST LEAVE.
THERE'S A MONSTER ATTACKING THE MALL!
ISN'T THIS RIGHT IN YOUR WHEELHOUSE?
LOOK, BETH, THE THING IS--THIS IS NOT OUR MONSTER, AND THEREFORE NOT OUR PROBLEM.
I VOTE WE GET JERRY, AND LEAVE ON THIS ONE.
WELL... I SUPPOSE?

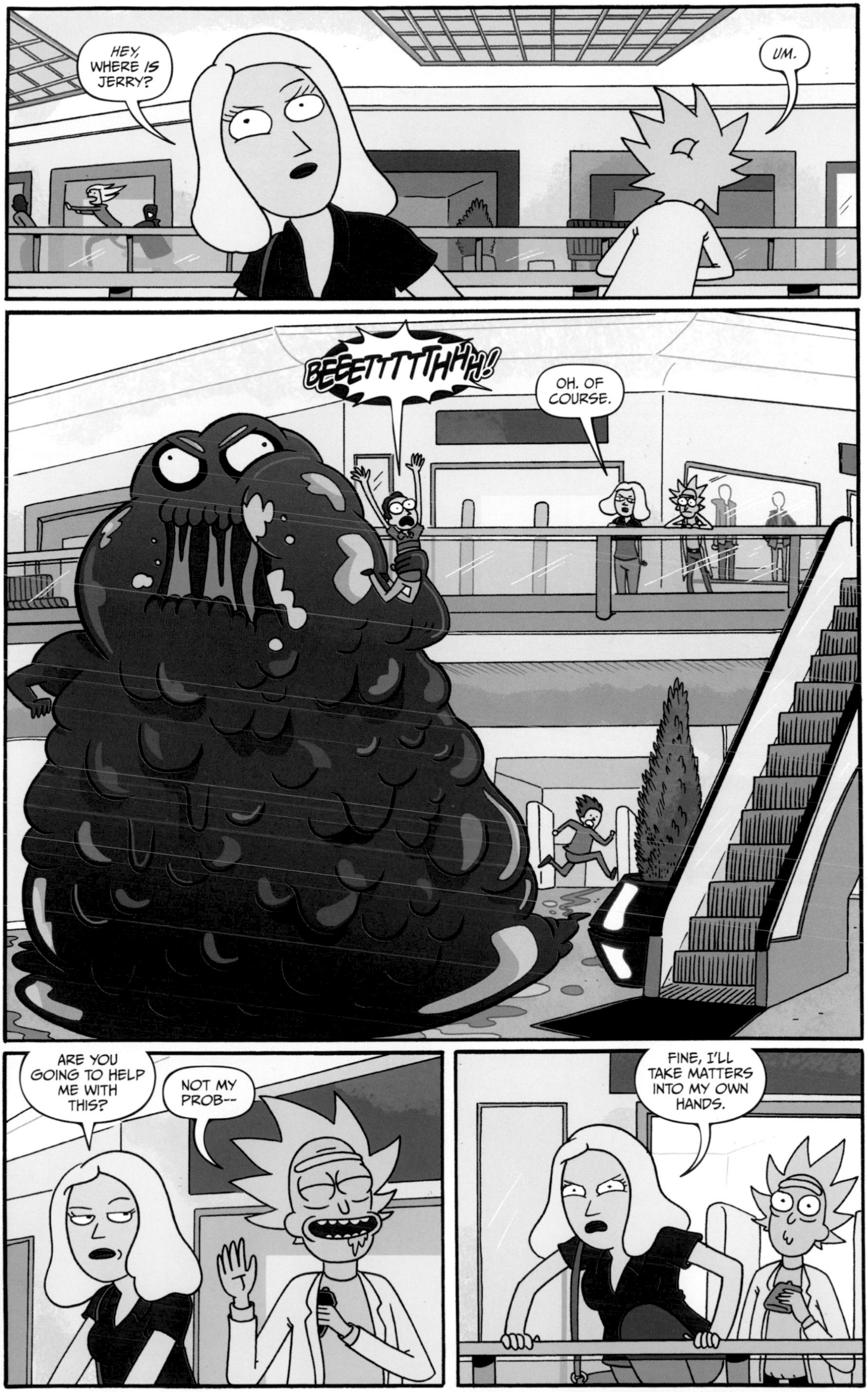
HEY, WHERE IS JERRY?
UM.
BEEEETTTTTHHHH!
OH. OF COURSE.
ARE YOU GOING TO HELP ME WITH THIS?
NOT MY PROB--
FINE, I'LL TAKE MATTERS INTO MY OWN HANDS.

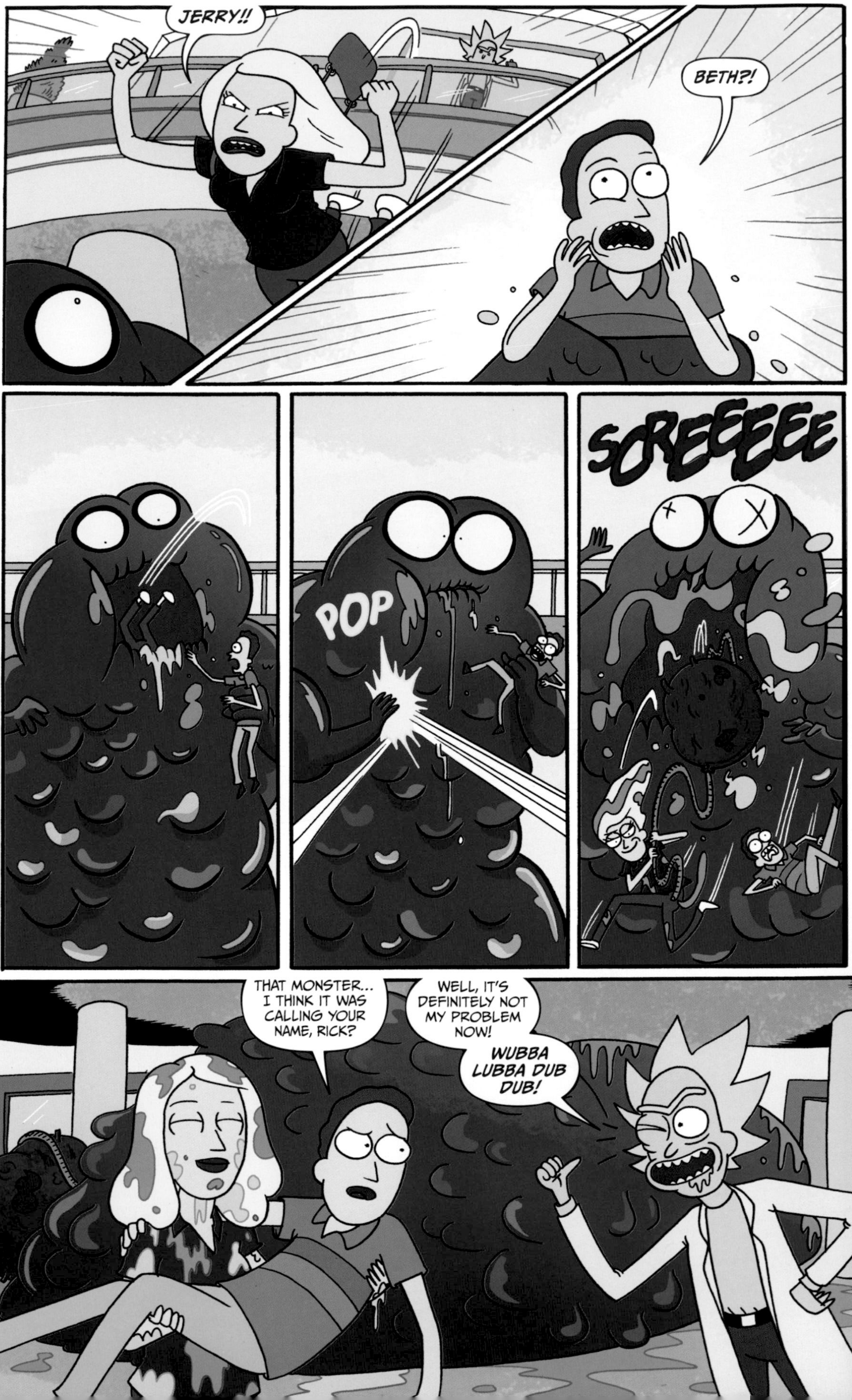
JERRY!!
BETH?!
POP
SCREEEEEE
THAT MONSTER... I THINK IT WAS CALLING YOUR NAME, RICK?
WELL, IT'S DEFINITELY NOT MY PROBLEM NOW!
WUBBA LUBBA DUB DUB!

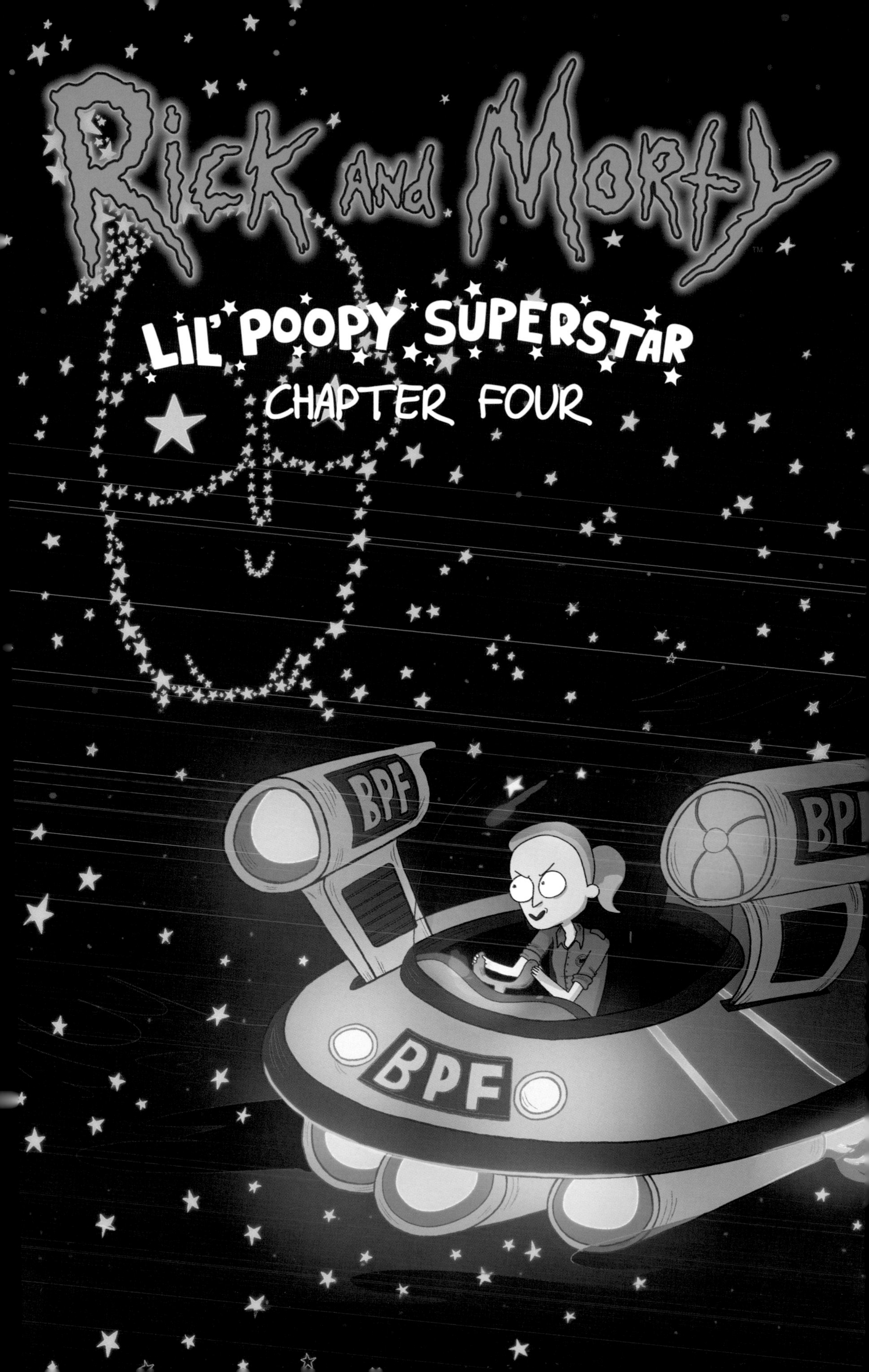
Rick and Morty™
LIL' POOPY SUPERSTAR
CHAPTER FOUR
BPF
BP
BPF

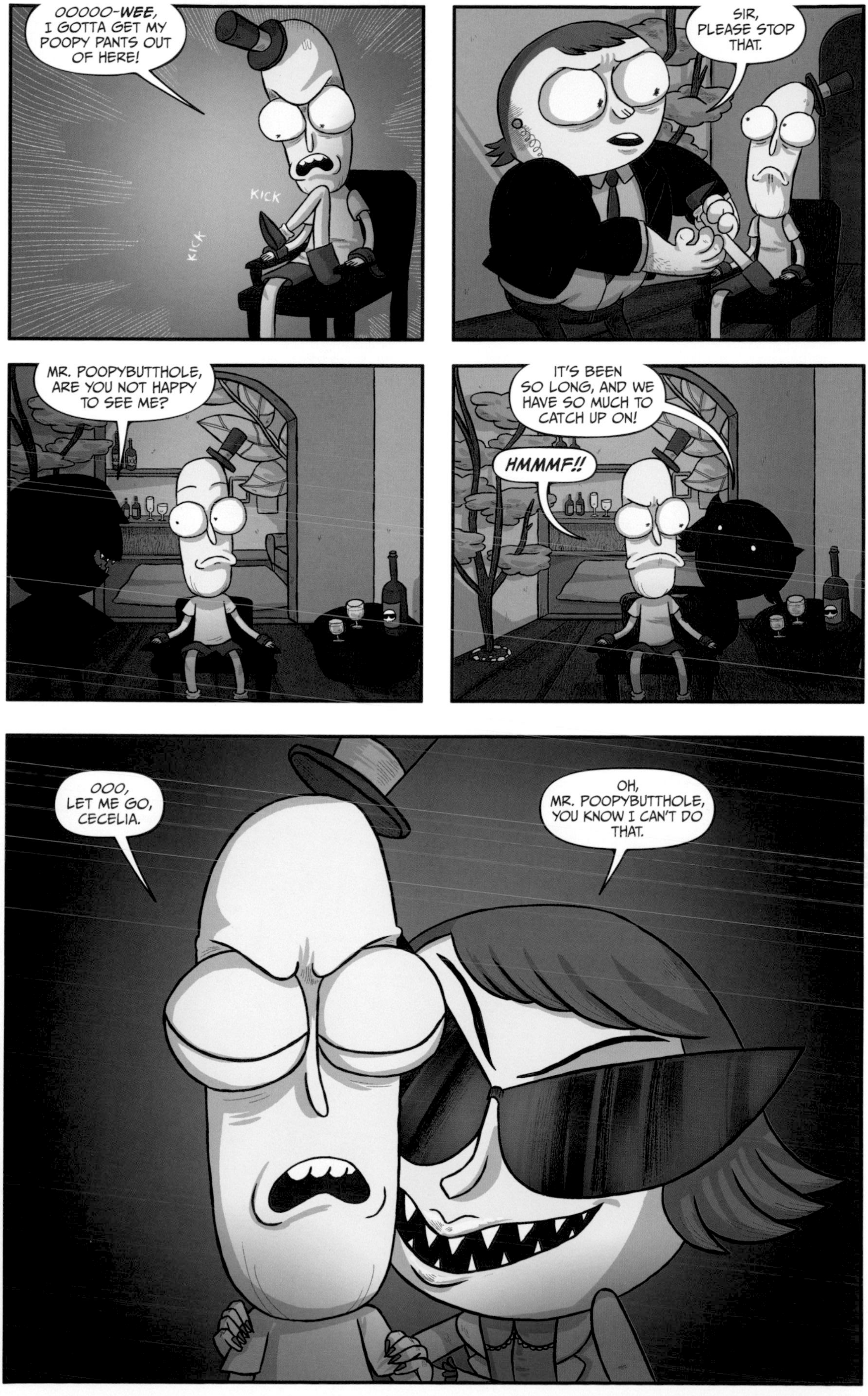
OOOOO-WEE, I GOTTA GET MY POOPY PANTS OUT OF HERE!
KICK
KICK
SIR, PLEASE STOP THAT.
MR. POOPYBUTTHOLE, ARE YOU NOT HAPPY TO SEE ME?
IT'S BEEN SO LONG, AND WE HAVE SO MUCH TO CATCH UP ON!
HMMMF!!
OOO, LET ME GO, CECELIA.
OH, MR. POOPYBUTTHOLE, YOU KNOW I CAN'T DO THAT.

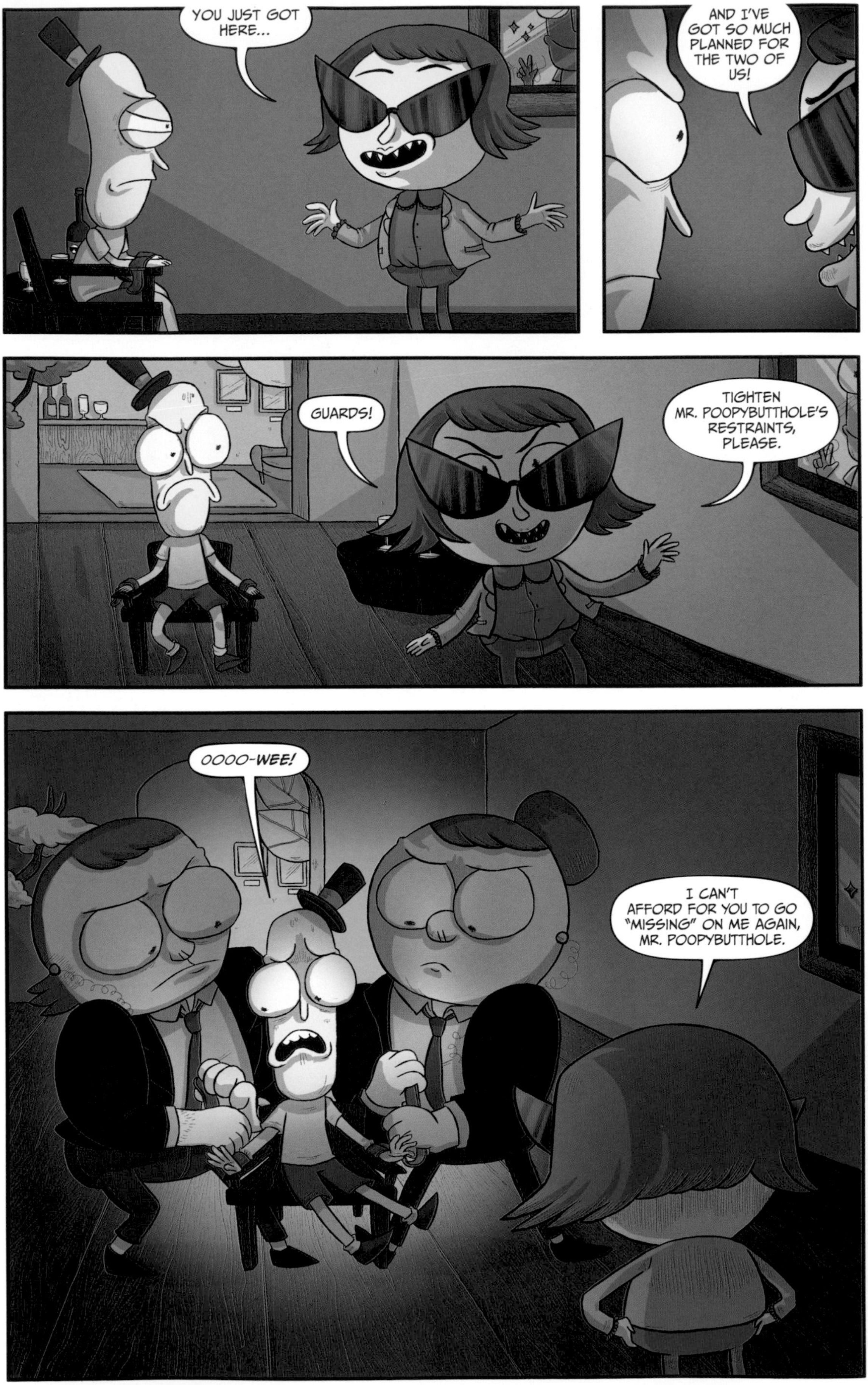
YOU JUST GOT HERE...
AND I'VE GOT SO MUCH PLANNED FOR THE TWO OF US!
GUARDS!
TIGHTEN MR. POOPYBUTTHOLE'S RESTRAINTS, PLEASE.
OOOO-WEE!
I CAN'T AFFORD FOR YOU TO GO "MISSING" ON ME AGAIN, MR. POOPYBUTTHOLE.

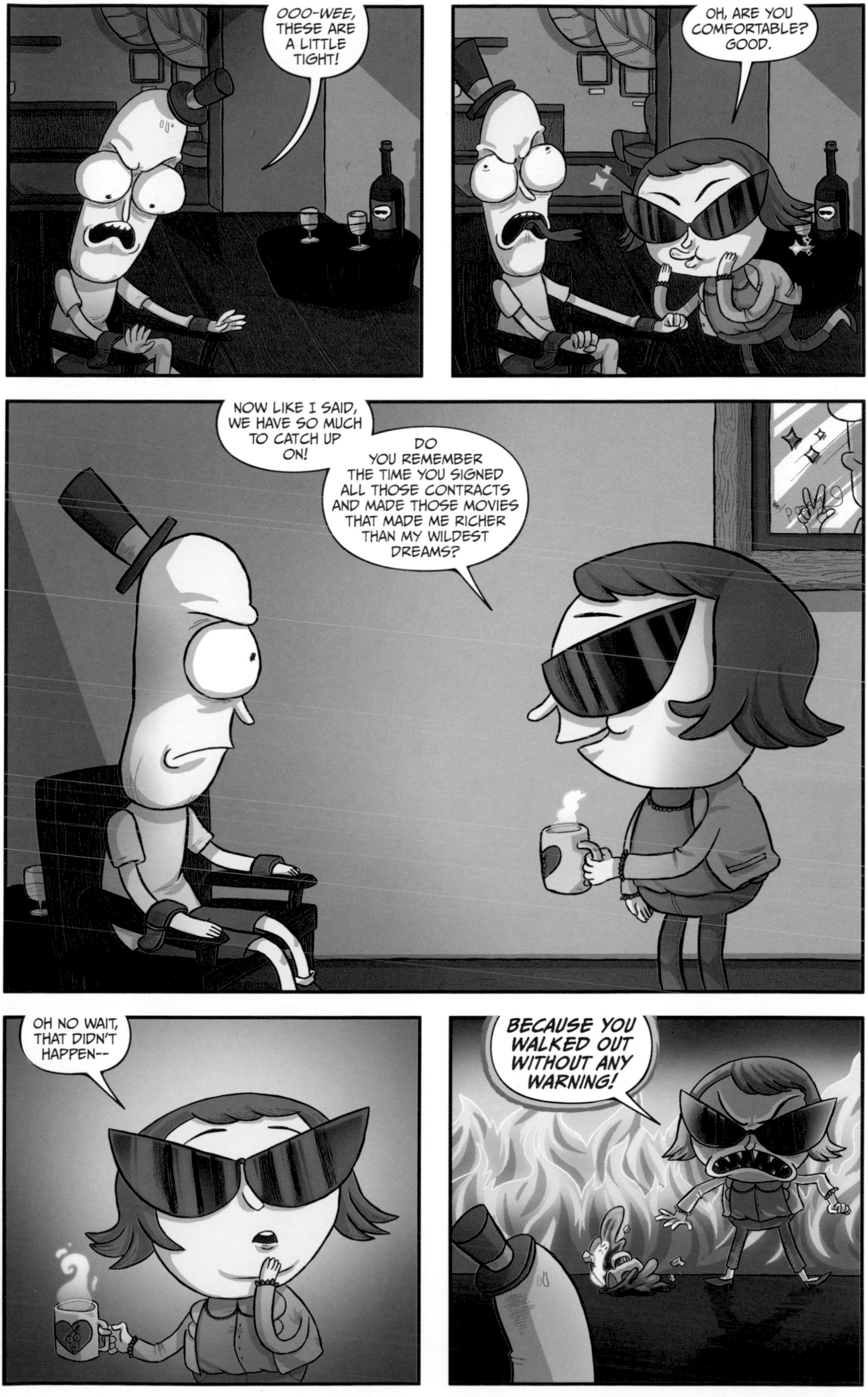
OOO-WEE, THESE ARE A LITTLE TIGHT!
OH, ARE YOU COMFORTABLE? GOOD.
NOW LIKE I SAID, WE HAVE SO MUCH TO CATCH UP ON!
DO YOU REMEMBER THE TIME YOU SIGNED ALL THOSE CONTRACTS AND MADE THOSE MOVIES THAT MADE ME RICHER THAN MY WILDEST DREAMS?
OH NO WAIT, THAT DIDN'T HAPPEN--
BECAUSE YOU WALKED OUT WITHOUT ANY WARNING!

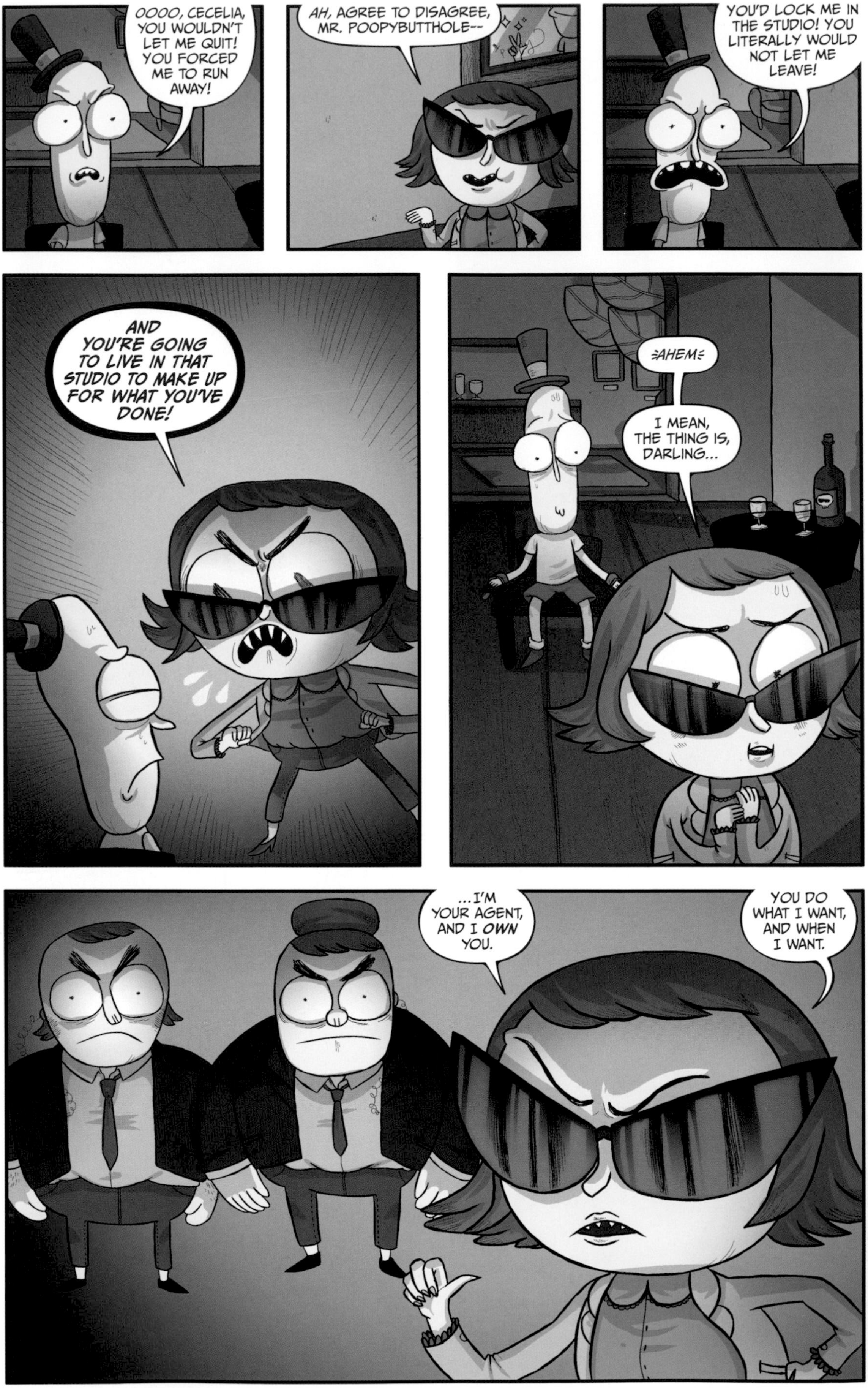
OOOO, CECELIA, YOU WOULDN'T LET ME QUIT! YOU FORCED ME TO RUN AWAY!
AH, AGREE TO DISAGREE, MR. POOPYBUTTHOLE--
YOU'D LOCK ME IN THE STUDIO! YOU LITERALLY WOULD NOT LET ME LEAVE!
AND YOU'RE GOING TO LIVE IN THAT STUDIO TO MAKE UP FOR WHAT YOU'VE DONE!
AHEM
I MEAN, THE THING IS, DARLING...
...I'M YOUR AGENT, AND I OWN YOU.
YOU DO WHAT I WANT, AND WHEN I WANT.

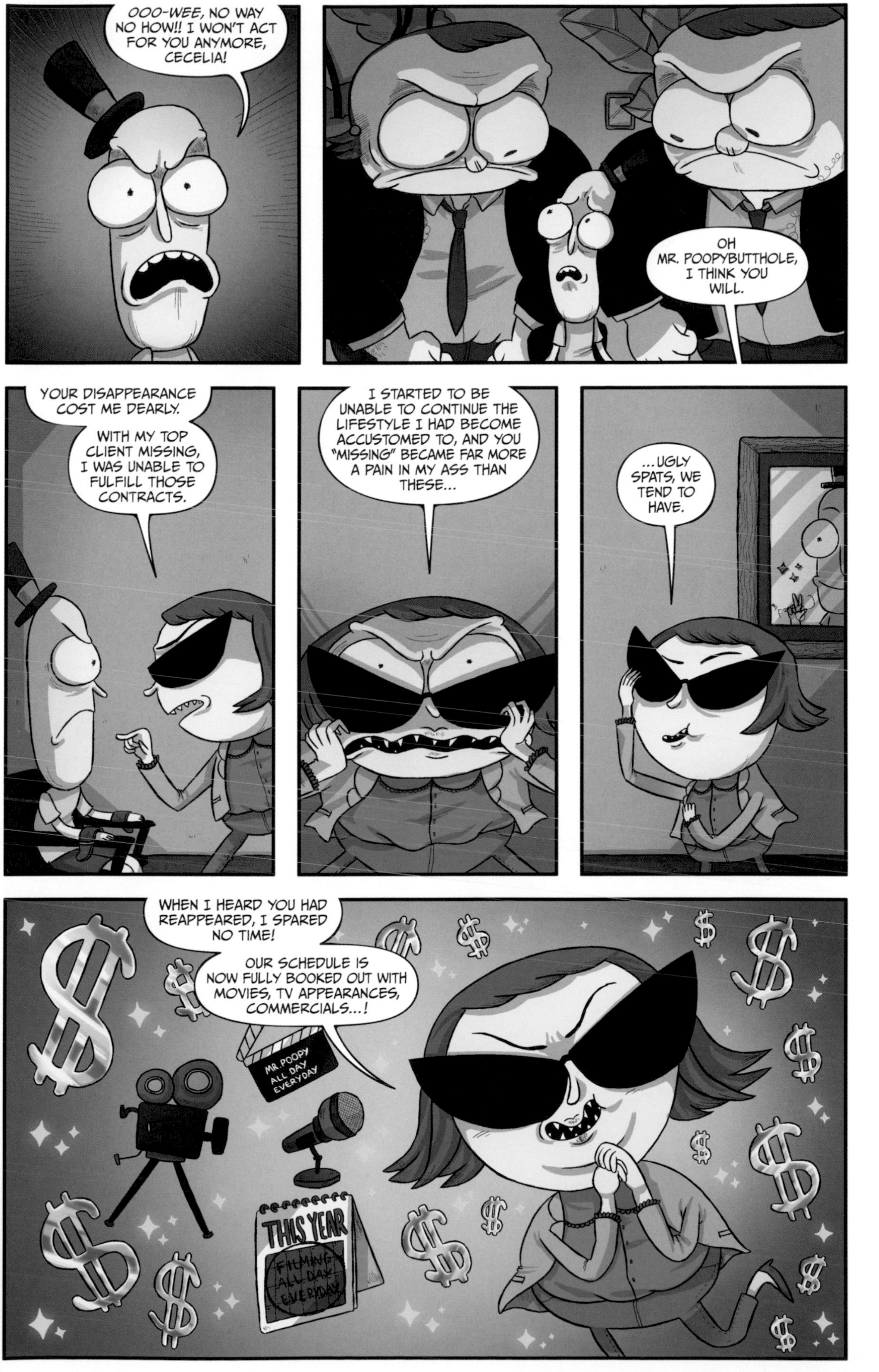
OOO-WEE, NO WAY NO HOW!! I WON'T ACT FOR YOU ANYMORE, CECELIA!
OH MR. POOPYBUTTHOLE, I THINK YOU WILL.
YOUR DISAPPEARANCE COST ME DEARLY.
WITH MY TOP CLIENT MISSING, I WAS UNABLE TO FULFILL THOSE CONTRACTS.
I STARTED TO BE UNABLE TO CONTINUE THE LIFESTYLE I HAD BECOME ACCUSTOMED TO, AND YOU "MISSING" BECAME FAR MORE A PAIN IN MY ASS THAN THESE...
...UGLY SPATS, WE TEND TO HAVE.
WHEN I HEARD YOU HAD REAPPEARED, I SPARED NO TIME!
OUR SCHEDULE IS NOW FULLY BOOKED OUT WITH MOVIES, TV APPEARANCES, COMMERCIALS...!
MR. POOPY ALL DAY EVERYDAY
THIS YEAR
FILMING ALL DAY EVERYDAY

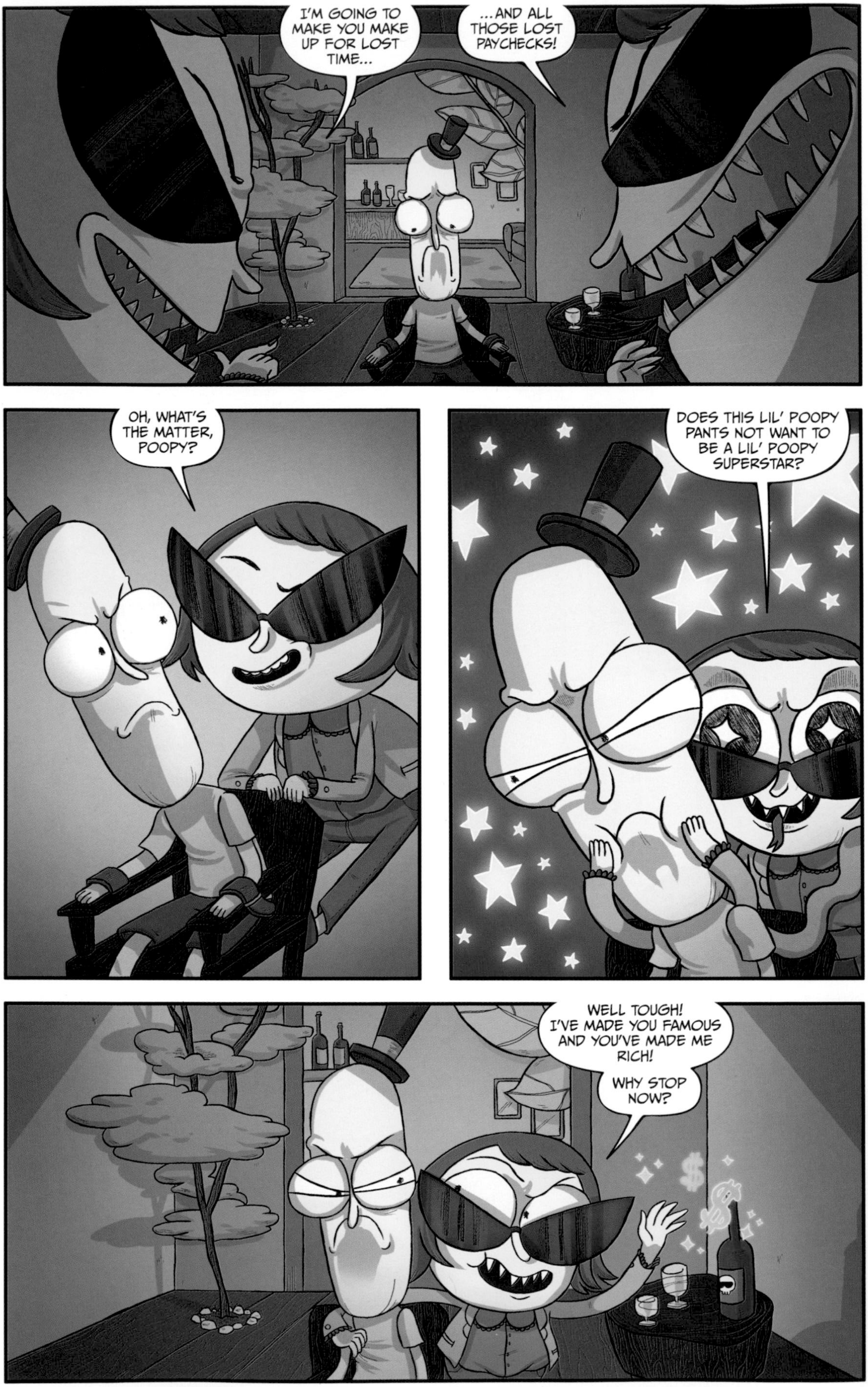
I'M GOING TO MAKE YOU MAKE UP FOR LOST TIME...
...AND ALL THOSE LOST PAYCHECKS!
OH, WHAT'S THE MATTER, POOPY?
DOES THIS LIL' POOPY PANTS NOT WANT TO BE A LIL' POOPY SUPERSTAR?
WELL TOUGH! I'VE MADE YOU FAMOUS AND YOU'VE MADE ME RICH!
WHY STOP NOW?

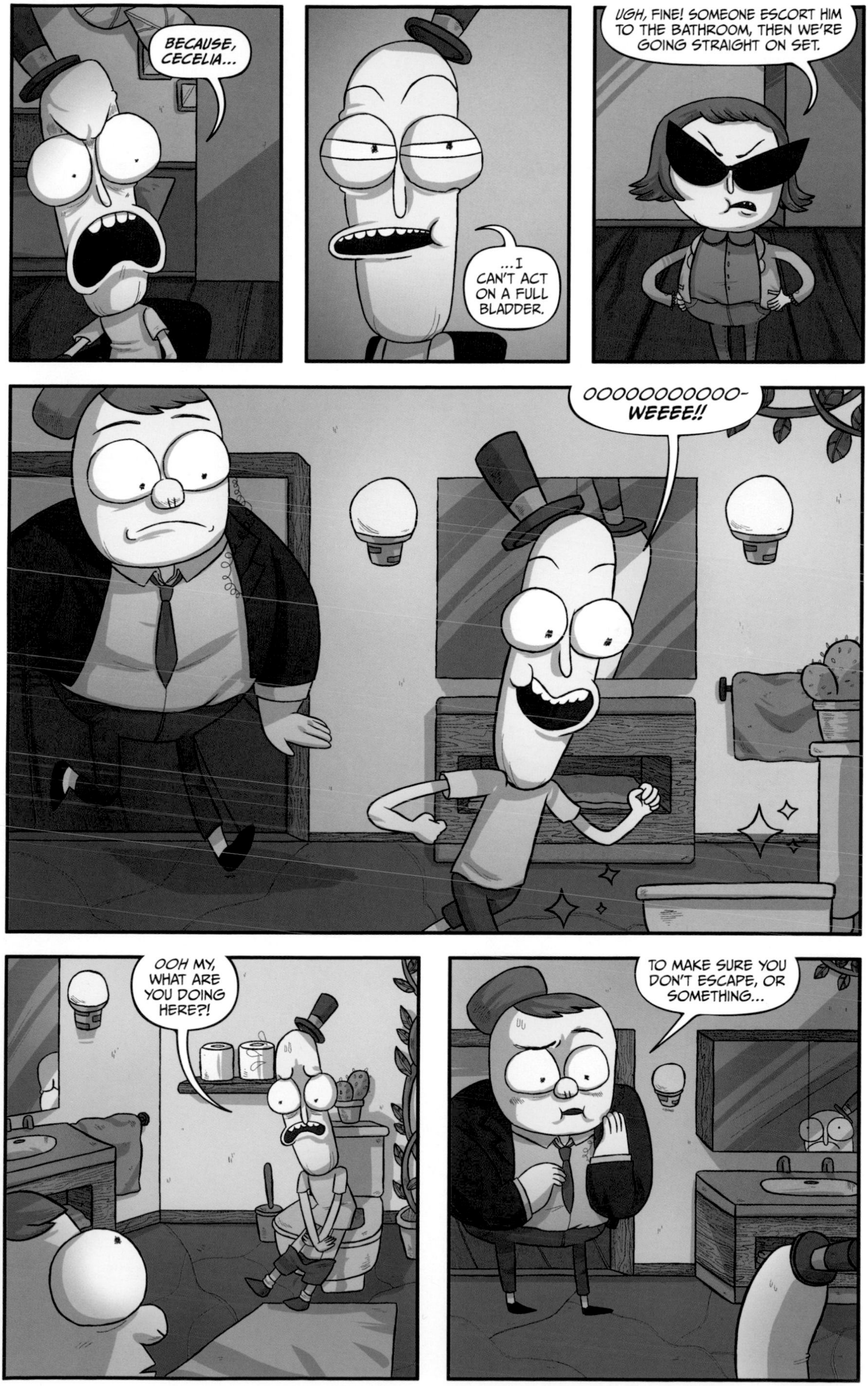
BECAUSE, CECELIA...
...I CAN'T ACT ON A FULL BLADDER.
UGH, FINE! SOMEONE ESCORT HIM TO THE BATHROOM, THEN WE'RE GOING STRAIGHT ON SET.
OOOOOOOOOOO-WEEEE!!
OOH MY, WHAT ARE YOU DOING HERE?!
TO MAKE SURE YOU DON'T ESCAPE, OR SOMETHING...

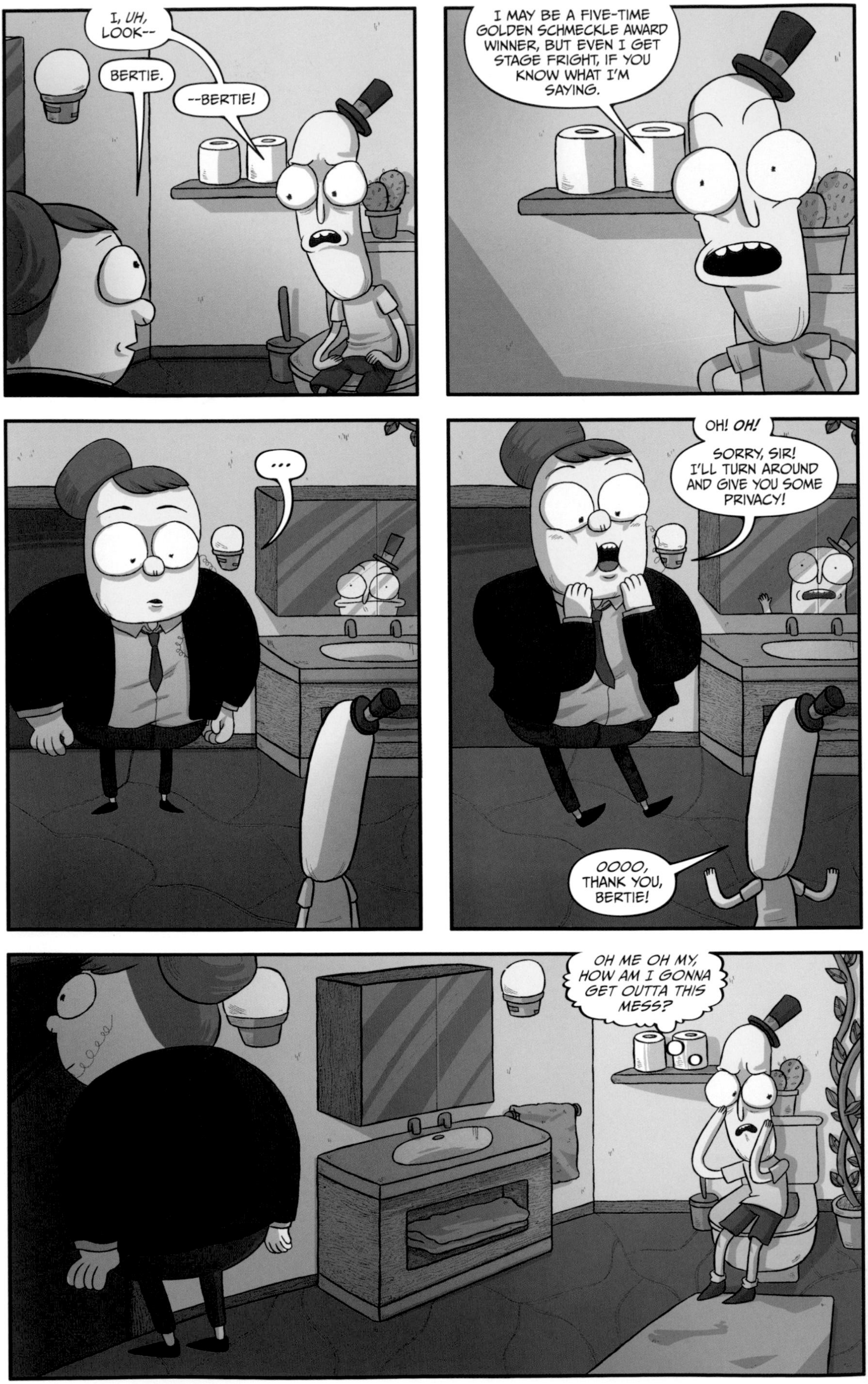
I, UH, LOOK--
BERTIE.
--BERTIE!
I MAY BE A FIVE-TIME GOLDEN SCHMECKLE AWARD WINNER, BUT EVEN I GET STAGE FRIGHT, IF YOU KNOW WHAT I'M SAYING.
...
OH! OH!
SORRY, SIR! I'LL TURN AROUND AND GIVE YOU SOME PRIVACY!
OOOO, THANK YOU, BERTIE!
OH ME OH MY, HOW AM I GONNA GET OUTTA THIS MESS?

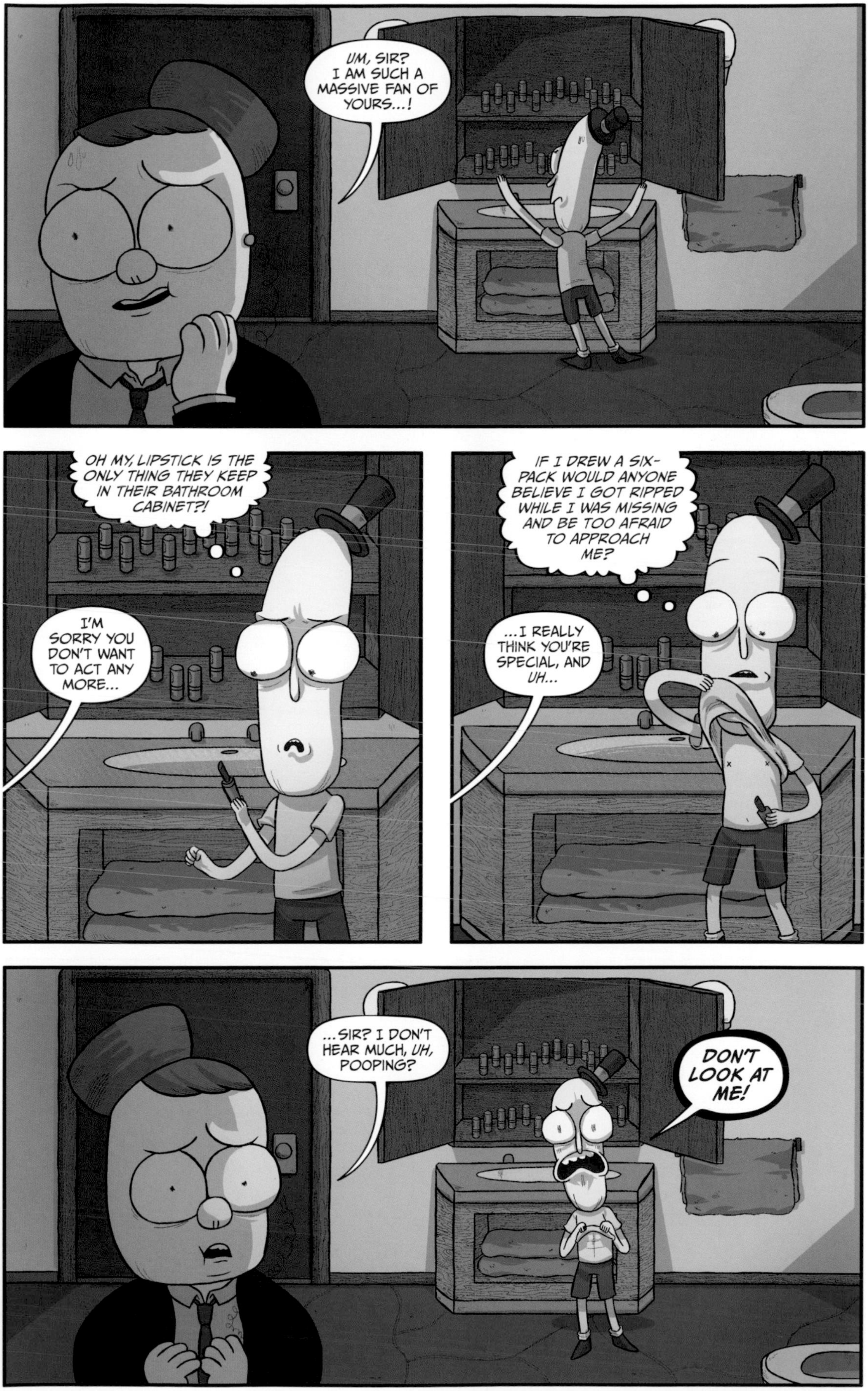
UM, SIR? I AM SUCH A MASSIVE FAN OF YOURS...!
OH MY, LIPSTICK IS THE ONLY THING THEY KEEP IN THEIR BATHROOM CABINET?!
I'M SORRY YOU DON'T WANT TO ACT ANY MORE...
IF I DREW A SIX-PACK WOULD ANYONE BELIEVE I GOT RIPPED WHILE I WAS MISSING AND BE TOO AFRAID TO APPROACH ME?
...I REALLY THINK YOU'RE SPECIAL, AND UH...
...SIR? I DON'T HEAR MUCH, UH, POOPING?
DON'T LOOK AT ME!

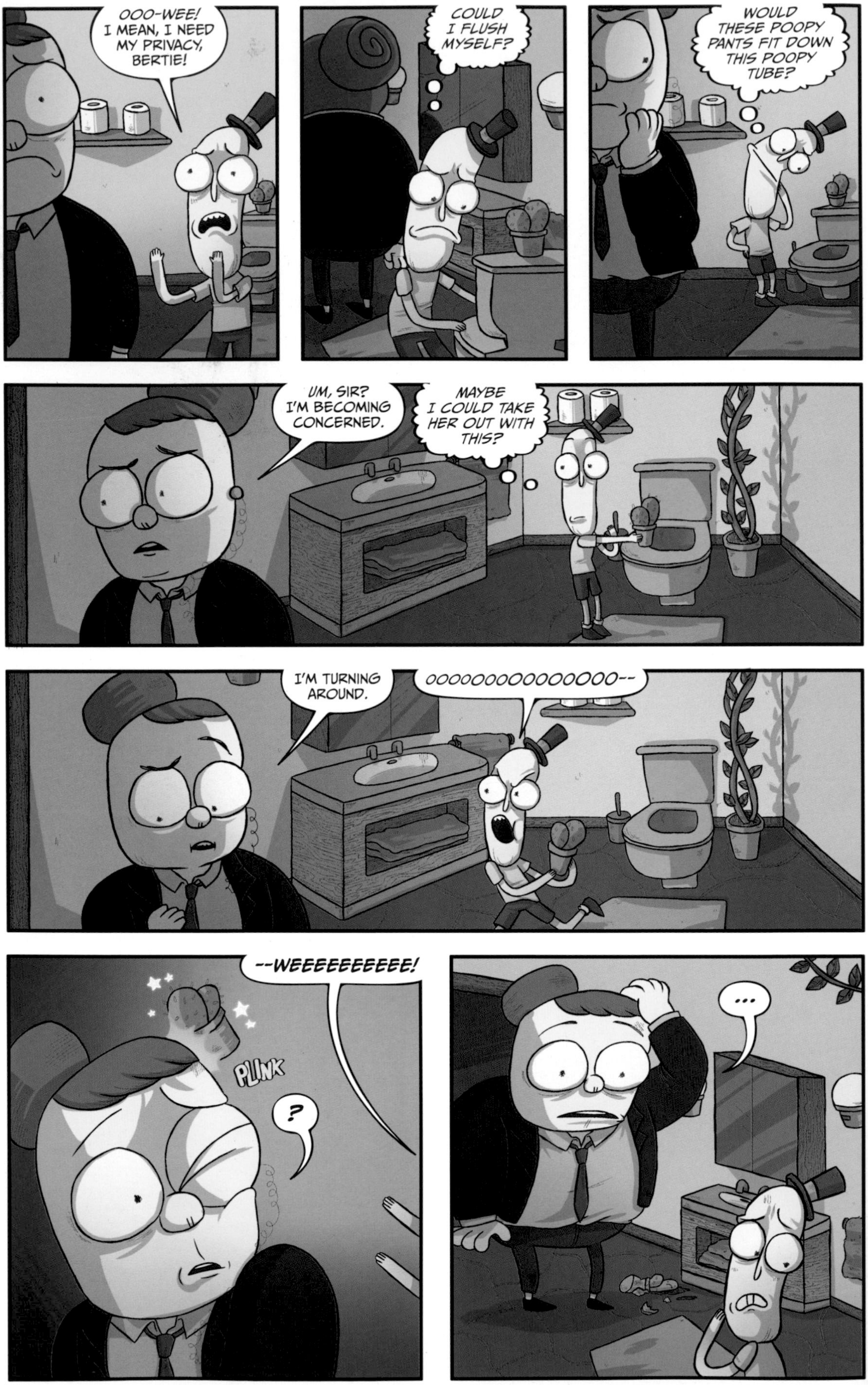
OOO-WEE! I MEAN, I NEED MY PRIVACY, BERTIE!
COULD I FLUSH MYSELF?
WOULD THESE POOPY PANTS FIT DOWN THIS POOPY TUBE?
UM, SIR? I'M BECOMING CONCERNED.
MAYBE I COULD TAKE HER OUT WITH THIS?
I'M TURNING AROUND.
OOOOOOOOOOOOOOO--
--WEEEEEEEEEE!
PLINK
?
...

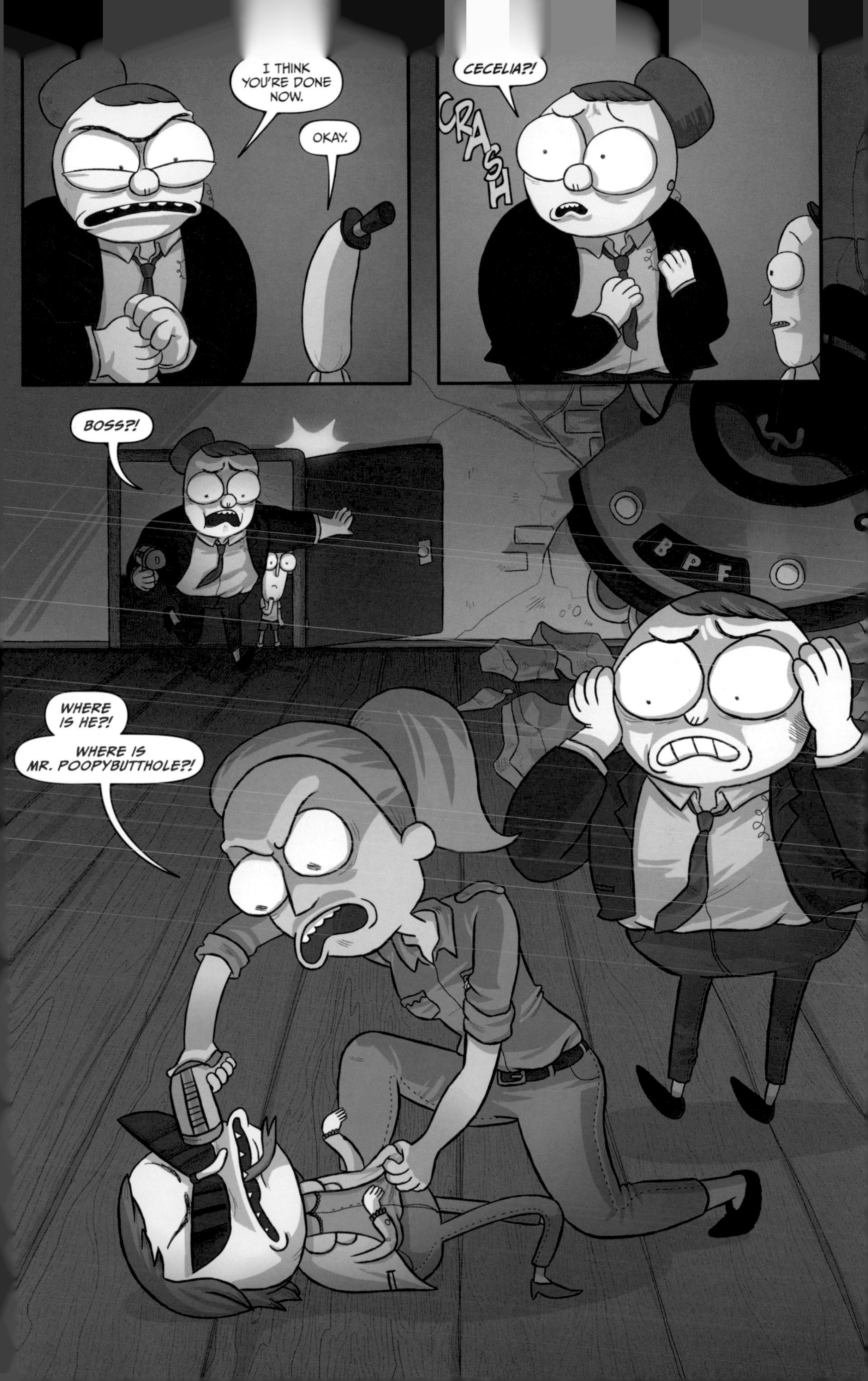
I THINK YOU'RE DONE NOW.
OKAY.
CECELIA?!
CRASH
BOSS?!
B P E
WHERE IS HE?!
WHERE IS MR. POOPYBUTTHOLE?!

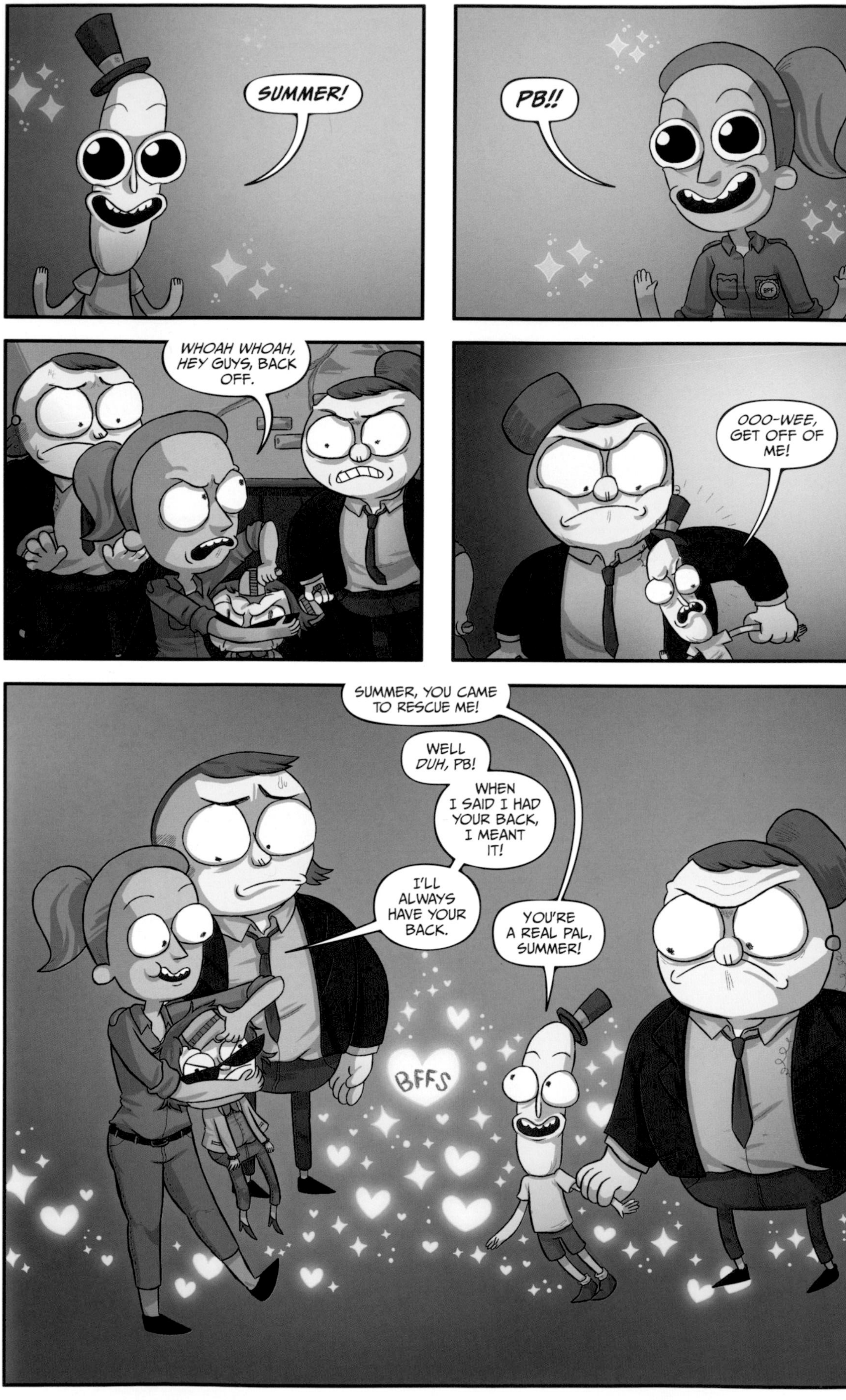
SUMMER!
PB!!
WHOAH WHOAH, HEY GUYS, BACK OFF.
OOO-WEE, GET OFF OF ME!
SUMMER, YOU CAME TO RESCUE ME!
WELL *DUH*, PB!
WHEN I SAID I HAD YOUR BACK, I MEANT IT!
I'LL ALWAYS HAVE YOUR BACK.
YOU'RE A REAL PAL, SUMMER!
BFFS

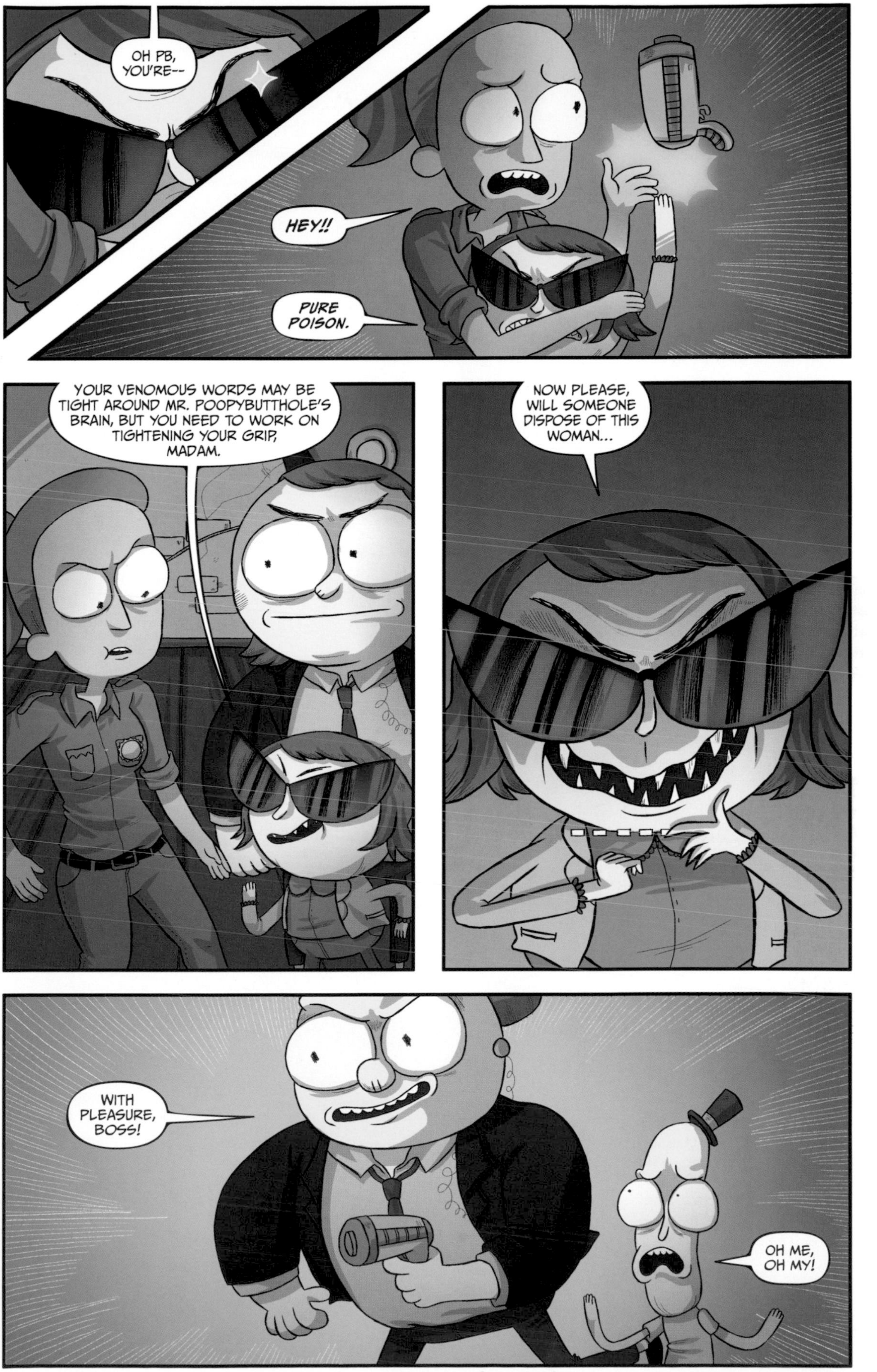
OH PB, YOU'RE--
HEY!!
PURE POISON.
YOUR VENOMOUS WORDS MAY BE TIGHT AROUND MR. POOPYBUTTHOLE'S BRAIN, BUT YOU NEED TO WORK ON TIGHTENING YOUR GRIP, MADAM.
NOW PLEASE, WILL SOMEONE DISPOSE OF THIS WOMAN...
WITH PLEASURE, BOSS!
OH ME, OH MY!

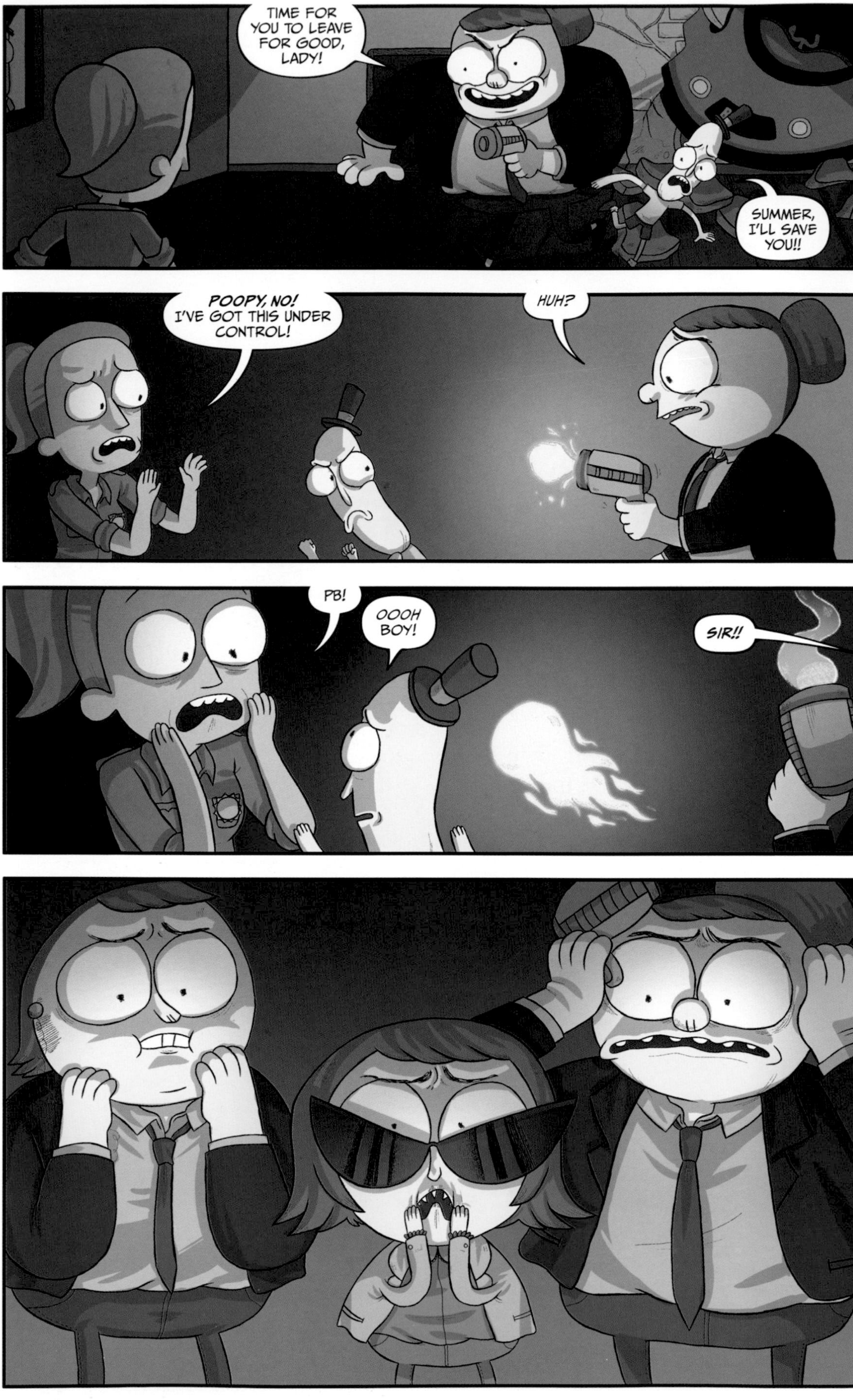
TIME FOR YOU TO LEAVE FOR GOOD, LADY!
SUMMER, I'LL SAVE YOU!!
POOPY, NO! I'VE GOT THIS UNDER CONTROL!
HUH?
PB!
OOOH BOY!
SIR!!

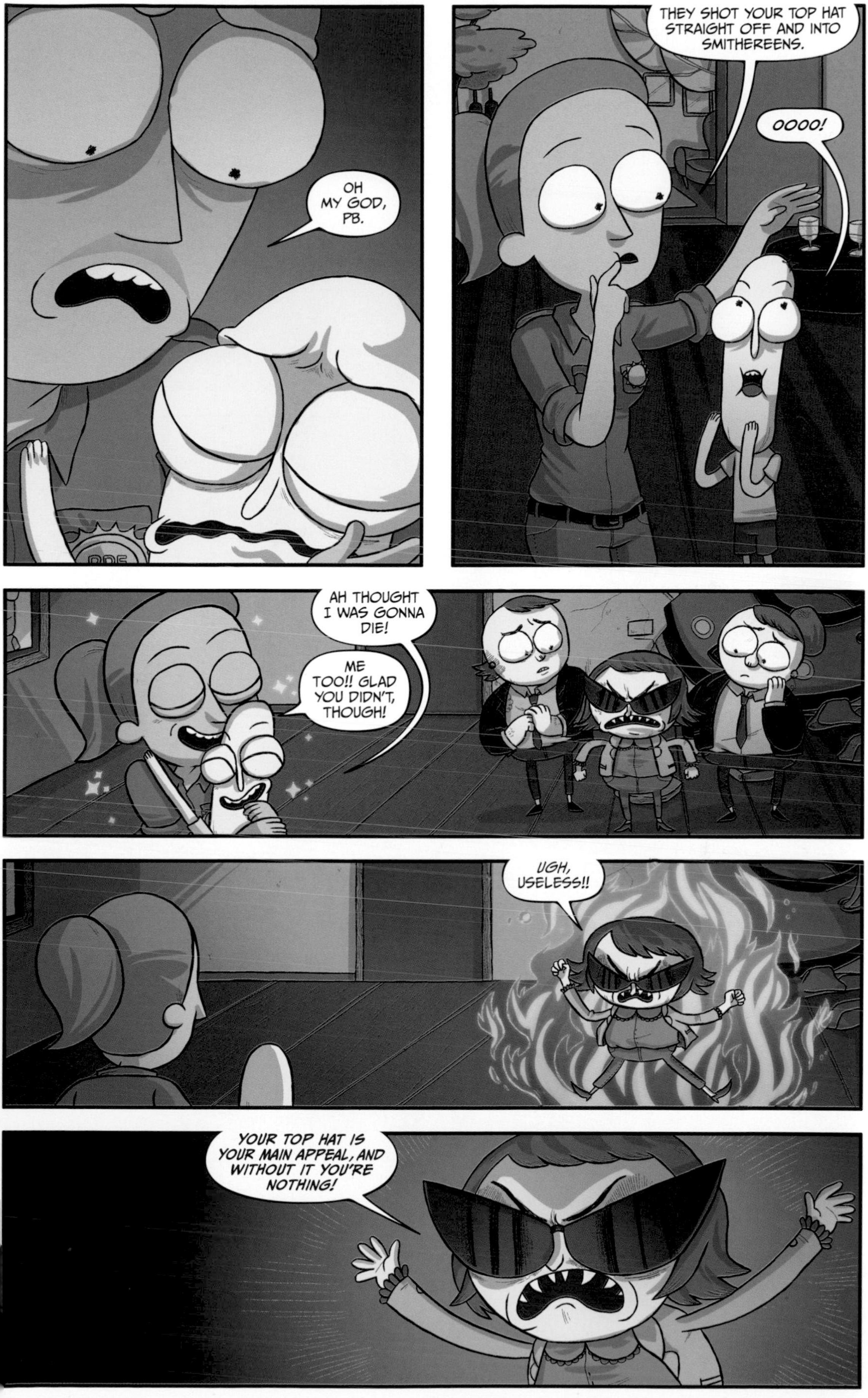
OH MY GOD, PB.
THEY SHOT YOUR TOP HAT STRAIGHT OFF AND INTO SMITHEREENS.
OOOO!
AH THOUGHT I WAS GONNA DIE!
ME TOO!! GLAD YOU DIDN'T, THOUGH!
UGH, USELESS!!
YOUR TOP HAT IS YOUR MAIN APPEAL, AND WITHOUT IT YOU'RE NOTHING!

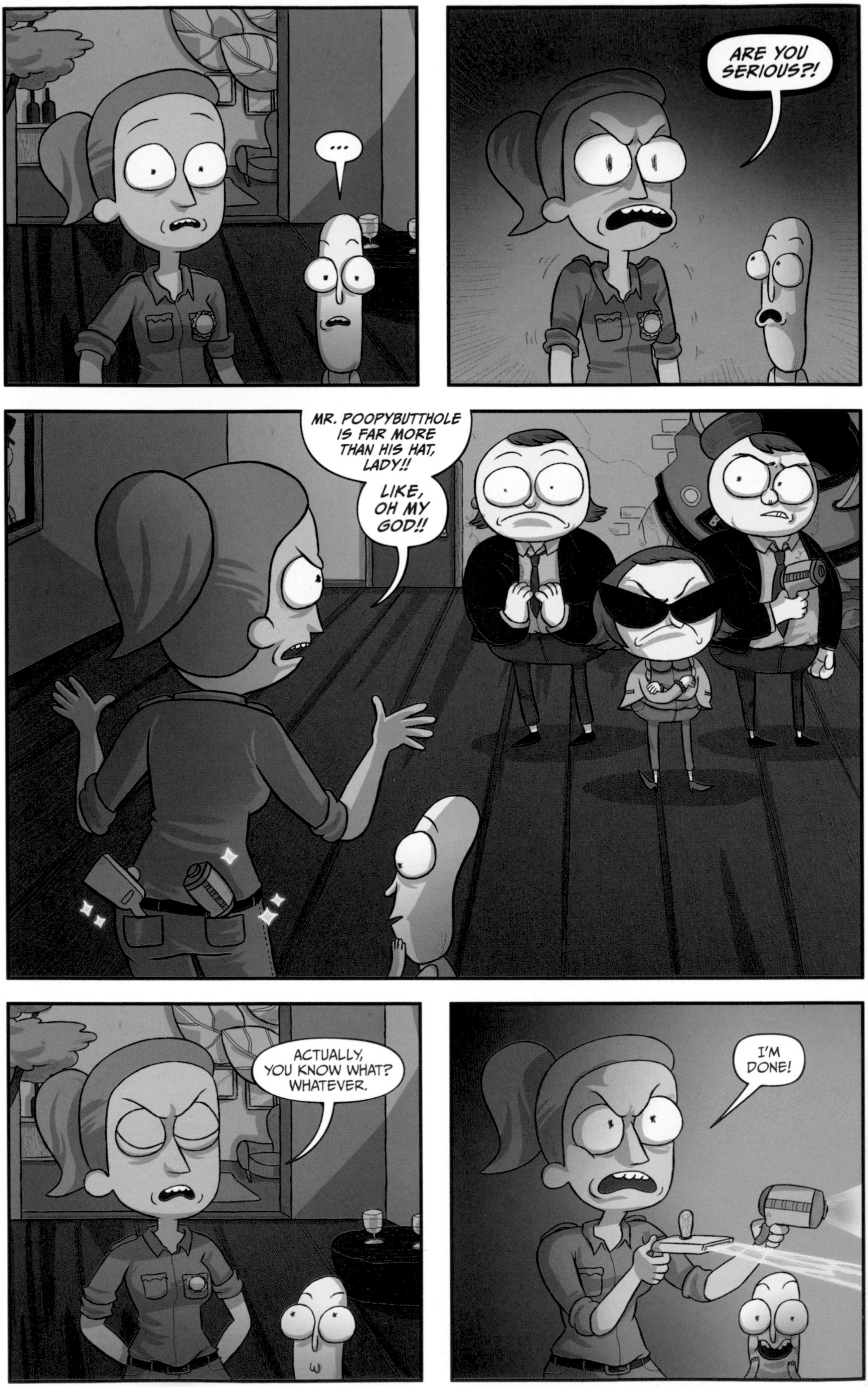
...
ARE YOU SERIOUS?!
MR. POOPYBUTTHOLE IS FAR MORE THAN HIS HAT, LADY!!
LIKE, OH MY GOD!!
ACTUALLY, YOU KNOW WHAT? WHATEVER.
I'M DONE!

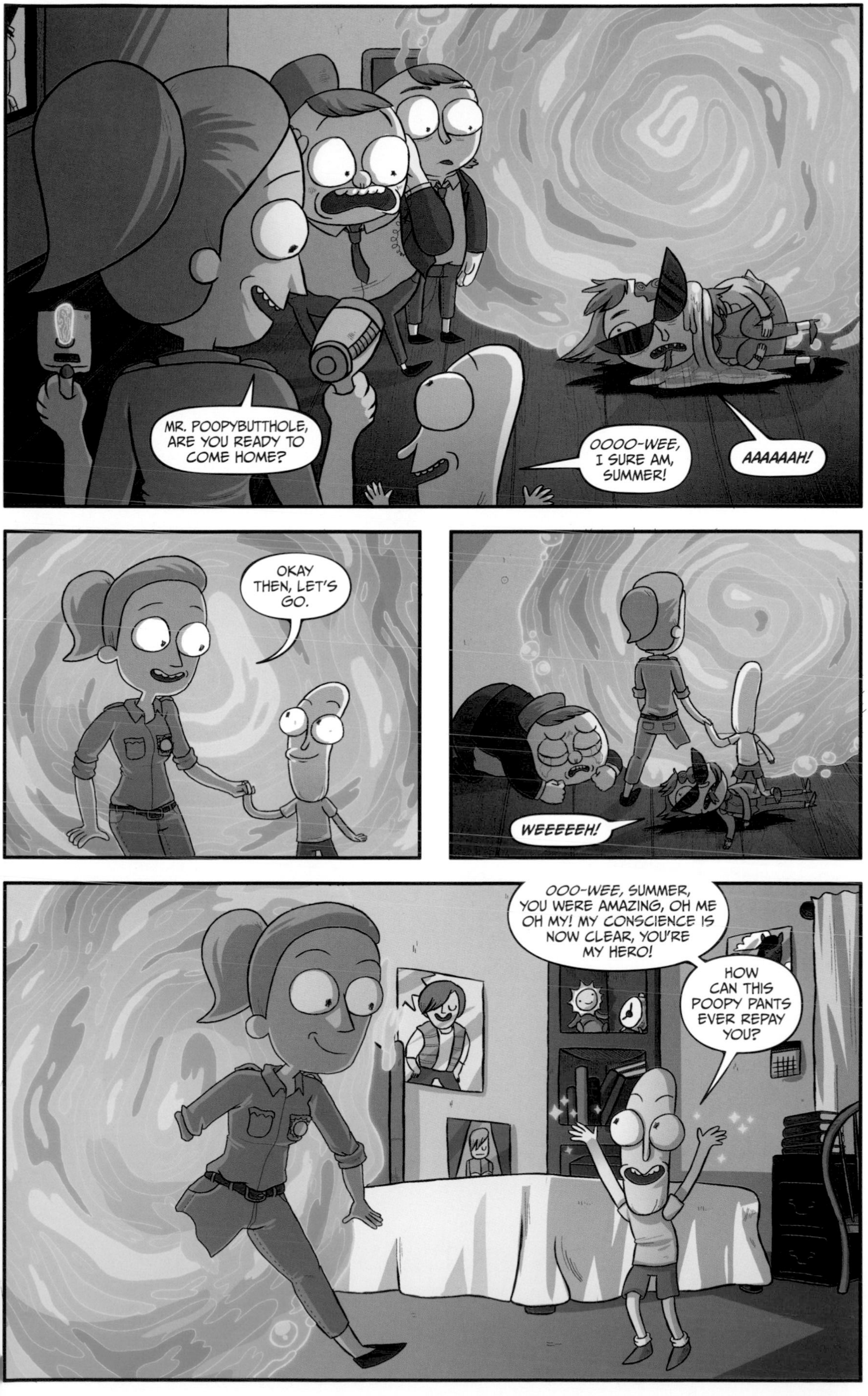
MR. POOPYBUTTHOLE, ARE YOU READY TO COME HOME?
OOOO-WEE, I SURE AM, SUMMER!
AAAAAAH!
OKAY THEN, LET'S GO.
WEEEEEH!
OOO-WEE, SUMMER, YOU WERE AMAZING, OH ME OH MY! MY CONSCIENCE IS NOW CLEAR, YOU'RE MY HERO!
HOW CAN THIS POOPY PANTS EVER REPAY YOU?

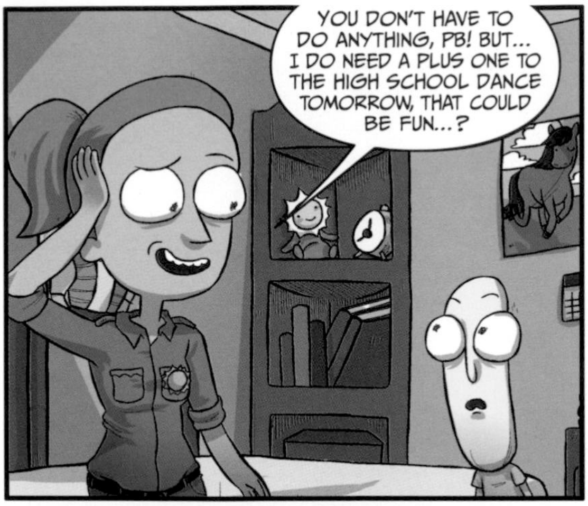
YOU DON'T HAVE TO DO ANYTHING, PB! BUT... I DO NEED A PLUS ONE TO THE HIGH SCHOOL DANCE TOMORROW, THAT COULD BE FUN...?

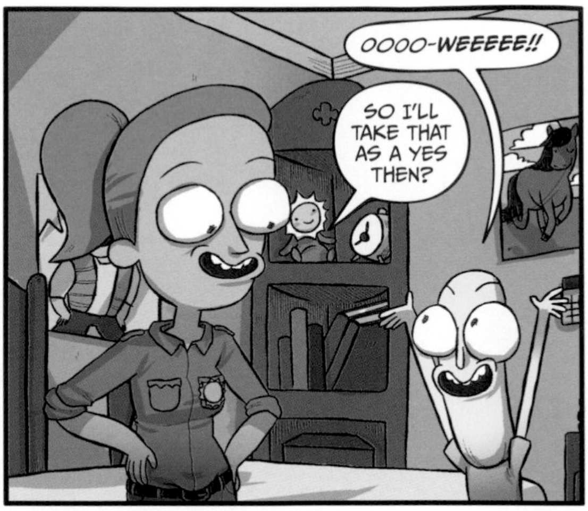
SO I'LL TAKE THAT AS A YES THEN?
OOOO-WEEEEE!!

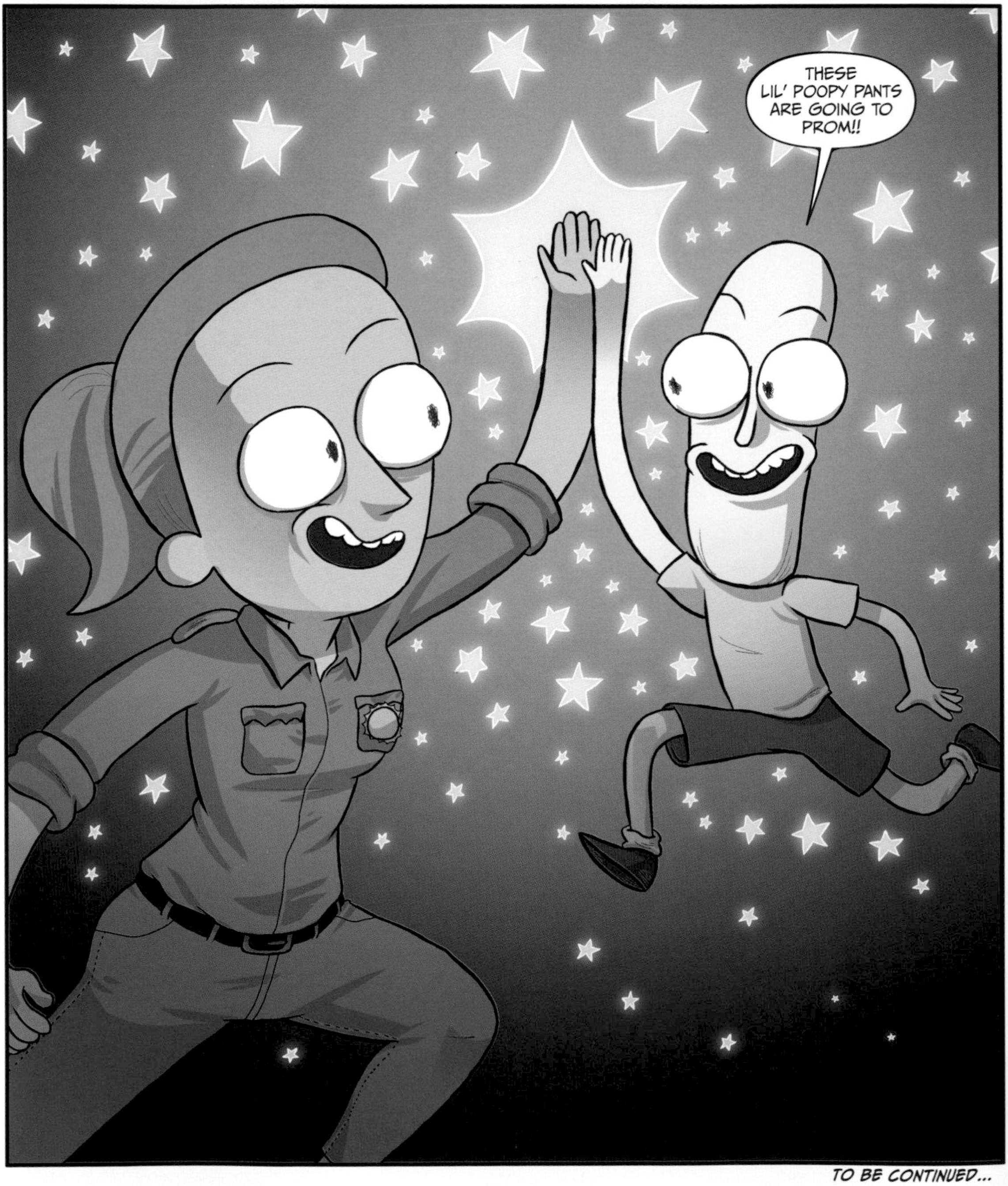
THESE LIL' POOPY PANTS ARE GOING TO PROM!!

TO BE CONTINUED...

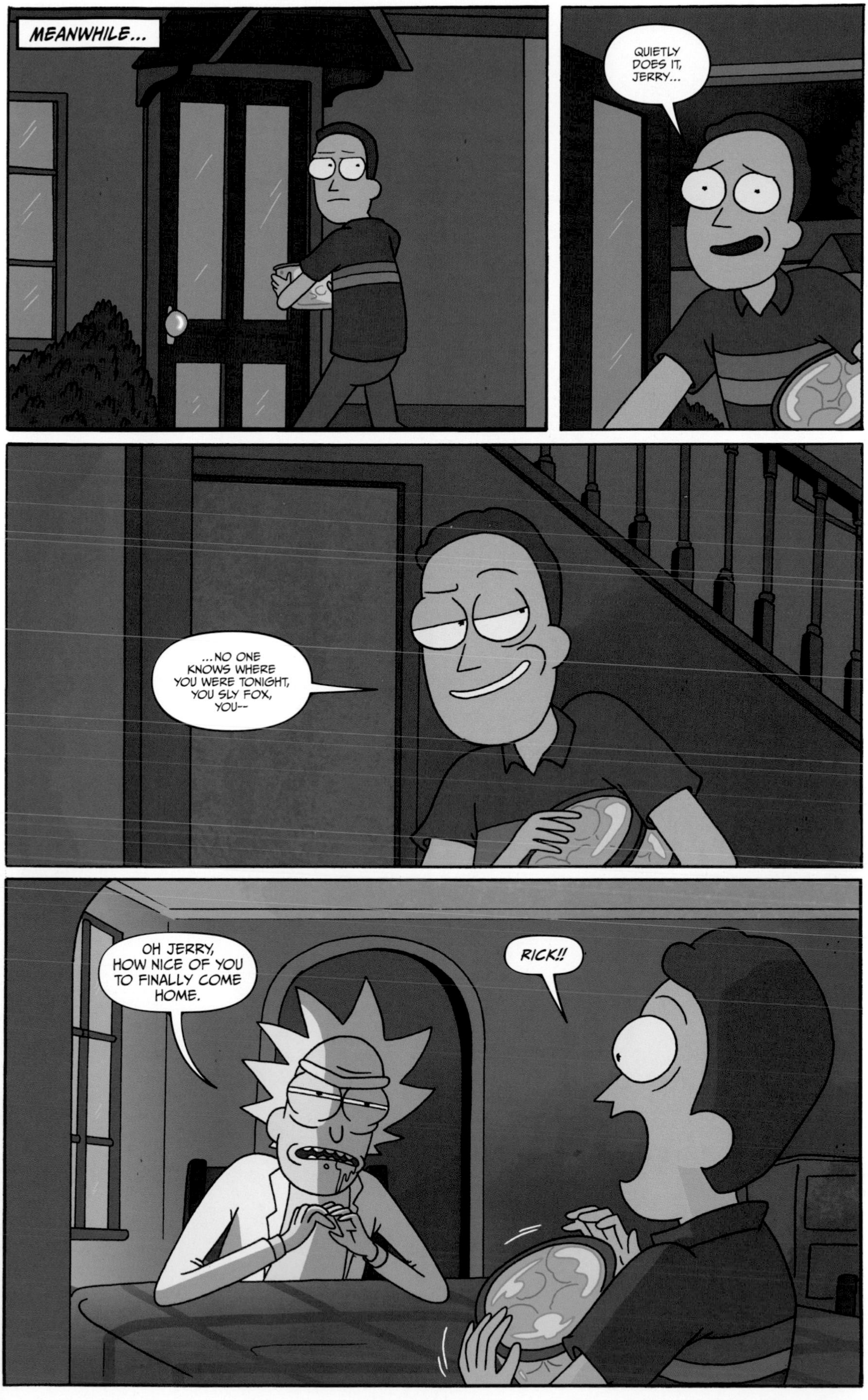
MEANWHILE...
QUIETLY DOES IT, JERRY...
...NO ONE KNOWS WHERE YOU WERE TONIGHT, YOU SLY FOX, YOU--
OH JERRY, HOW NICE OF YOU TO FINALLY COME HOME.
RICK!!

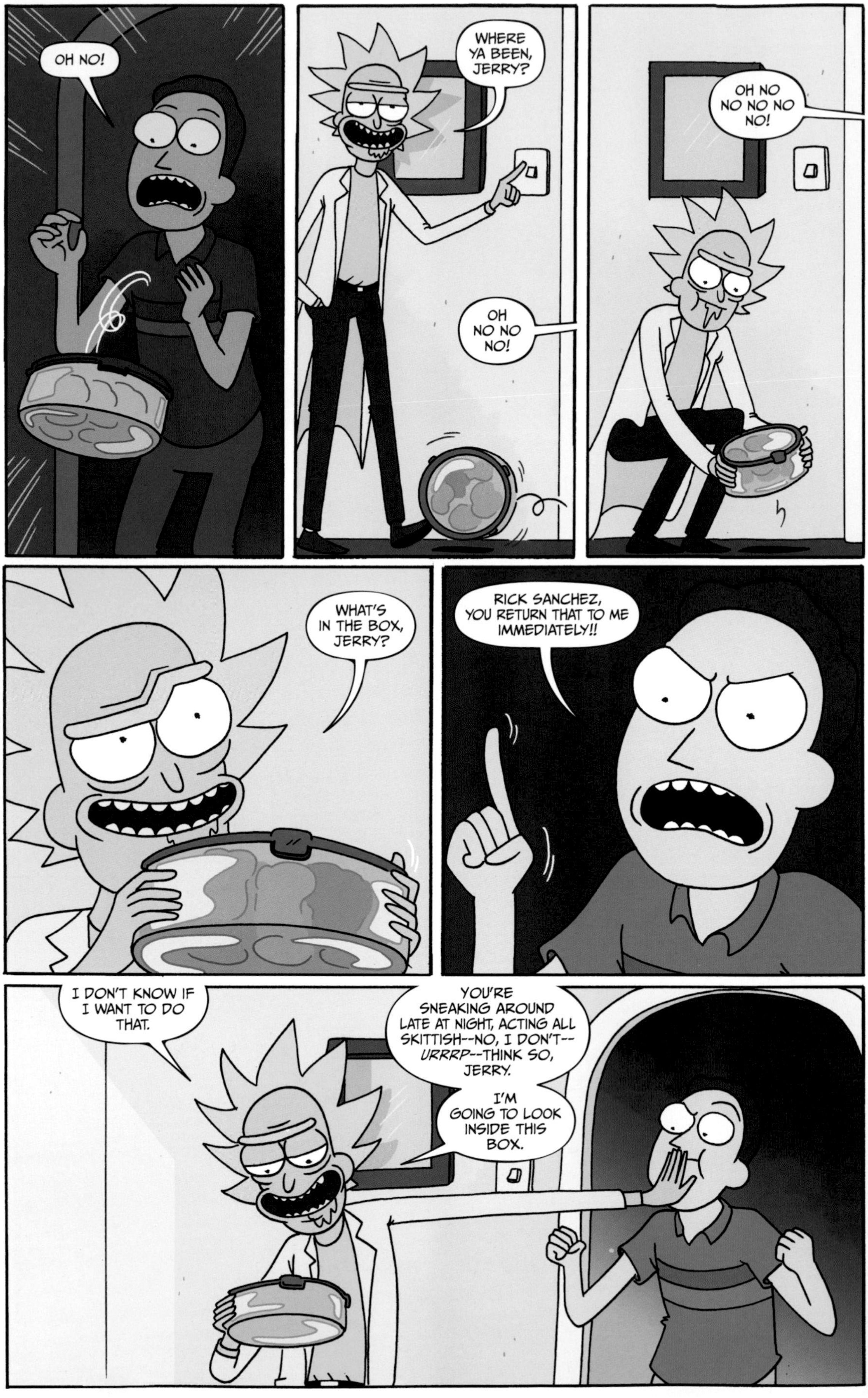

OH NO!
WHERE YA BEEN, JERRY?
OH NO NO NO!
OH NO NO NO NO NO!
WHAT'S IN THE BOX, JERRY?
RICK SANCHEZ, YOU RETURN THAT TO ME IMMEDIATELY!!
I DON'T KNOW IF I WANT TO DO THAT.
YOU'RE SNEAKING AROUND LATE AT NIGHT, ACTING ALL SKITTISH--NO, I DON'T--URRRP--THINK SO, JERRY.
I'M GOING TO LOOK INSIDE THIS BOX.

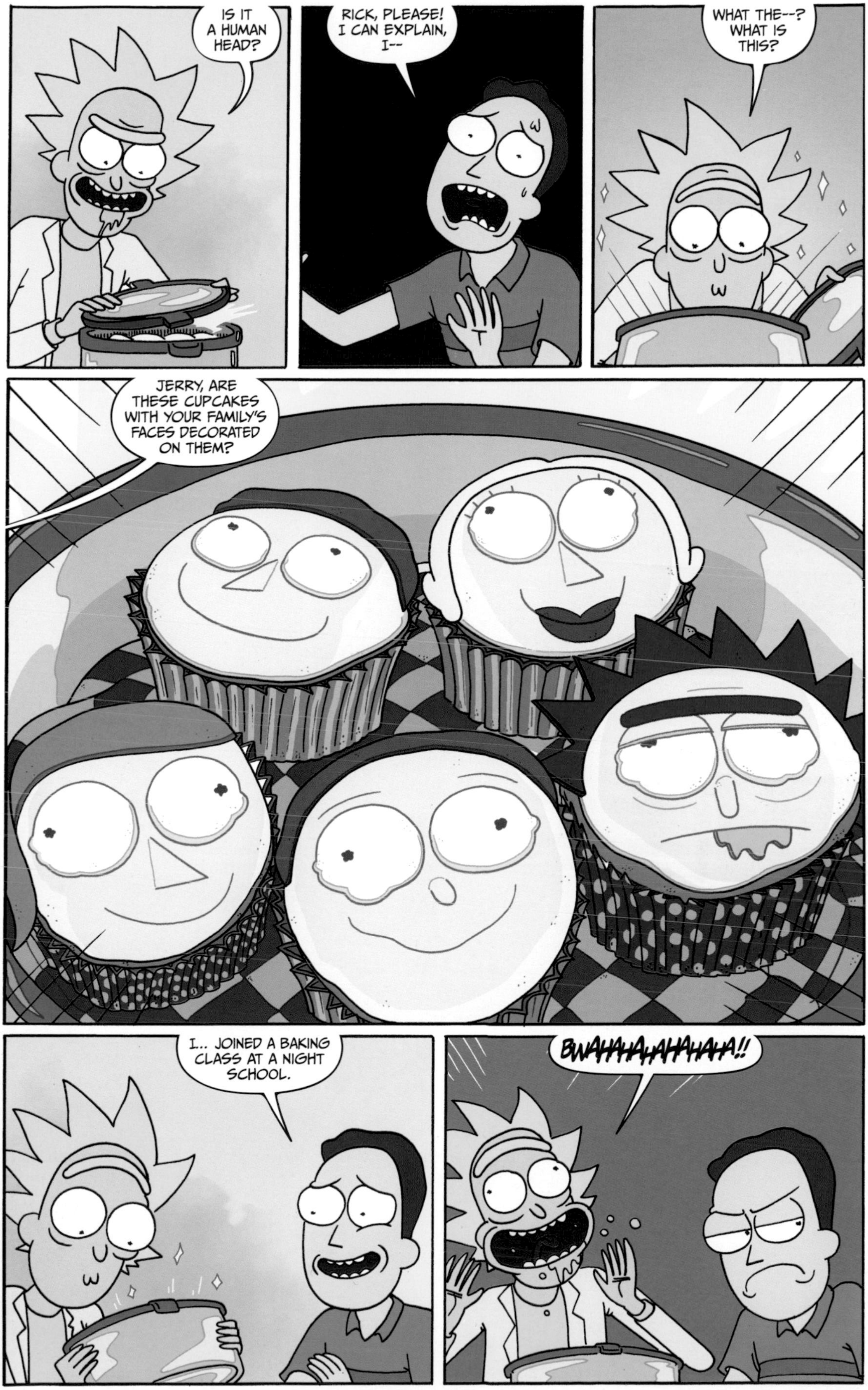
IS IT A HUMAN HEAD?
RICK, PLEASE! I CAN EXPLAIN, I--
WHAT THE--? WHAT IS THIS?
JERRY, ARE THESE CUPCAKES WITH YOUR FAMILY'S FACES DECORATED ON THEM?
I... JOINED A BAKING CLASS AT A NIGHT SCHOOL.
BWAHAHAHAHAHAHA!!

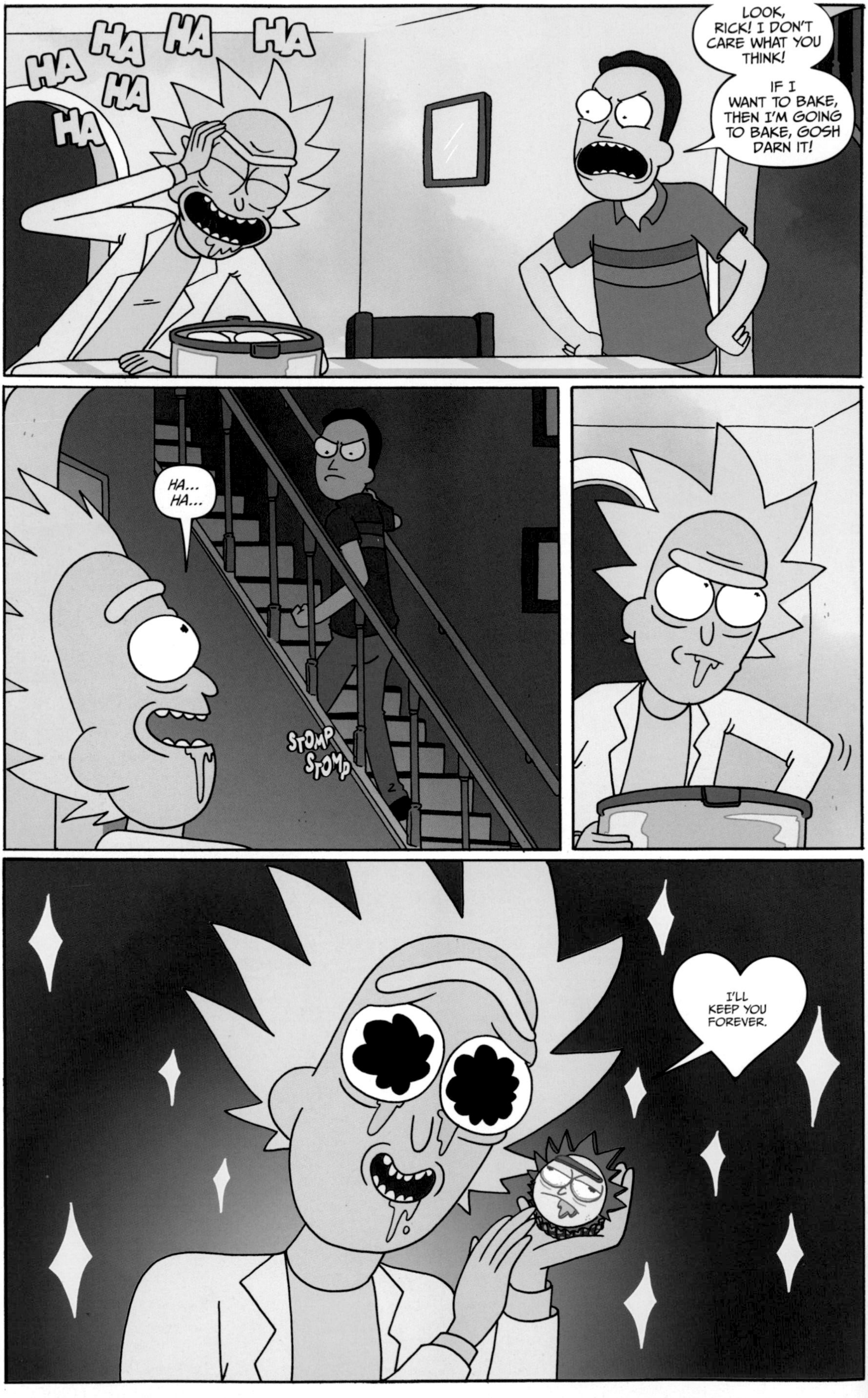
HA HA HA HA HA HA
LOOK, RICK! I DON'T CARE WHAT YOU THINK!
IF I WANT TO BAKE, THEN I'M GOING TO BAKE, GOSH DARN IT!
HA... HA...
STOMP STOMP
I'LL KEEP YOU FOREVER.

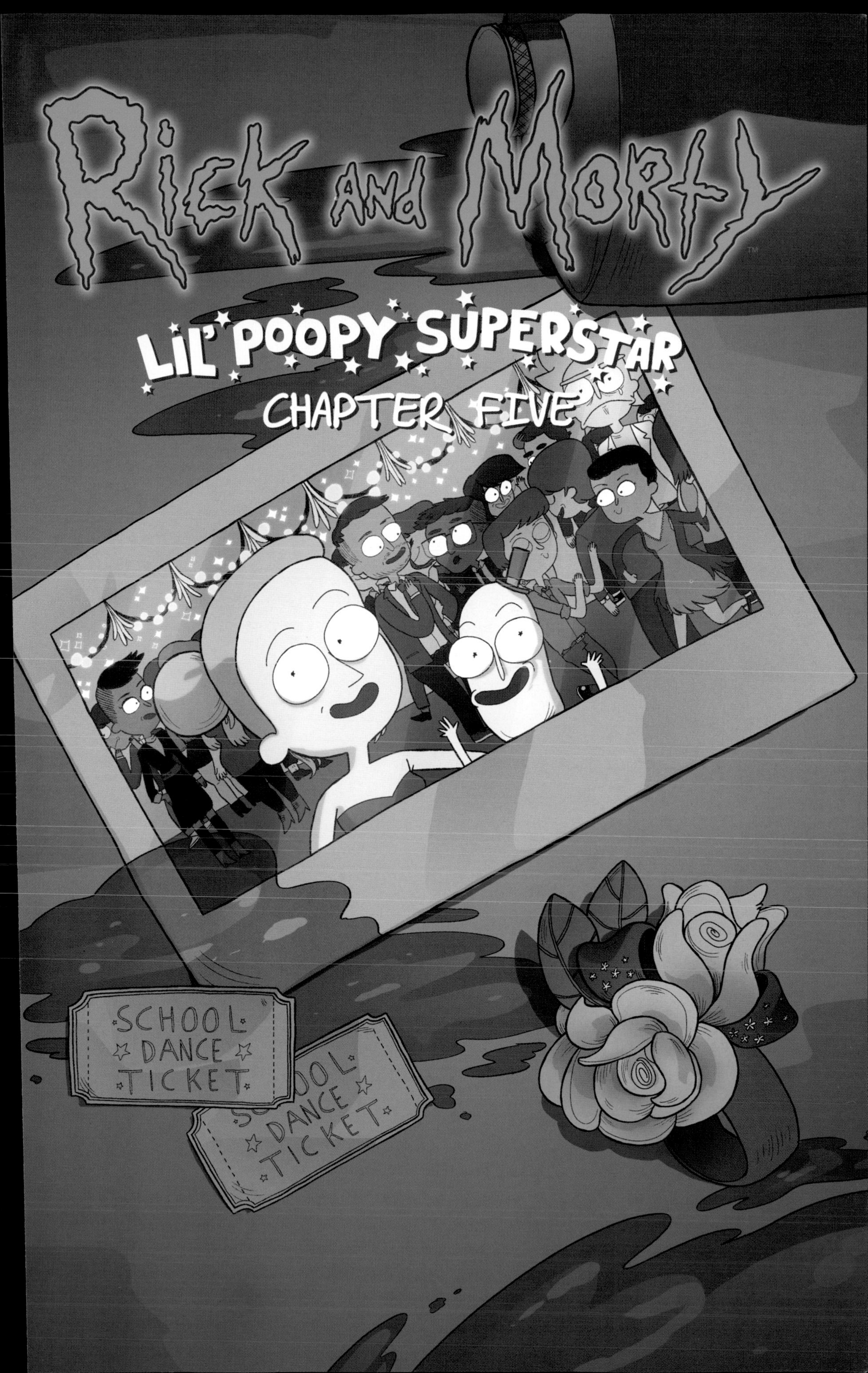
Rick and Morty™
LIL' POOPY SUPERSTAR
CHAPTER FIVE
SCHOOL DANCE TICKET
SCHOOL DANCE TICKET

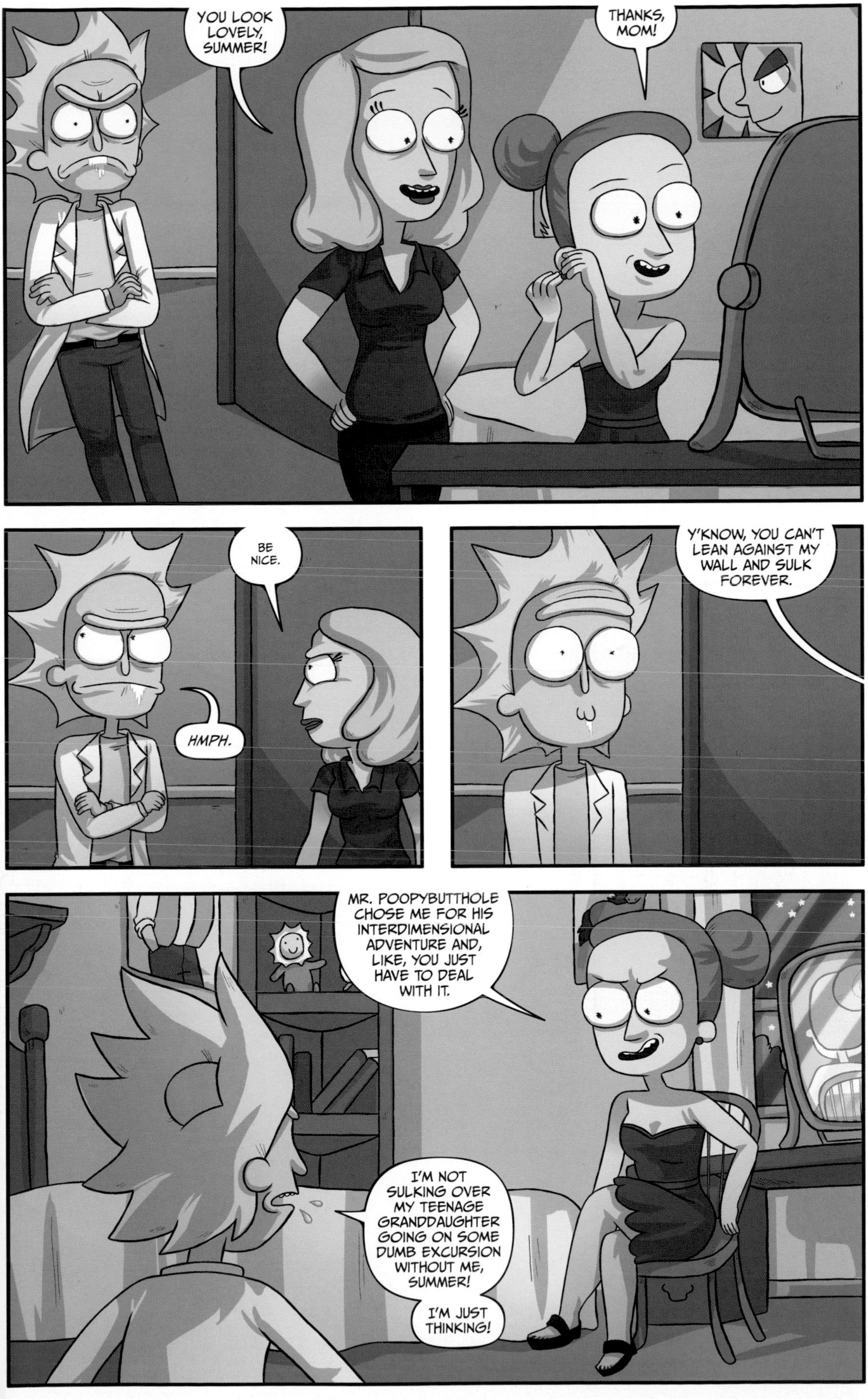
YOU LOOK LOVELY, SUMMER!
THANKS, MOM!
BE NICE.
HMPH.
Y'KNOW, YOU CAN'T LEAN AGAINST MY WALL AND SULK FOREVER.
MR. POOPYBUTTHOLE CHOSE ME FOR HIS INTERDIMENSIONAL ADVENTURE AND, LIKE, YOU JUST HAVE TO DEAL WITH IT.
I'M NOT SULKING OVER MY TEENAGE GRANDDAUGHTER GOING ON SOME DUMB EXCURSION WITHOUT ME, SUMMER!
I'M JUST THINKING!

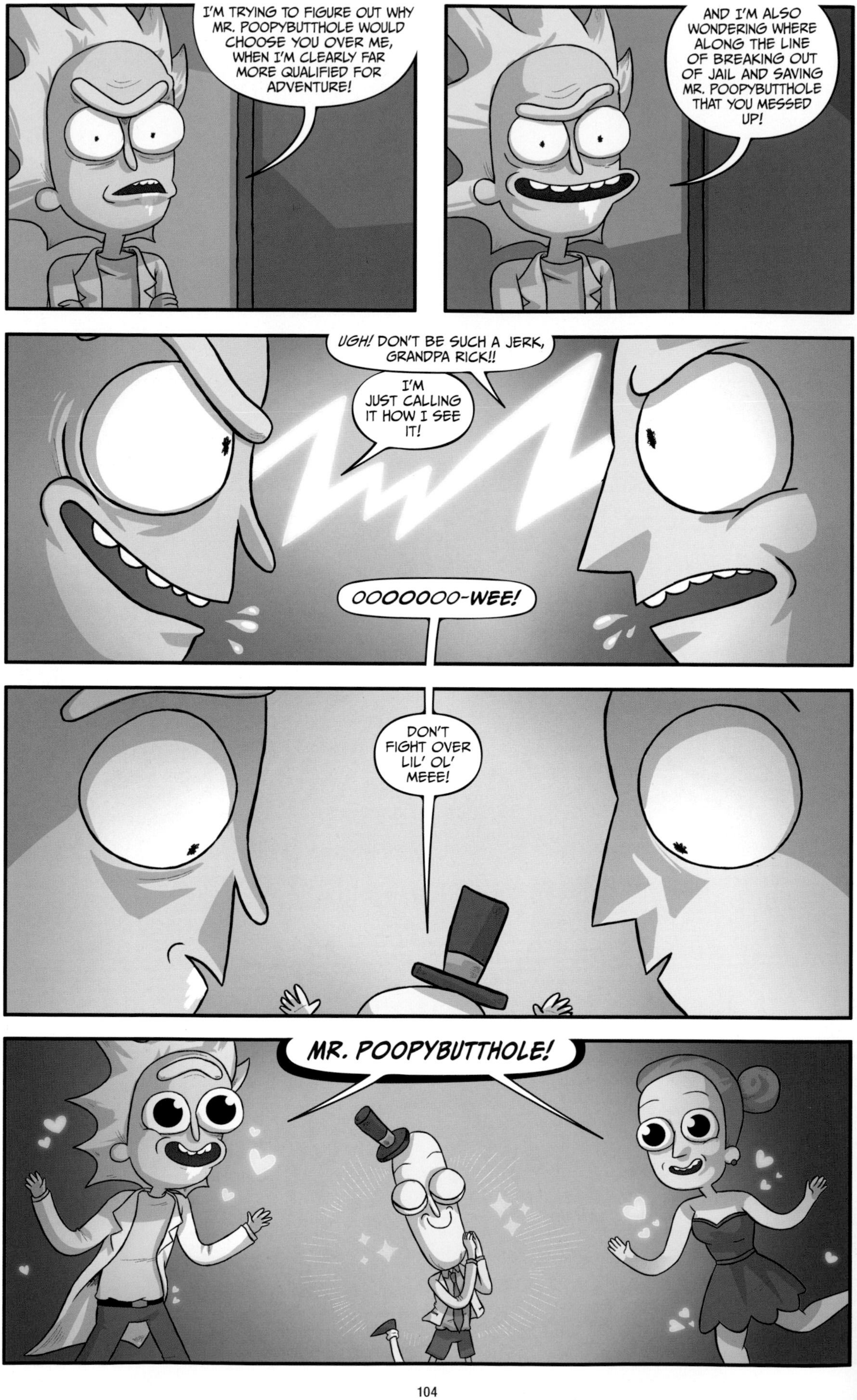
I'M TRYING TO FIGURE OUT WHY MR. POOPYBUTTHOLE WOULD CHOOSE YOU OVER ME, WHEN I'M CLEARLY FAR MORE QUALIFIED FOR ADVENTURE!
AND I'M ALSO WONDERING WHERE ALONG THE LINE OF BREAKING OUT OF JAIL AND SAVING MR. POOPYBUTTHOLE THAT YOU MESSED UP!
UGH! DON'T BE SUCH A JERK, GRANDPA RICK!!
I'M JUST CALLING IT HOW I SEE IT!
OOOOOOO-WEE!
DON'T FIGHT OVER LIL' OL' MEEE!
MR. POOPYBUTTHOLE!

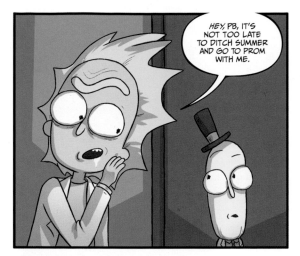

HEY, PB, IT'S NOT TOO LATE TO DITCH SUMMER AND GO TO PROM WITH ME.

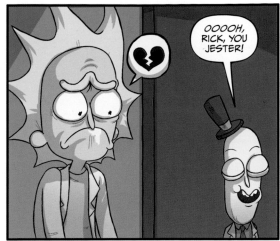

OOOOH, RICK, YOU JESTER!

MR. POOPYBUTTHOLE!! YOU'RE, LIKE, TOO SWEET!

NOW NOW, SUMMER, I'VE PLAYED PROM KING IN MANY MOVIES.

THIS LIL' POOPY PANTS IS A PROM PROFESSIONAL AND WE'RE GONNA DO PROM RIGHT!

ARE YOU READY TO GO?

I SUUURRRE AM!

BYE, GRANDPA RICK!

BYE!

THERE IS NO WAY SUMMER DIDN'T SCREW ANYTHING UP!

SO I GUESS *ONCE AGAIN* IT'S UP TO ME TO FIX EVERYTHING!

HEY, I LIKE YOUR NEW HAT.

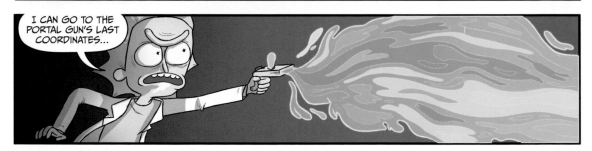

I CAN GO TO THE PORTAL GUN'S LAST COORDINATES...

H.H.H.S SCHOOL DANCE

SCHOOL PROM

...AND CHECK OUT THE INEVITABLE SHIT SHOW SUMMER LEFT BEHIND!

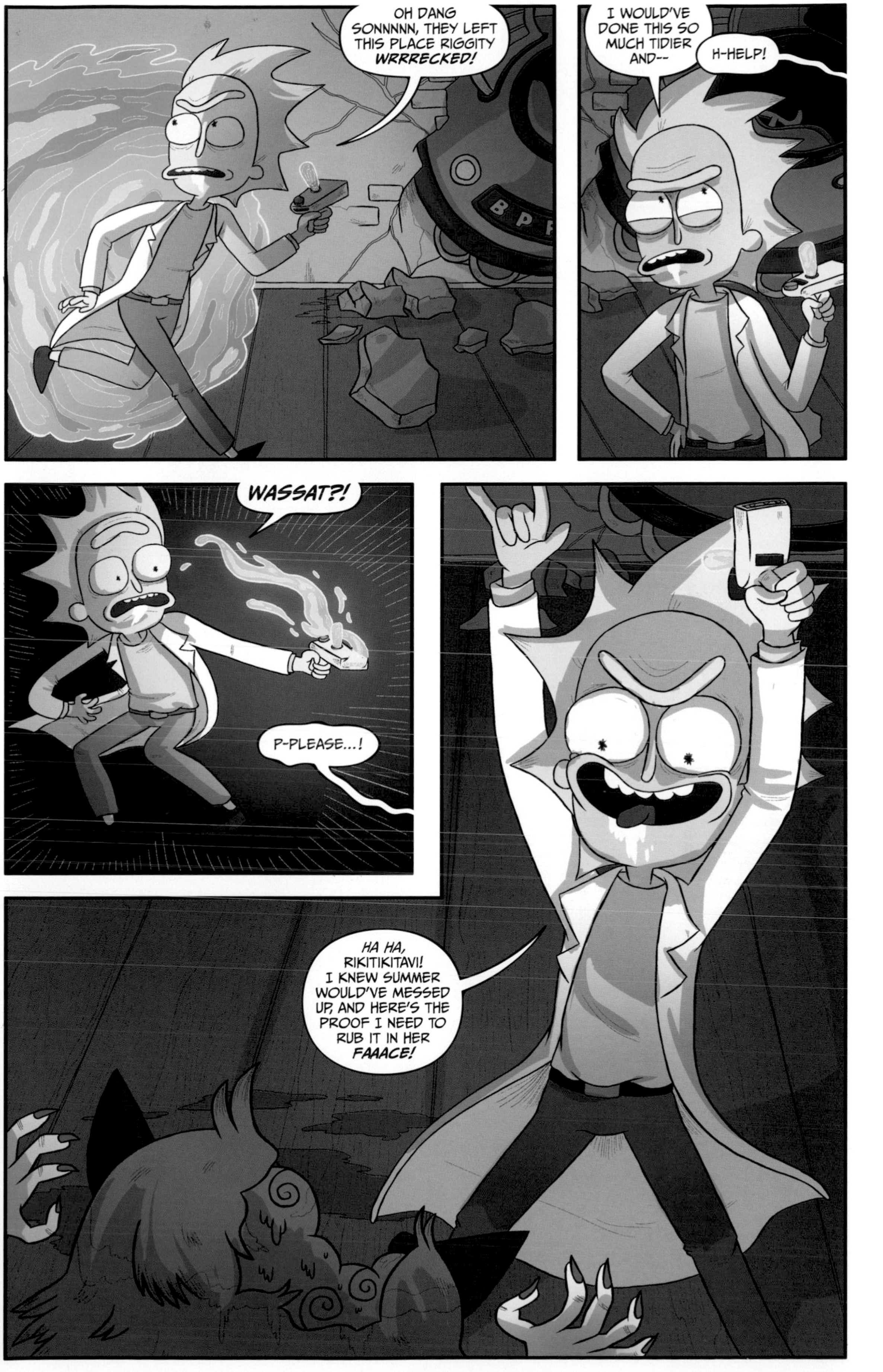

OH DANG SONNNNN, THEY LEFT THIS PLACE RIGGITY WRRRECKED!
I WOULD'VE DONE THIS SO MUCH TIDIER AND--
H-HELP!
WASSAT?!
P-PLEASE...!
HA HA, RIKITIKITAVI! I KNEW SUMMER WOULD'VE MESSED UP, AND HERE'S THE PROOF I NEED TO RUB IT IN HER FAAACE!

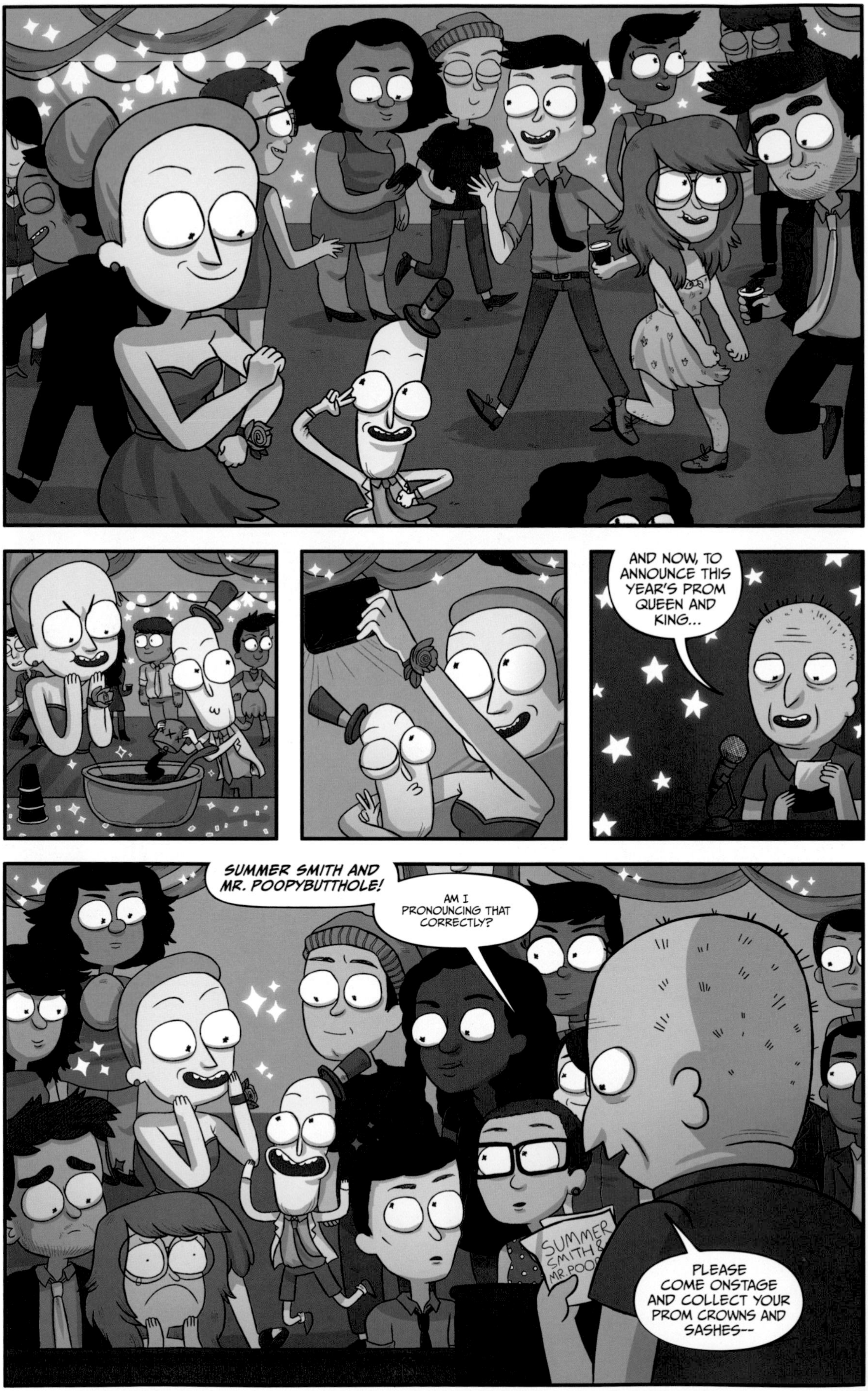
AND NOW, TO ANNOUNCE THIS YEAR'S PROM QUEEN AND KING...
SUMMER SMITH AND MR. POOPYBUTTHOLE!
AM I PRONOUNCING THAT CORRECTLY?
SUMMER SMITH &
PLEASE COME ONSTAGE AND COLLECT YOUR PROM CROWNS AND SASHES--

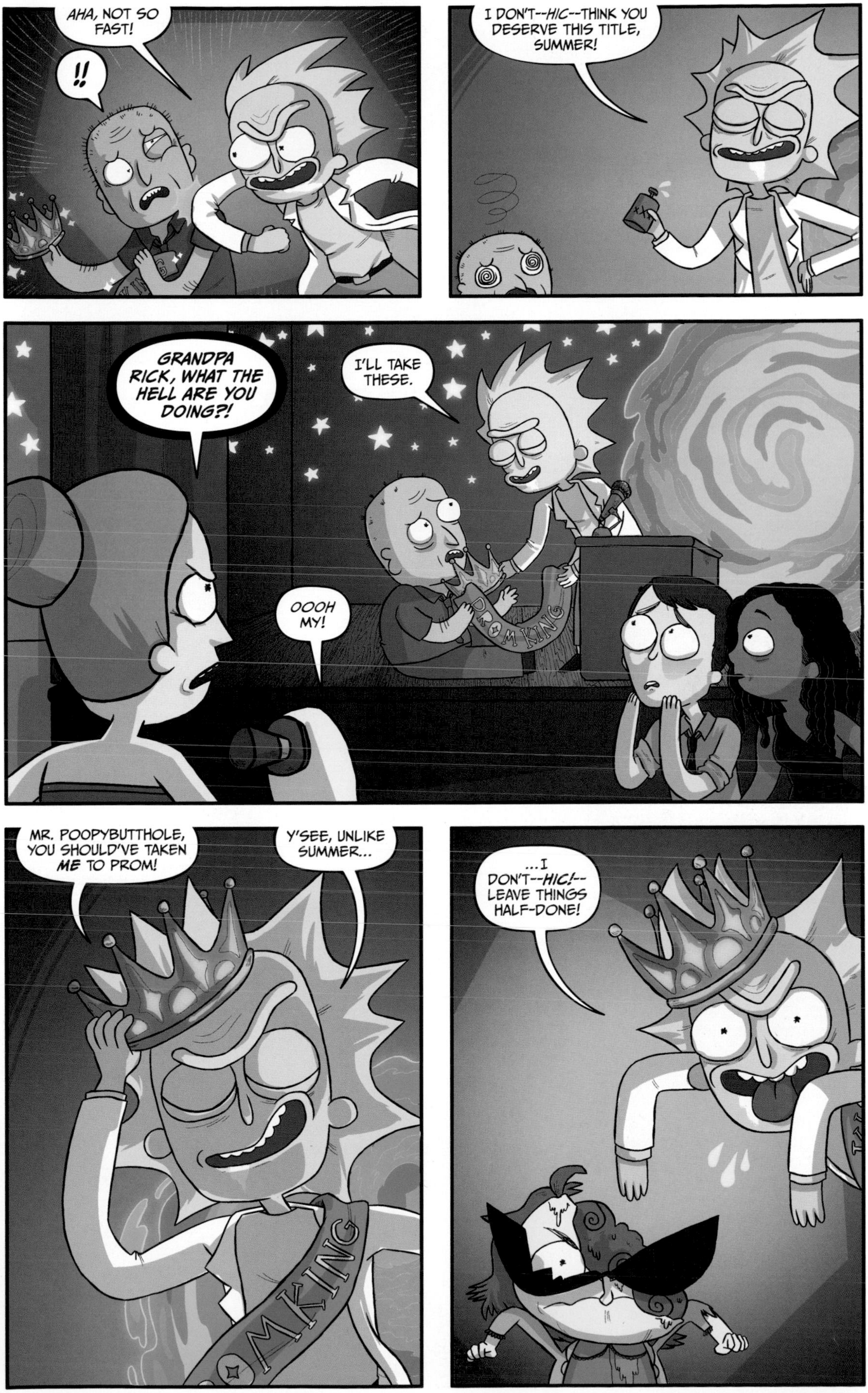

AHA, NOT SO FAST!
!!
I DON'T--HIC--THINK YOU DESERVE THIS TITLE, SUMMER!
GRANDPA RICK, WHAT THE HELL ARE YOU DOING?!
I'LL TAKE THESE.
PROM KING
OOOH MY!
MR. POOPYBUTTHOLE, YOU SHOULD'VE TAKEN ME TO PROM!
Y'SEE, UNLIKE SUMMER...
...I DON'T--HIC!--LEAVE THINGS HALF-DONE!

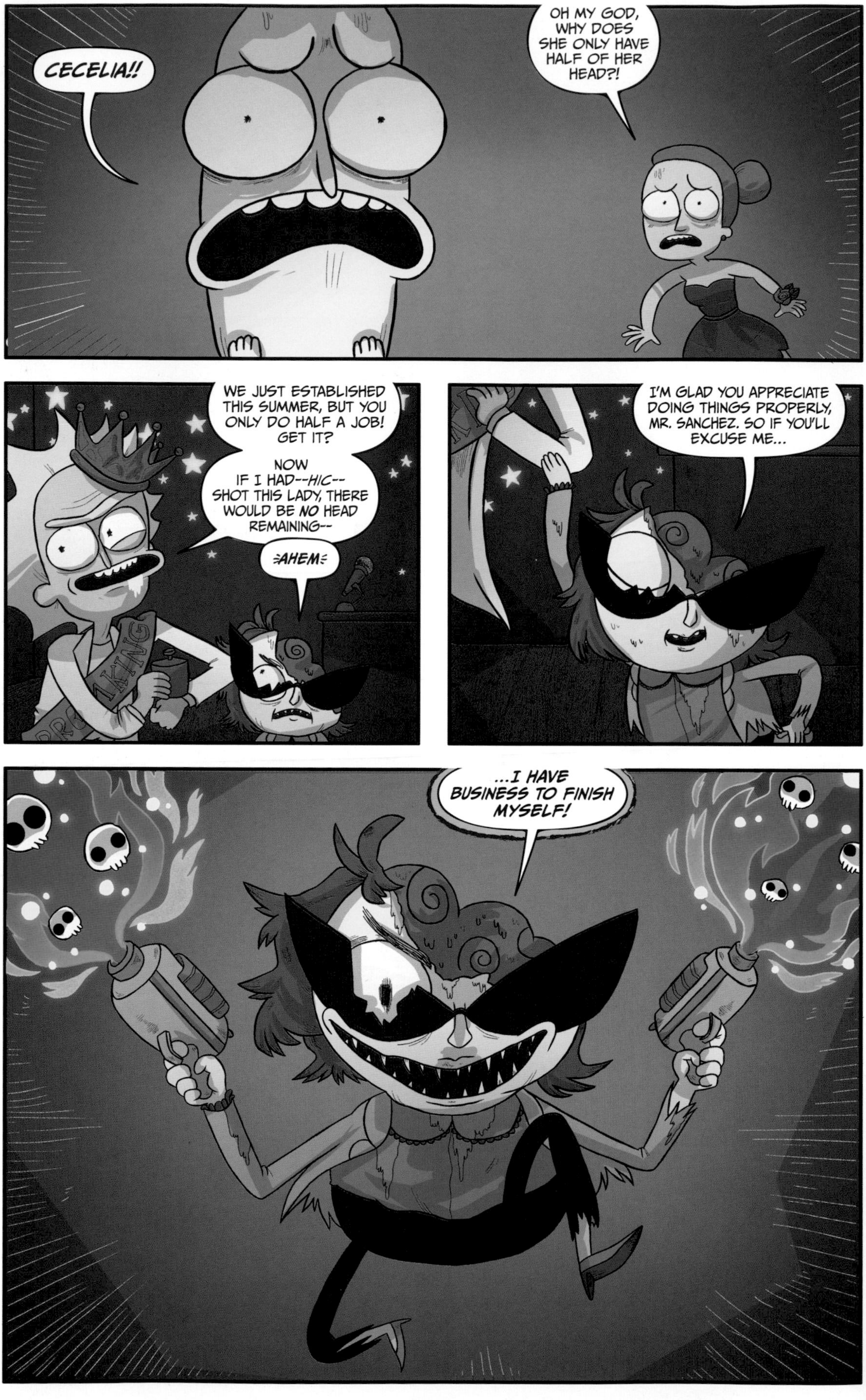
CECELIA!!
OH MY GOD, WHY DOES SHE ONLY HAVE HALF OF HER HEAD?!
WE JUST ESTABLISHED THIS SUMMER, BUT YOU ONLY DO HALF A JOB! GET IT?
NOW IF I HAD--HIC--SHOT THIS LADY, THERE WOULD BE NO HEAD REMAINING--
AHEM
PROM KING
I'M GLAD YOU APPRECIATE DOING THINGS PROPERLY, MR. SANCHEZ. SO IF YOU'LL EXCUSE ME...
...I HAVE BUSINESS TO FINISH MYSELF!

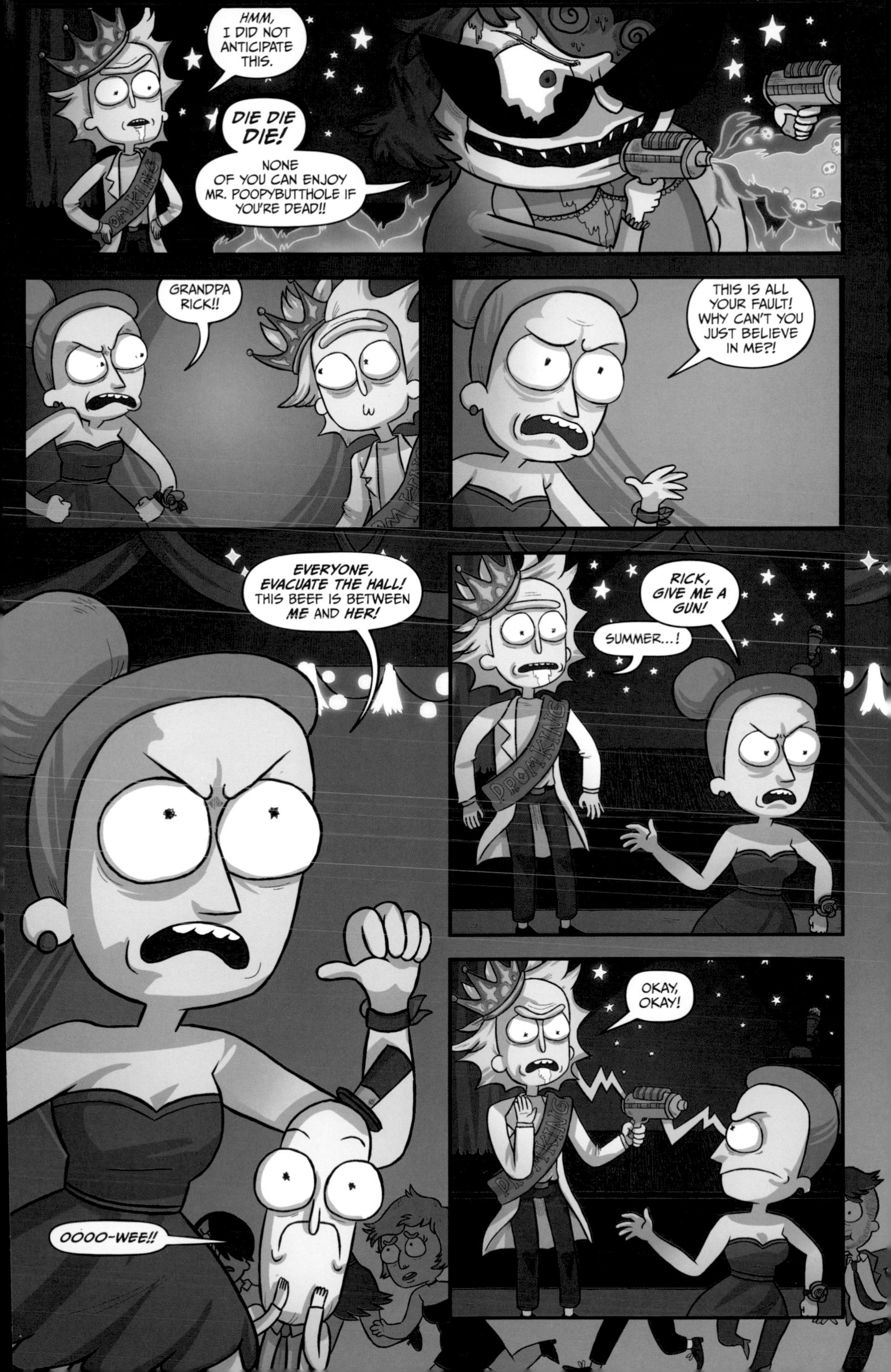
HMM, I DID NOT ANTICIPATE THIS.
DIE DIE DIE!
NONE OF YOU CAN ENJOY MR. POOPYBUTTHOLE IF YOU'RE DEAD!!
GRANDPA RICK!!
THIS IS ALL YOUR FAULT! WHY CAN'T YOU JUST BELIEVE IN ME?!
EVERYONE, EVACUATE THE HALL! THIS BEEF IS BETWEEN ME AND HER!
OOOO-WEE!!
RICK, GIVE ME A GUN!
SUMMER...!
PROM KING
OKAY, OKAY!

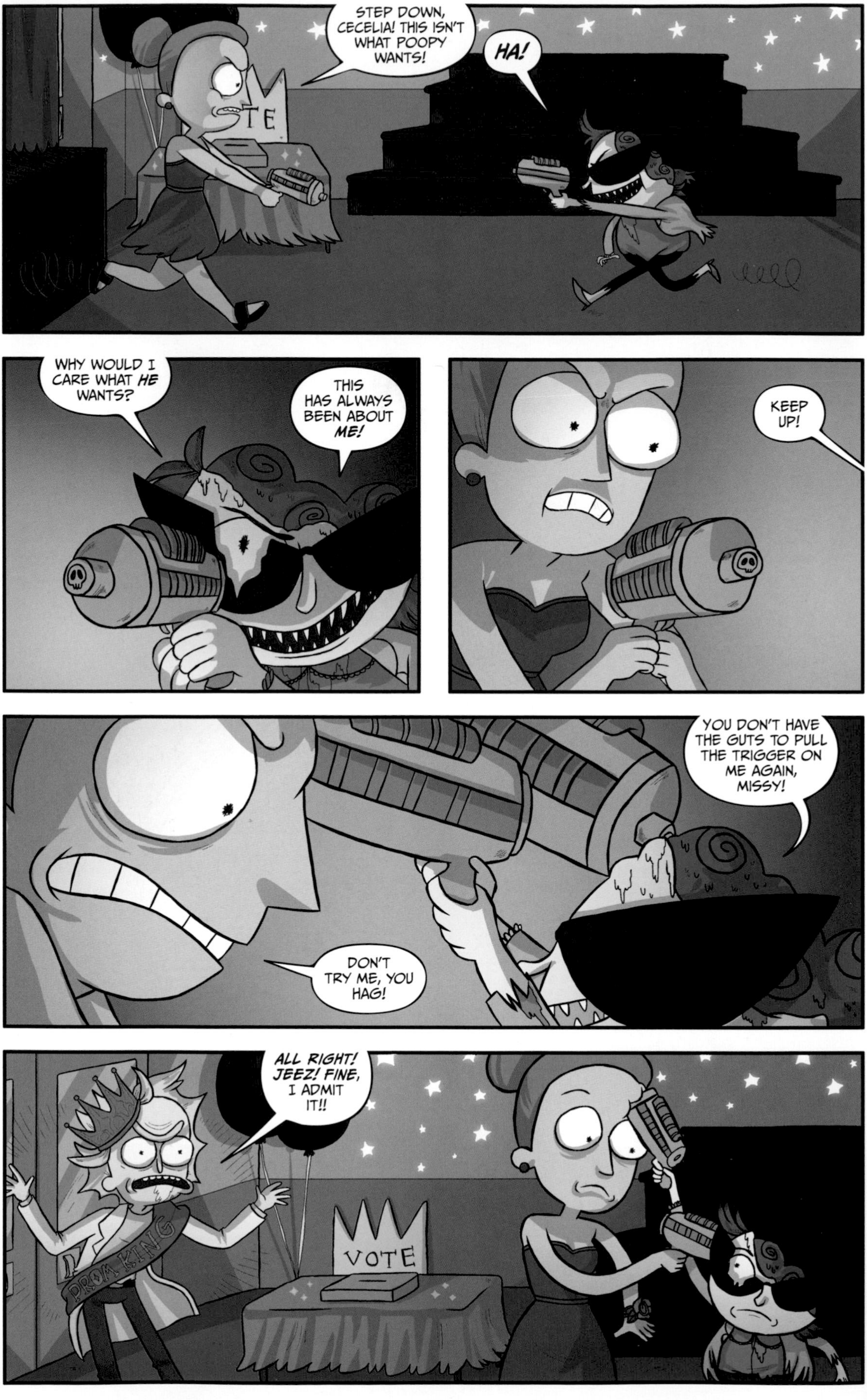
STEP DOWN, CECELIA! THIS ISN'T WHAT POOPY WANTS!
HA!
TE
WHY WOULD I CARE WHAT HE WANTS?
THIS HAS ALWAYS BEEN ABOUT ME!
KEEP UP!
YOU DON'T HAVE THE GUTS TO PULL THE TRIGGER ON ME AGAIN, MISSY!
DON'T TRY ME, YOU HAG!
ALL RIGHT! JEEZ! FINE, I ADMIT IT!!
PROM KING
VOTE

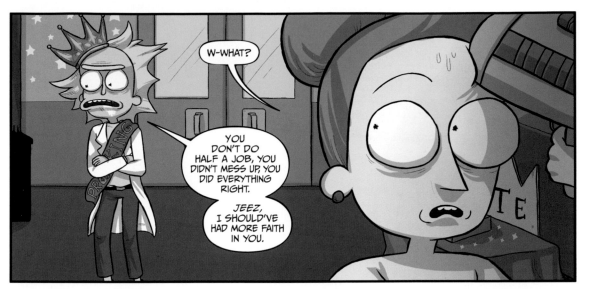

W-WHAT?

YOU DON'T DO HALF A JOB, YOU DIDN'T MESS UP, YOU DID EVERYTHING RIGHT.

JEEZ, I SHOULD'VE HAD MORE FAITH IN YOU.

I WAS PISSED THAT MR. POOPYBUTTHOLE CHOSE YOU OVER ME... I GUESS WHAT I'M TRYING TO--HIC--SAY, IS THAT I'M SORRY.

...

OH C'MON, SUMMER, YOU KNOW THAT MUST'VE BEEN HARD FOR ME!

AREN'T YOU GOING TO SAY ANYTHING?!

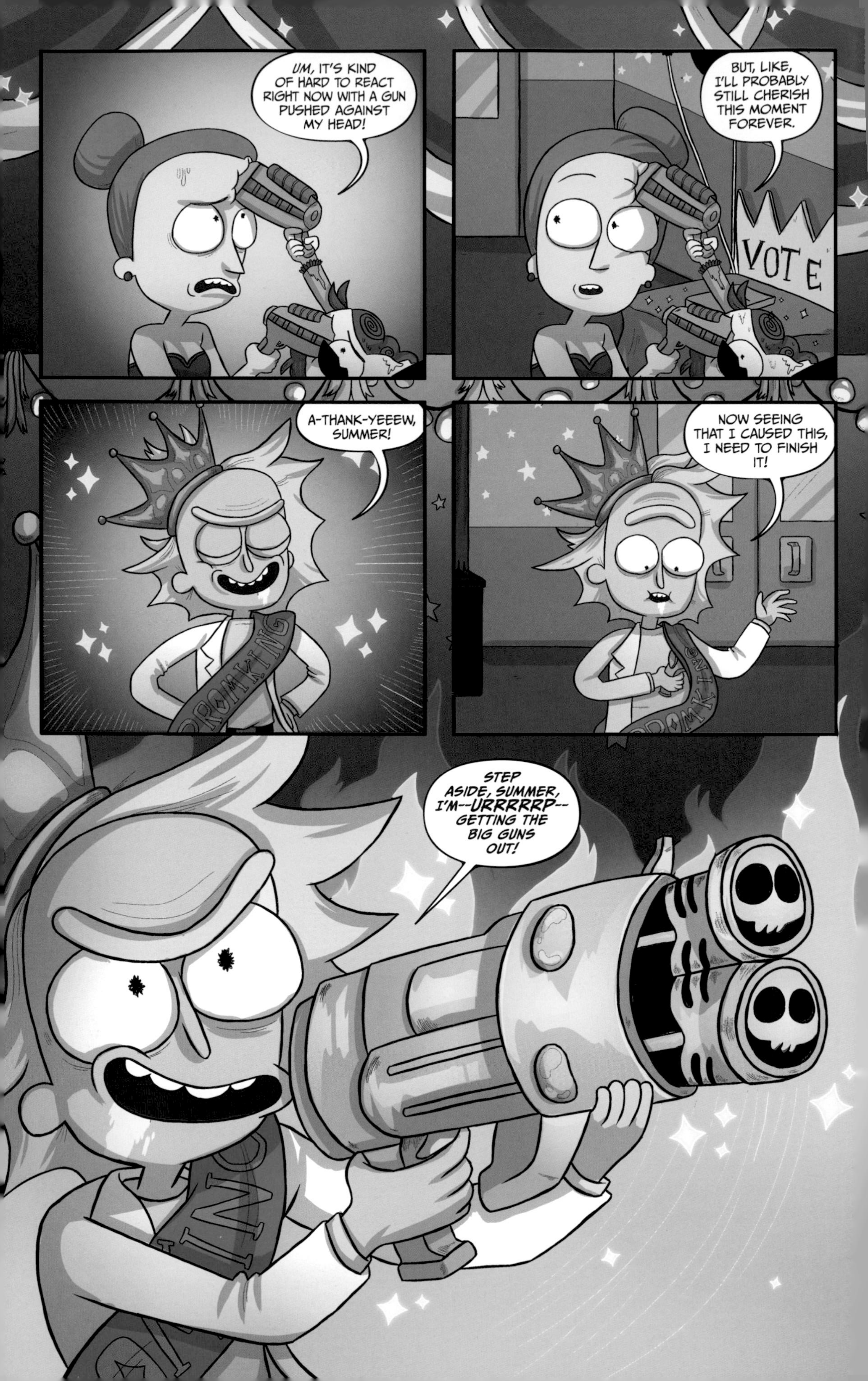
UM, IT'S KIND OF HARD TO REACT RIGHT NOW WITH A GUN PUSHED AGAINST MY HEAD!
BUT, LIKE, I'LL PROBABLY STILL CHERISH THIS MOMENT FOREVER.
VOTE
A-THANK-YEEEW, SUMMER!
PROM KING
NOW SEEING THAT I CAUSED THIS, I NEED TO FINISH IT!
PROM KING
STEP ASIDE, SUMMER, I'M--URRRRRP--GETTING THE BIG GUNS OUT!

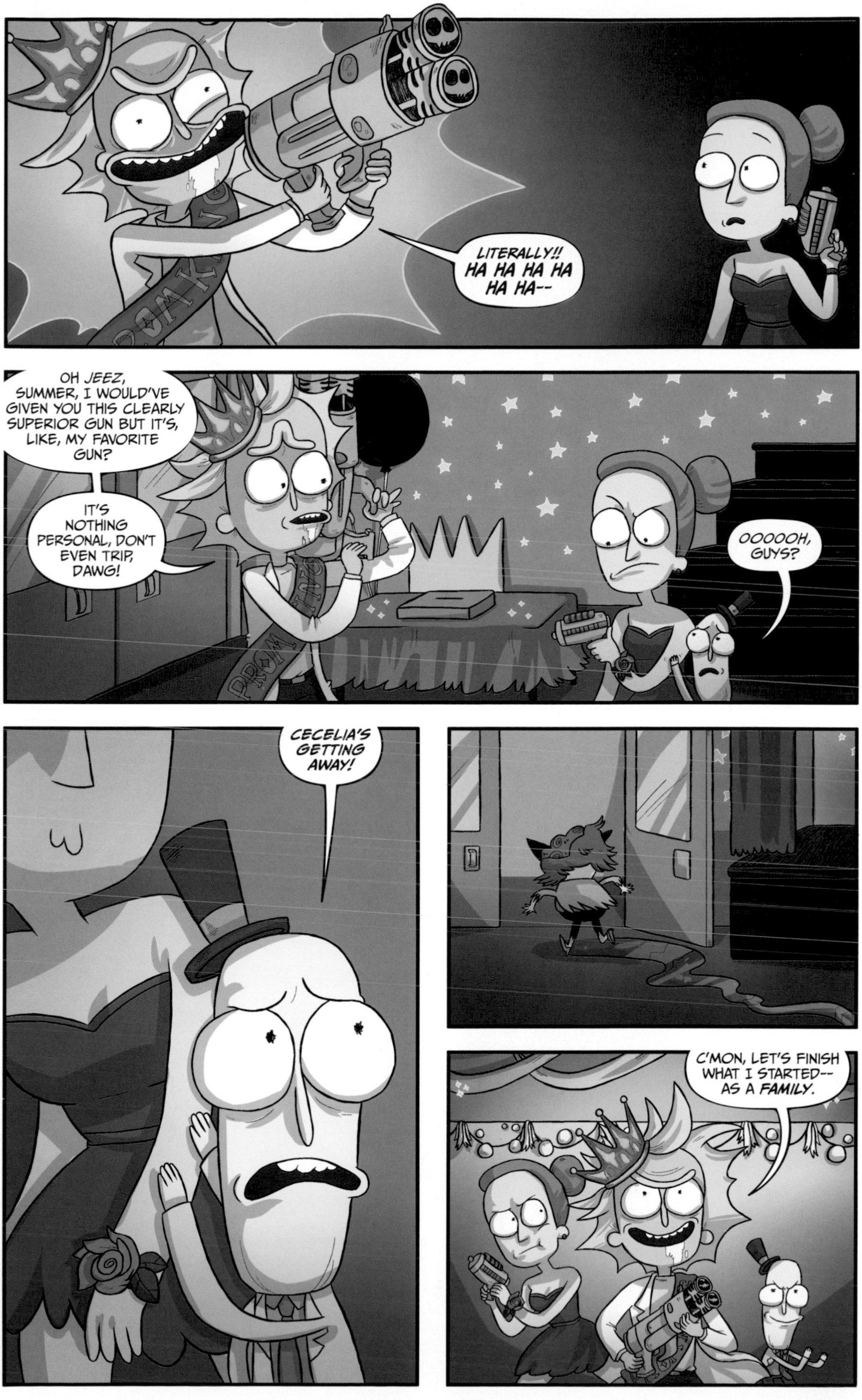

LITERALLY!! HA HA HA HA HA HA--
PROM KING
OH JEEZ, SUMMER, I WOULD'VE GIVEN YOU THIS CLEARLY SUPERIOR GUN BUT IT'S, LIKE, MY FAVORITE GUN?
IT'S NOTHING PERSONAL, DON'T EVEN TRIP, DAWG!
OOOOOH, GUYS?
PROM KING
CECELIA'S GETTING AWAY!
C'MON, LET'S FINISH WHAT I STARTED-- AS A FAMILY.

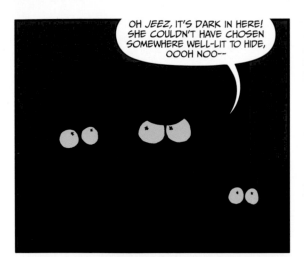

OH *JEEZ*, IT'S DARK IN HERE! SHE COULDN'T HAVE CHOSEN SOMEWHERE WELL-LIT TO HIDE, OOOH NOO--

LET'S SPLIT UP, THAT WAY WE CAN, LIKE, COVER MORE GROUND!

SCHOOLPROM

SCHOOL PROM

OOOO OOOO

WEEEE EEE!

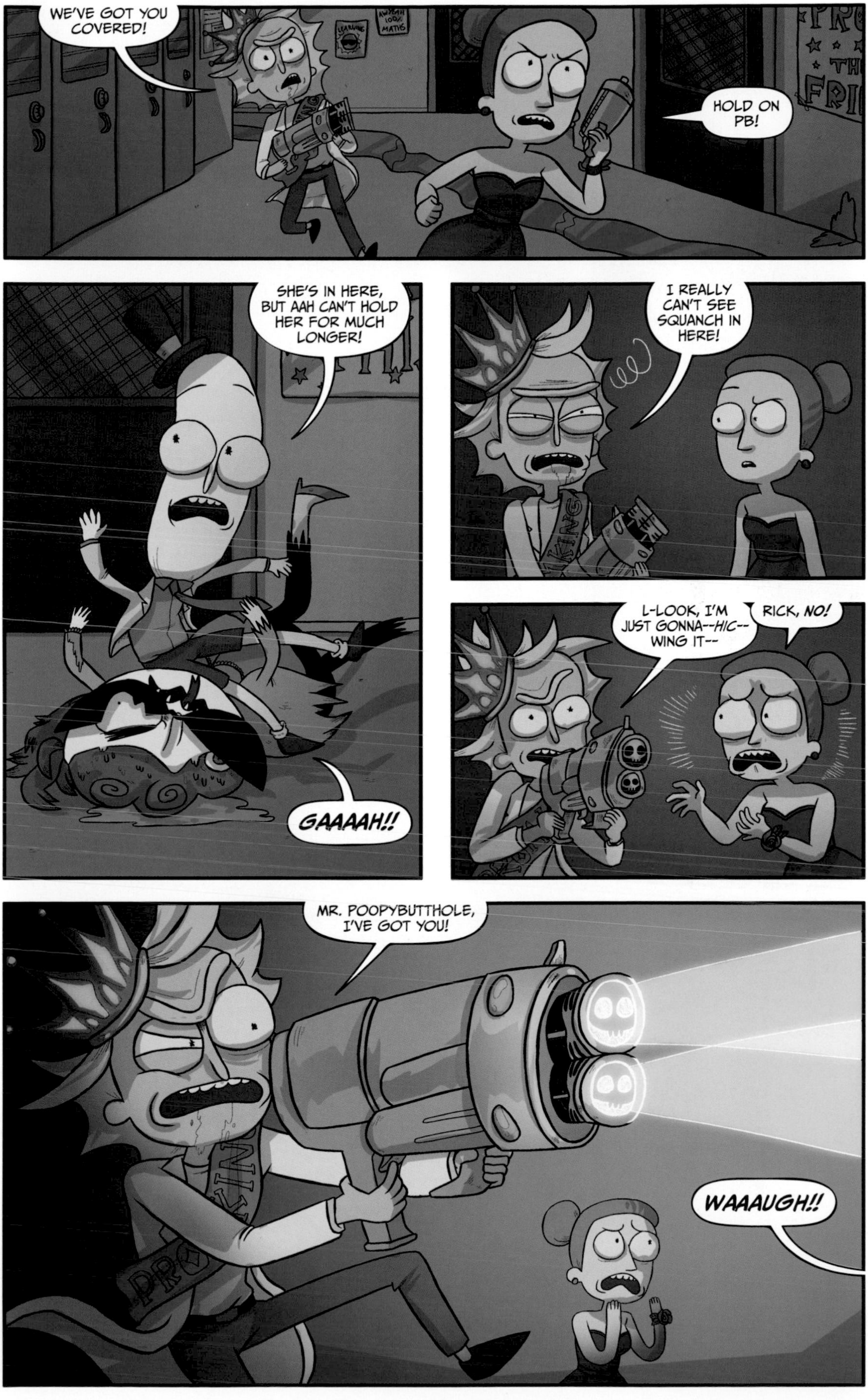
WE'VE GOT YOU COVERED!
HOLD ON PB!
SHE'S IN HERE, BUT AAH CAN'T HOLD HER FOR MUCH LONGER!
GAAAAH!!
I REALLY CAN'T SEE SQUANCH IN HERE!
L-LOOK, I'M JUST GONNA--*HIC*-- WING IT--
RICK, *NO!*
MR. POOPYBUTTHOLE, I'VE GOT YOU!
WAAAUGH!!

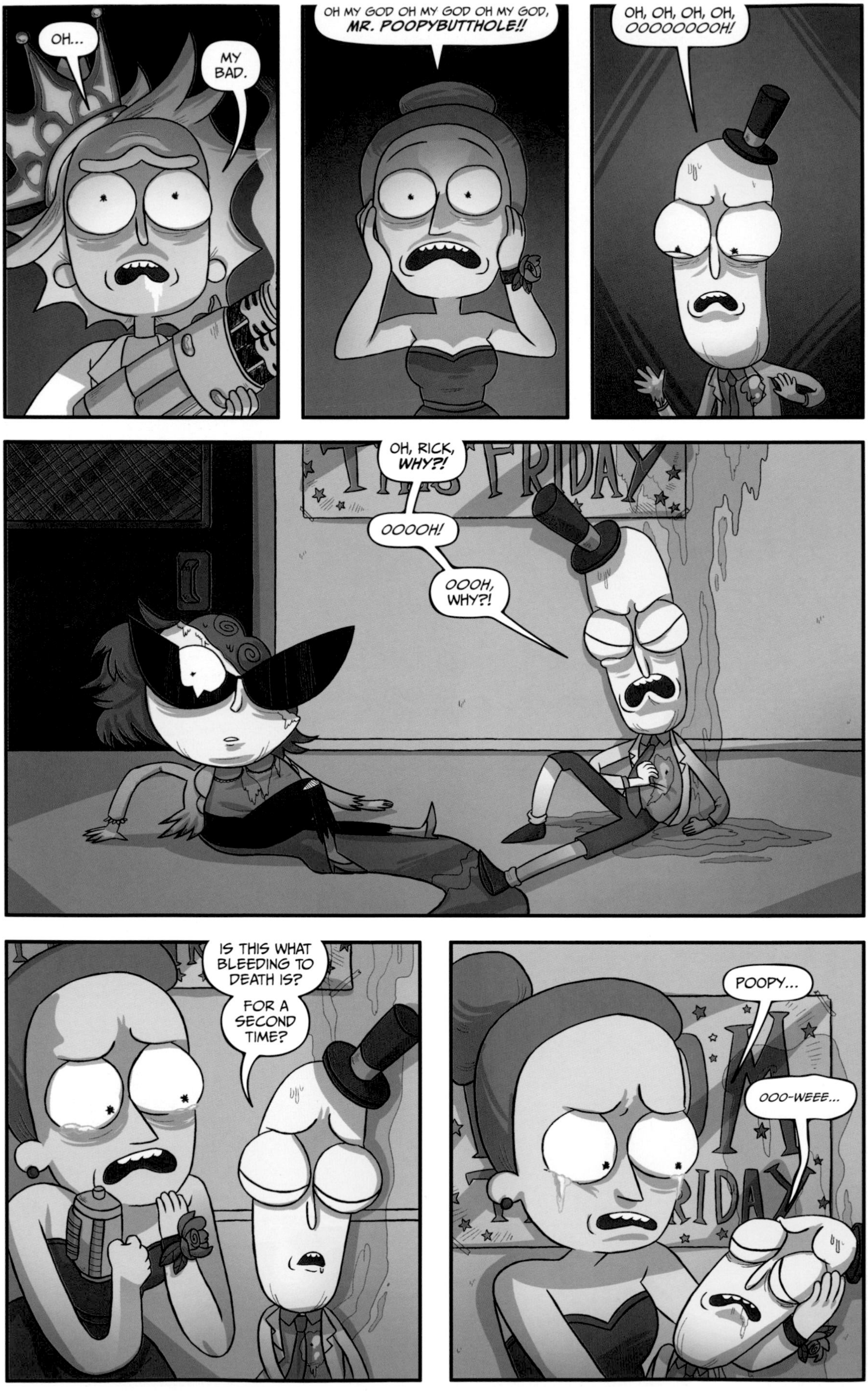
OH...
MY BAD.
OH MY GOD OH MY GOD OH MY GOD, MR. POOPYBUTTHOLE!!
OH, OH, OH, OH, OOOOOOOOH!
THIS FRIDAY
OH, RICK, WHY?!
OOOOH!
OOOH, WHY?!
IS THIS WHAT BLEEDING TO DEATH IS?
FOR A SECOND TIME?
POOPY...
OOO-WEEE...

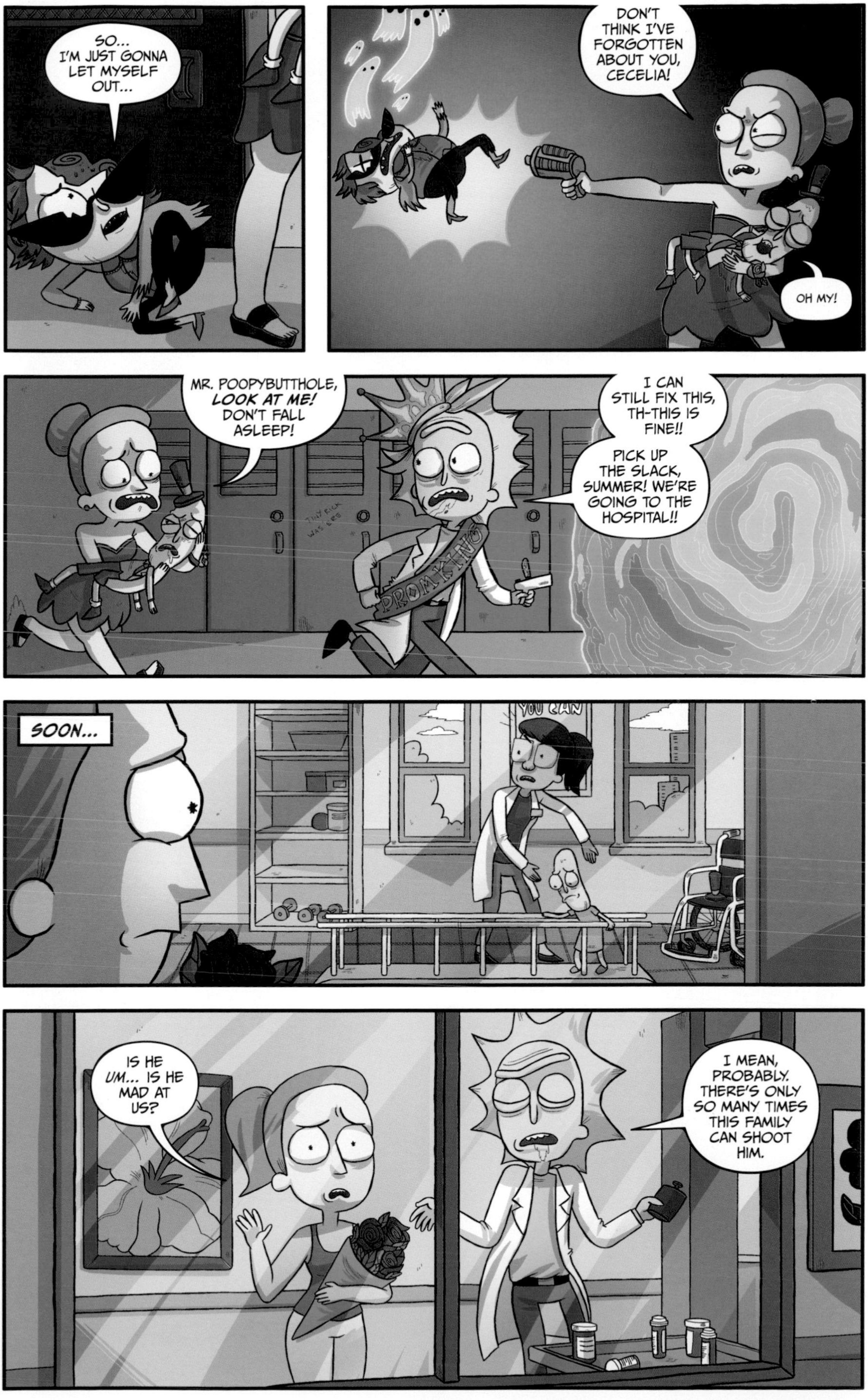
SO... I'M JUST GONNA LET MYSELF OUT...
DON'T THINK I'VE FORGOTTEN ABOUT YOU, CECELIA!
OH MY!
MR. POOPYBUTTHOLE, **LOOK AT ME!** DON'T FALL ASLEEP!
I CAN STILL FIX THIS, TH-THIS IS FINE!!
PICK UP THE SLACK, SUMMER! WE'RE GOING TO THE HOSPITAL!!
PROMKING
SOON...
YOU CAN
IS HE *UM...* IS HE MAD AT US?
I MEAN, PROBABLY. THERE'S ONLY SO MANY TIMES THIS FAMILY CAN SHOOT HIM.

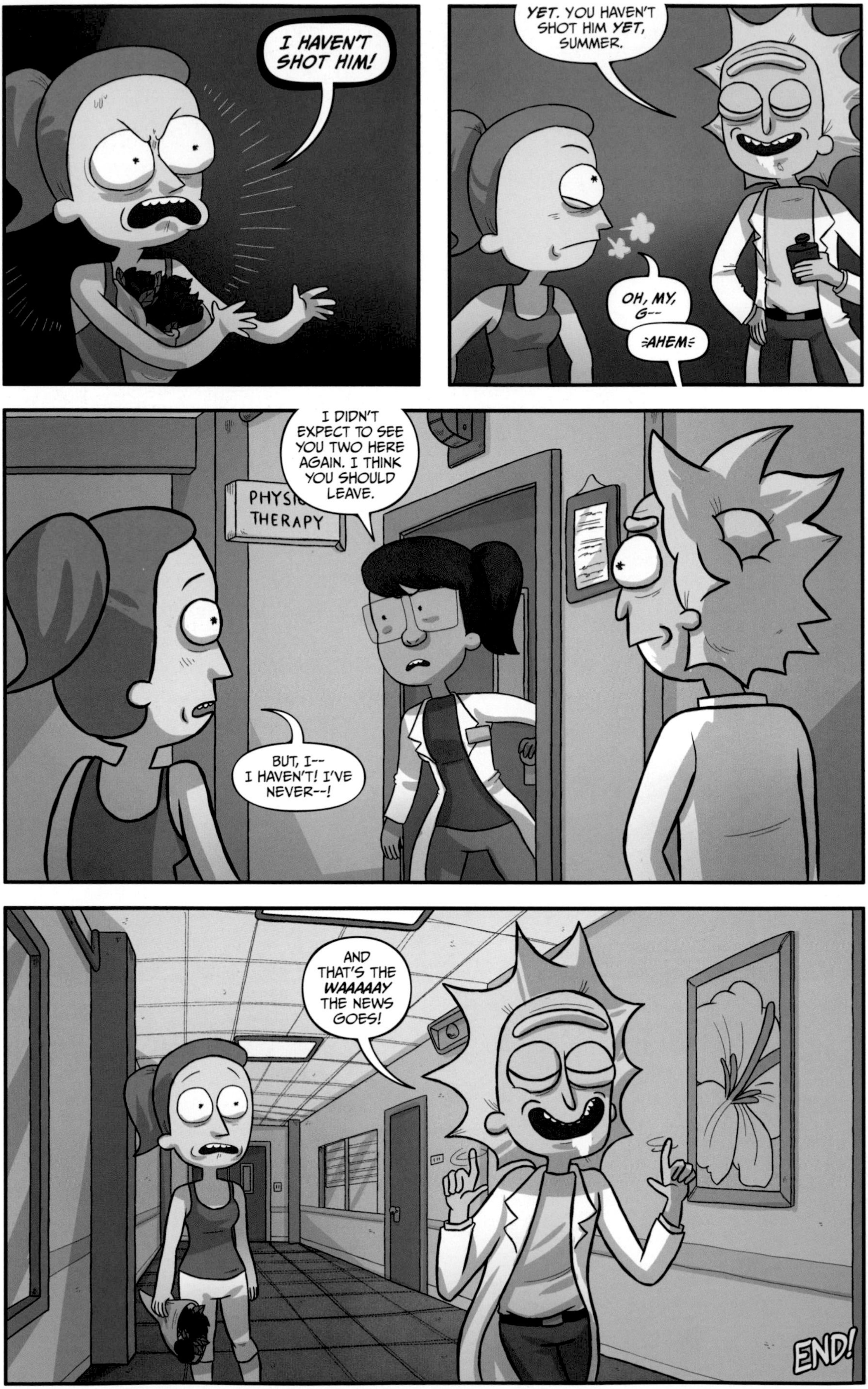

I HAVEN'T SHOT HIM!
YET. YOU HAVEN'T SHOT HIM YET, SUMMER.
OH, MY, G--
AHEM
I DIDN'T EXPECT TO SEE YOU TWO HERE AGAIN. I THINK YOU SHOULD LEAVE.
THERAPY
BUT, I-- I HAVEN'T! I'VE NEVER--!
AND THAT'S THE WAAAAAY THE NEWS GOES!
END!

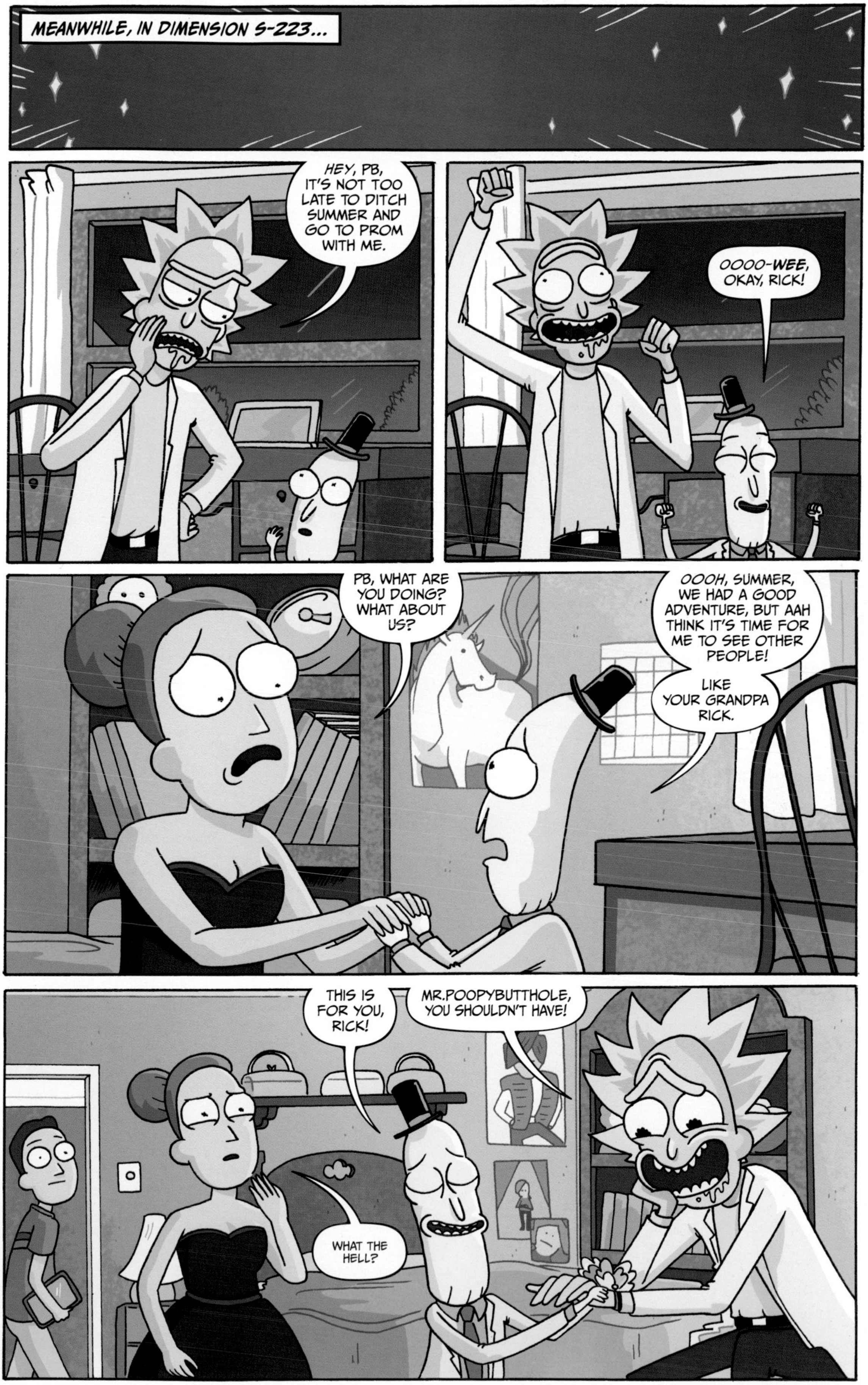

MEANWHILE, IN DIMENSION S-223...
HEY, PB, IT'S NOT TOO LATE TO DITCH SUMMER AND GO TO PROM WITH ME.
OOOO-WEE, OKAY, RICK!
PB, WHAT ARE YOU DOING? WHAT ABOUT US?
OOOH, SUMMER, WE HAD A GOOD ADVENTURE, BUT AAH THINK IT'S TIME FOR ME TO SEE OTHER PEOPLE!
LIKE YOUR GRANDPA RICK.
THIS IS FOR YOU, RICK!
MR.POOPYBUTTHOLE, YOU SHOULDN'T HAVE!
WHAT THE HELL?

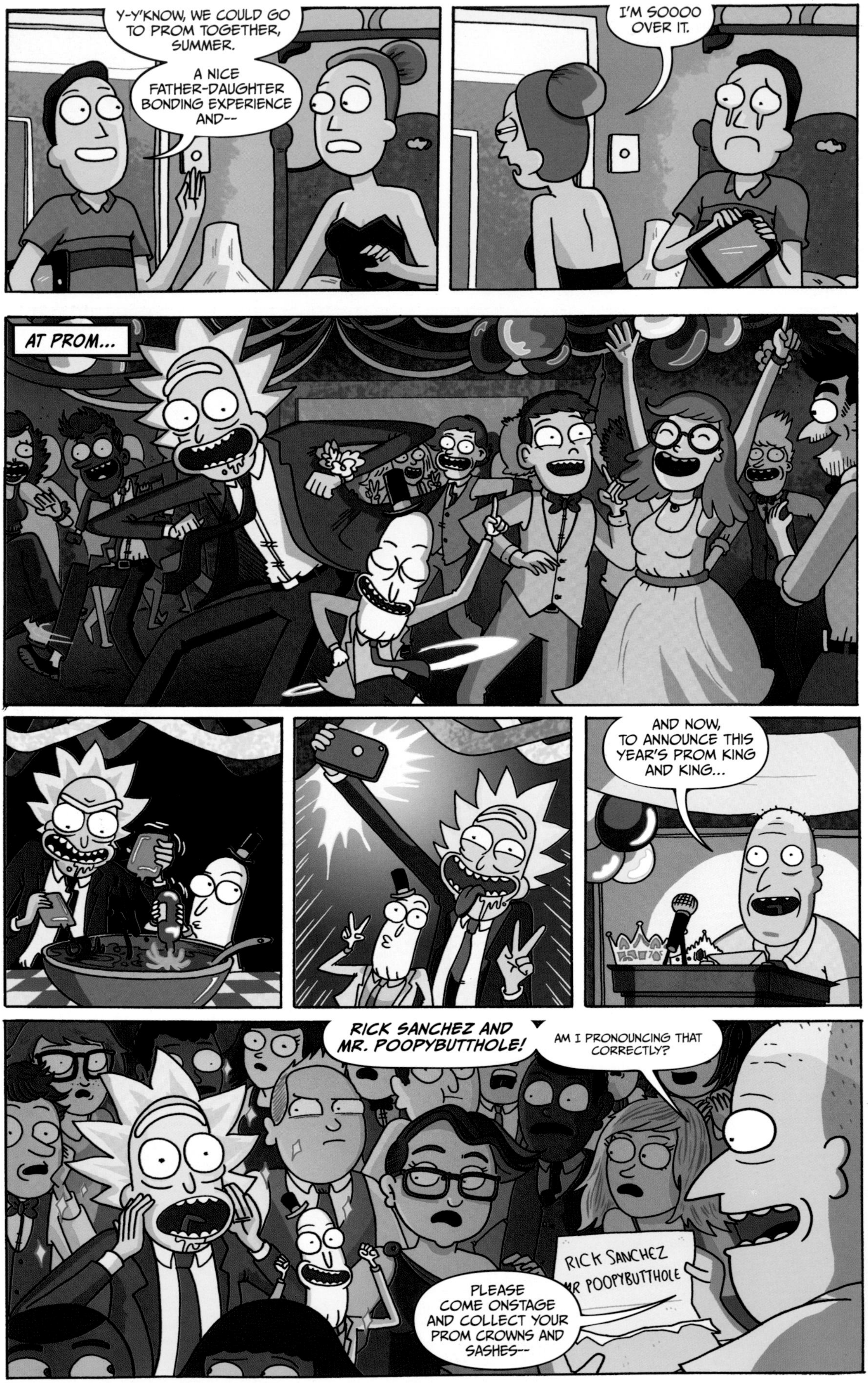
Y-Y'KNOW, WE COULD GO TO PROM TOGETHER, SUMMER.
A NICE FATHER-DAUGHTER BONDING EXPERIENCE AND--
I'M SOOOO OVER IT.
AT PROM...
AND NOW, TO ANNOUNCE THIS YEAR'S PROM KING AND KING...
RICK SANCHEZ AND MR. POOPYBUTTHOLE!
AM I PRONOUNCING THAT CORRECTLY?
RICK SANCHEZ
MR POOPYBUTTHOLE
PLEASE COME ONSTAGE AND COLLECT YOUR PROM CROWNS AND SASHES--

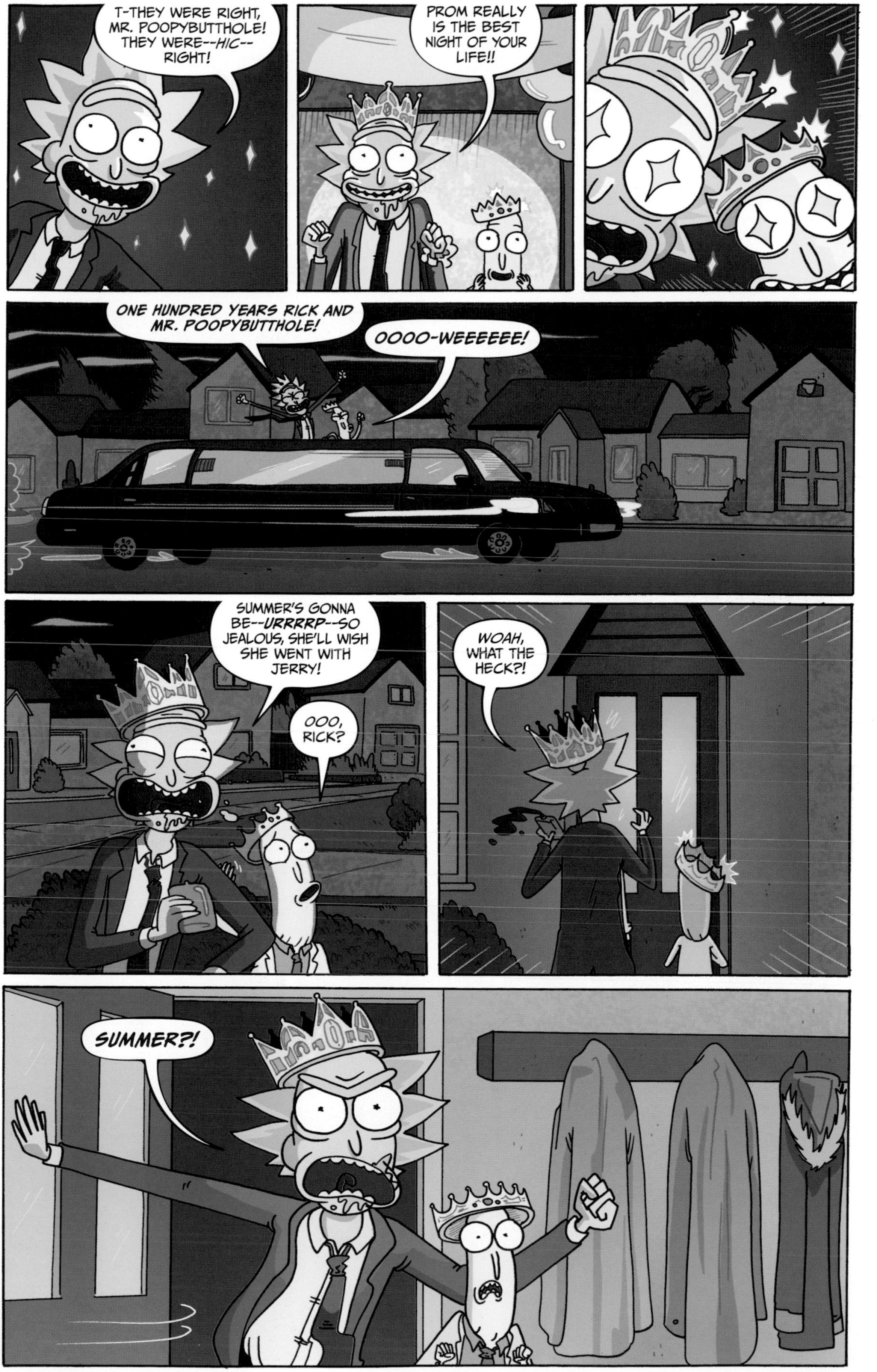
T-THEY WERE RIGHT, MR. POOPYBUTTHOLE! THEY WERE--HIC--RIGHT!
PROM REALLY IS THE BEST NIGHT OF YOUR LIFE!!
ONE HUNDRED YEARS RICK AND MR. POOPYBUTTHOLE!
OOOO-WEEEEEE!
SUMMER'S GONNA BE--URRRRP--SO JEALOUS, SHE'LL WISH SHE WENT WITH JERRY!
OOO, RICK?
WOAH, WHAT THE HECK?!
SUMMER?!

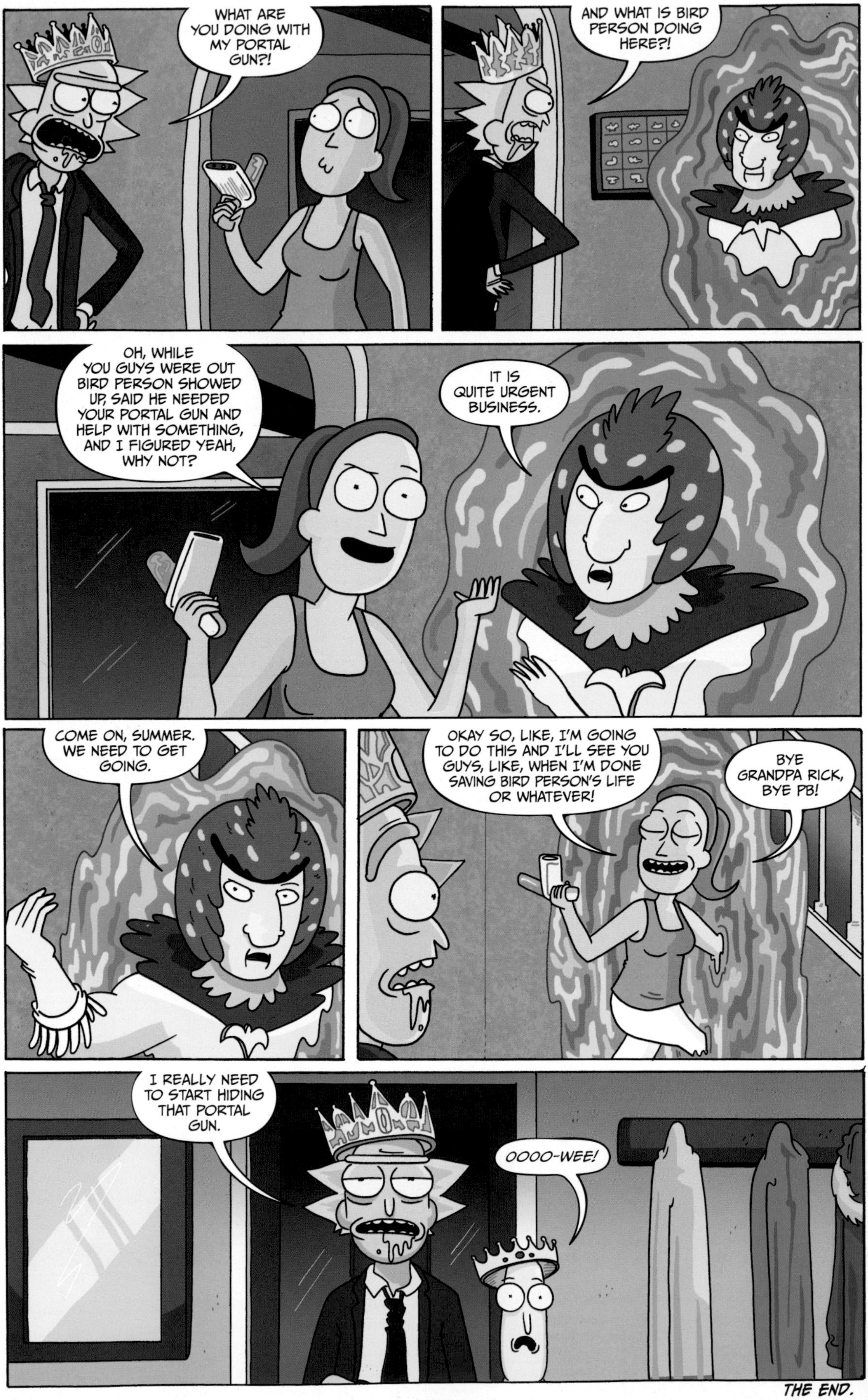
WHAT ARE YOU DOING WITH MY PORTAL GUN?!
AND WHAT IS BIRD PERSON DOING HERE?!
OH, WHILE YOU GUYS WERE OUT BIRD PERSON SHOWED UP, SAID HE NEEDED YOUR PORTAL GUN AND HELP WITH SOMETHING, AND I FIGURED YEAH, WHY NOT?
IT IS QUITE URGENT BUSINESS.
COME ON, SUMMER. WE NEED TO GET GOING.
OKAY SO, LIKE, I'M GOING TO DO THIS AND I'LL SEE YOU GUYS, LIKE, WHEN I'M DONE SAVING BIRD PERSON'S LIFE OR WHATEVER!
BYE GRANDPA RICK, BYE PB!
I REALLY NEED TO START HIDING THAT PORTAL GUN.
OOOO-WEE!
THE END.

DAN HARMON is the Emmy® winning creator/executive producer of the comedy series *Community* as well as the co-creator/executive producer of Adult Swim's *Rick and Morty.*

Harmon's pursuit of minimal work for maximum reward took him from stand-up to improv to sketch comedy, then finally to Los Angeles, where he began writing feature screenplays with fellow Milwaukeean Rob Schrab. As part of his deal with Robert Zemeckis at Imagemovers, Harmon co-wrote the feature film *Monster House*. Following this, Harmon co-wrote the Ben Stiller-directed pilot *Heat Vision and Jack*, starring Jack Black and Owen Wilson.

Disillusioned by the legitimate industry, Harmon began attending classes at nearby Glendale Community College. At the same time, Harmon and Schrab founded Channel 101, an untelevised non-profit audience-controlled network for undiscovered filmmakers, many of whom used it to launch mainstream careers, including the boys behind SNL's Digital Shorts. Harmon, along with Schrab, partnered with Sarah Silverman to create her Comedy Central series, *The Sarah Silverman Program*, where he served as head writer for the first season.

Harmon went on to create, write, and perform in the short-lived VH1 sketch series *Acceptable TV* before eventually creating the critically acclaimed and fan-favorite comedy *Community*. The show originally aired on NBC for five seasons before being acquired by Yahoo, which premiered season six of the show in March 2015. In 2009, he won an Emmy for Outstanding Music and Lyrics for the opening number of the 81st Annual Academy Awards.

Along with Justin Roiland, Harmon created the breakout Adult Swim animated series *Rick and Morty*. The show premiered in December 2013 and quickly became a ratings hit. Harmon and Roiland have wrapped up season two, which premiered in 2015.

In 2014, Harmon was the star of the documentary *Harmontown*, which premiered at the SXSW Film Festival and chronicled his 20-city stand-up/podcast tour of the same name. The documentary was released theatrically in October 2014.

JUSTIN ROILAND grew up in Manteca, California, where he did the basic stuff children do. Later in life he traveled to Los Angeles. Once settled in, he created several popular online shorts for Channel 101. Some notable examples of his work (both animated and live action) include *House of Cosbys* and *Two Girls One Cup: The Show.*

Justin is afraid of his mortality and hopes the things he creates will make lots of people happy. Then maybe when modern civilization collapses into chaos, people will remember him and they'll help him survive the bloodshed and violence. Global economic collapse is looming. It's going to be horrible, and honestly, a swift death might be preferable than living in the hell that awaits mankind.

Justin also really hates writing about himself in the third person. I hate this. That's right. It's me. I've been writing this whole thing. Hi. The cat's out of the bag. It's just you and me now. There never was a third person. If you want to know anything about me, just ask. Sorry this wasn't more informative.

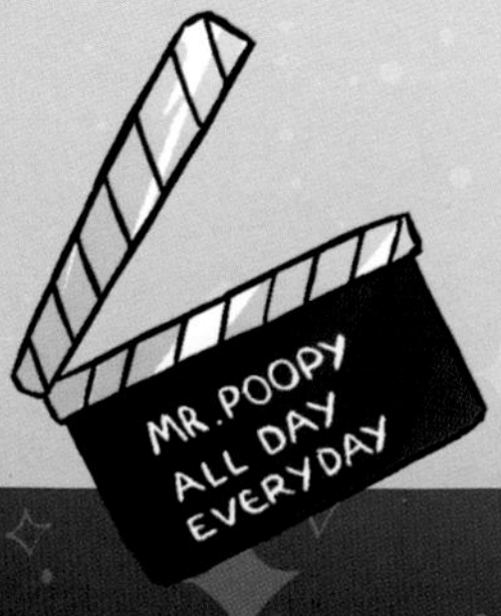
MR. POOPY
ALL DAY
EVERYDAY

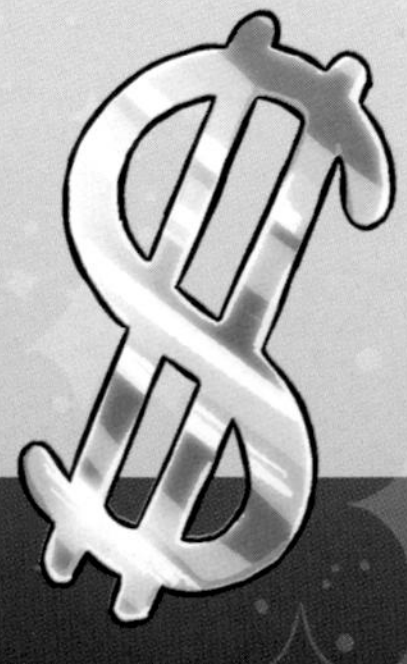

SARAH GRALEY is a writer and comic artist currently living in the UK with four cats, and one cat-like boy. When she is not working on comics, she is playing video games or singing songs in her pop band with her partner—but she's probably still thinking about comics at the same time. If you cut her, she might bleed ink (but let's not find out). Her new Oni Press book, *Kim Reaper*, debuts April 2017!

MARC ELLERBY is a comics illustrator living in Essex, UK. He has worked on such titles as *Doctor Who*, *Regular Show*, and *The Amazing World of Gumball*. His own comics (which you should totally check out!) are *Chloe Noonan: Monster Hunter* and *Ellerbisms*. You can read some comics if you like at marcellerby.com.

MILDRED LOUIS studied animation at Sheridan College in Canada. Mildred then began to find herself falling in love with comics as a visual storytelling medium. Currently she's working on an ongoing magical girl-inspired webcomic series titled *Agents of the Realm*, as well as a queer high fantasy graphic novel titled *Bound Blades* with its first chapter already released, and plans to continue in 2017. In her free time, she enjoys punching and kicking (in the appropriate kickboxing environments), and perusing food blogs right before bed.

CHRIS CRANK has worked on several recent Oni Press books like *The Sixth Gun*, *Brides of Helheim*, *Terrible Lizard*, and others. Maybe you've seen his letters in *Revival*, *Hack/Slash*, *God Hates Astronauts*, or *Dark Engine* from Image. Or perhaps you've read *Lady Killer* or *Sundowners* from Dark Horse. Heck, you might even be reading the award winning *Battlepug* at battlepug.com right now!

KIM REAPER

BY SARAH GRALEY

PART-TIME GRIM REAPER. FULL-TIME CUTIE.

This April, Kim and Becka take on the underworld.

ONI PRESS
www.onipress.com